Patricia A. McKillip
and the Art of Fantasy
World-Building

CRITICAL EXPLORATIONS IN SCIENCE FICTION AND FANTASY
(a series edited by Donald E. Palumbo and C.W. Sullivan III)

1 *Worlds Apart? Dualism and Transgression in Contemporary Female Dystopias* (Dunja M. Mohr, 2005)

2 *Tolkien and Shakespeare: Essays on Shared Themes and Language* (ed. Janet Brennan Croft, 2007)

3 *Culture, Identities and Technology in the* Star Wars *Films: Essays on the Two Trilogies* (ed. Carl Silvio, Tony M. Vinci, 2007)

4 *The Influence of* Star Trek *on Television, Film and Culture* (ed. Lincoln Geraghty, 2008)

5 *Hugo Gernsback and the Century of Science Fiction* (Gary Westfahl, 2007)

6 *One Earth, One People: The Mythopoeic Fantasy Series of Ursula K. Le Guin, Lloyd Alexander, Madeleine L'Engle and Orson Scott Card* (Marek Oziewicz, 2008)

7 *The Evolution of Tolkien's Mythology: A Study of the History of Middle-earth* (Elizabeth A. Whittingham, 2008)

8 *H. Beam Piper: A Biography* (John F. Carr, 2008)

9 *Dreams and Nightmares: Science and Technology in Myth and Fiction* (Mordecai Roshwald, 2008)

10 *Lilith in a New Light: Essays on the George MacDonald Fantasy Novel* (ed. Lucas H. Harriman, 2008)

11 *Feminist Narrative and the Supernatural: The Function of Fantastic Devices in Seven Recent Novels* (Katherine J. Weese, 2008)

12 *The Science of Fiction and the Fiction of Science: Collected Essays on SF Storytelling and the Gnostic Imagination* (Frank McConnell, ed. Gary Westfahl, 2009)

13 *Kim Stanley Robinson Maps the Unimaginable: Critical Essays* (ed. William J. Burling, 2009)

14 *The Inter-Galactic Playground: A Critical Study of Children's and Teens' Science Fiction* (Farah Mendlesohn, 2009)

15 *Science Fiction from Québec: A Postcolonial Study* (Amy J. Ransom, 2009)

16 *Science Fiction and the Two Cultures: Essays on Bridging the Gap Between the Sciences and the Humanities* (ed. Gary Westfahl, George Slusser, 2009)

17 *Stephen R. Donaldson and the Modern Epic Vision: A Critical Study of the "Chronicles of Thomas Covenant" Novels* (Christine Barkley, 2009)

18 *Ursula K. Le Guin's Journey to Post-Feminism* (Amy M. Clarke, 2010)

19 *Portals of Power: Magical Agency and Transformation in Literary Fantasy* (Lori M. Campbell, 2010)

20 *The Animal Fable in Science Fiction and Fantasy* (Bruce Shaw, 2010)

21 *Illuminating* Torchwood*: Essays on Narrative, Character and Sexuality in the BBC Series* (ed. Andrew Ireland, 2010)

22 *Comics as a Nexus of Cultures: Essays on the Interplay of Media, Disciplines and International Perspectives* (ed. Mark Berninger, Jochen Ecke, Gideon Haberkorn, 2010)

23 *The Anatomy of Utopia: Narration, Estrangement and Ambiguity in More, Wells, Huxley and Clarke* (Károly Pintér, 2010)

24 *The Anticipation Novelists of 1950s French Science Fiction: Stepchildren of Voltaire* (Bradford Lyau, 2010)

25 *The* Twilight *Mystique: Critical Essays on the Novels and Films* (ed. Amy M. Clarke, Marijane Osborn, 2010)

26 *The Mythic Fantasy of Robert Holdstock: Critical Essays on the Fiction* (ed. Donald E. Morse, Kálmán Matolcsy, 2011)

27 *Science Fiction and the Prediction of the Future: Essays on Foresight and Fallacy* (ed. Gary Westfahl, Wong Kin Yuen, Amy Kit-sze Chan, 2011)

28 *Apocalypse in Australian Fiction and Film: A Critical Study* (Roslyn Weaver, 2011)

29 *British Science Fiction Film and Television: Critical Essays* (ed. Tobias Hochscherf, James Leggott, 2011)

30 *Cult Telefantasy Series: A Critical Analysis of* The Prisoner, Twin Peaks, The X-Files, Buffy the Vampire Slayer, Lost, Heroes, Doctor Who *and* Star Trek (Sue Short, 2011)

31 *The Postnational Fantasy: Essays on Postcolonialism, Cosmopolitics and Science Fiction* (ed. Masood Ashraf Raja, Jason W. Ellis and Swaralipi Nandi, 2011)

32 *Heinlein's Juvenile Novels: A Cultural Dictionary* (C.W. Sullivan III, 2011)

33 *Welsh Mythology and Folklore in Popular Culture: Essays on Adaptations in Literature, Film, Television and Digital Media* (ed. Audrey L. Becker and Kristin Noone, 2011)

34 *I See You: The Shifting Paradigms of James Cameron's* Avatar (Ellen Grabiner, 2012)

35 *Of Bread, Blood and* The Hunger Games: *Critical Essays on the Suzanne Collins Trilogy* (ed. Mary F. Pharr and Leisa A. Clark, 2012)

36 *The Sex Is Out of This World: Essays on the Carnal Side of Science Fiction* (ed. Sherry Ginn and Michael G. Cornelius, 2012)

37 *Lois McMaster Bujold: Essays on a Modern Master of Science Fiction and Fantasy* (ed. Janet Brennan Croft, 2013)

38 *Girls Transforming: Invisibility and Age-Shifting in Children's Fantasy Fiction Since the 1970s* (Sanna Lehtonen, 2013)

39 *Doctor Who in Time and Space: Essays on Themes, Characters, History and Fandom, 1963–2012* (ed. Gillian I. Leitch, 2013)

40 *The Worlds of Farscape: Essays on the Groundbreaking Television Series* (ed. Sherry Ginn, 2013)

41 *Orbiting Ray Bradbury's Mars: Biographical, Anthropological, Literary, Scientific and Other Perspectives* (ed. Gloria McMillan, 2013)

42 *The Heritage of Heinlein: A Critical Reading of the Fiction Television Series* (Thomas D. Clareson and Joe Sanders, 2014)

43 *The Past That Might Have Been, the Future That May Come: Women Writing Fantastic Fiction, 1960s to the Present* (Lauren J. Lacey, 2014)

44 *Environments in Science Fiction: Essays on Alternative Spaces* (ed. Susan M. Bernardo, 2014)

45 *Discworld and the Disciplines: Critical Approaches to the Terry Pratchett Works* (ed. Anne Hiebert Alton and William C. Spruiell, 2014)

46 *Nature and the Numinous in Mythopoeic Fantasy Literature* (Christopher Straw Brawley, 2014)

47 *J.R.R. Tolkien, Robert E. Howard and the Birth of Modern Fantasy* (Deke Parsons, 2014)

48 *The Monomyth in American Science Fiction Films: 28 Visions of the Hero's Journey* (Donald E. Palumbo, 2014)

49 *The Fantastic in Holocaust Literature and Film: Critical Perspectives* (ed. Judith B. Kerman and John Edgar Browning, 2014)

50 Star Wars *in the Public Square:* The Clone Wars *as Political Dialogue* (Derek R. Sweet, 2016)

51 *An Asimov Companion: Characters, Places and Terms in the Robot/Empire/Foundation Metaseries* (Donald E. Palumbo, 2016)

52 *Michael Moorcock: Fiction, Fantasy and the World's Pain* (Mark Scroggins, 2016)

53 *The Last Midnight: Essays on Apocalyptic Narratives in Millennial Media* (ed. Leisa A. Clark, Amanda Firestone and Mary F. Pharr, 2016)

54 *The Science Fiction Mythmakers: Religion, Science and Philosophy in Wells, Clarke, Dick and Herbert* (Jennifer Simkins, 2016)

55 *Gender and the Quest in British Science Fiction Television: An Analysis of* Doctor Who, Blake's 7, Red Dwarf *and* Torchwood (Tom Powers, 2016)

56 *Saving the World Through Science Fiction: James Gunn, Writer, Teacher and Scholar* (Michael R. Page, 2017)

57 *Wells Meets Deleuze: The Scientific Romances Reconsidered* (Michael Starr, 2017)

58 *Science Fiction and Futurism: Their Terms and Ideas* (Ace G. Pilkington, 2017)

59 Science Fiction in Classic Rock: Musical Explorations of Space, Technology and the Imagination, 1967–1982 (Robert McParland, 2017)

60 *Patricia A. McKillip and the Art of Fantasy World-Building* (Audrey Isabel Taylor, 2017)

Patricia A. McKillip and the Art of Fantasy World-Building

AUDREY ISABEL TAYLOR

CRITICAL EXPLORATIONS IN
SCIENCE FICTION AND FANTASY, 60
Series Editors Donald E. Palumbo *and* C.W. Sullivan III

McFarland & Company, Inc., Publishers
Jefferson, North Carolina

LIBRARY OF CONGRESS CATALOGUING-IN-PUBLICATION DATA

Names: Taylor, Audrey Isabel, 1984– author.
Title: Patricia A. McKillip and the art of fantasy world-building / Audrey Isabel Taylor.
Description: Jefferson, North Carolina : McFarland & Company, Inc., Publishers, 2017. | Series: Critical explorations in science fiction and fantasy ; 60 | Includes bibliographical references and index.
Identifiers: LCCN 2017032322 | ISBN 9781476665160 (softcover : acid free paper) ∞
Subjects: LCSH: McKillip, Patricia A. | Fantasy fiction, American—History and criticism. | Fantasy fiction, American—Authorship. | Imaginary places in literature. | Fiction—Technique.
Classification: LCC PS3563.C38 Z88 2017 | DDC 813/.54—dc23
LC record available at https://lccn.loc.gov/2017032322

BRITISH LIBRARY CATALOGUING DATA ARE AVAILABLE

ISBN (print) 978-1-4766-6516-0
ISBN (ebook) 978-1-4766-3145-5

© 2017 Audrey Isabel Taylor. All rights reserved

No part of this book may be reproduced or transmitted in any form or by any means, electronic or mechanical, including photocopying or recording, or by any information storage and retrieval system, without permission in writing from the publisher.

Front cover image © 2017 Shutterstock

Printed in the United States of America

McFarland & Company, Inc., Publishers
 Box 611, Jefferson, North Carolina 28640
  www.mcfarlandpub.com

To Chrissie and Stefan,
without whose immense patience,
expertise, and encouragement this book
would have been much the poorer.
(All deficiencies are, of course, my own)

Acknowledgments

First and foremost, thanks go to my family for their never-ending love and support. I would also like to thank all those at ICFA and in the field of SF/F more generally who were invaluable with their great kindness, expertise and help, in ways both large and small (especially Brian Attebery, Mark Bould, Sarah Brown, A.P. Canavan, Stefan Ekman, Edward James, Maureen Kincaid Speller, Christine Mains, and Rob Maslen). Furthermore, I gratefully acknowledge Chris Pak who looked at a very early version of this book and had some extremely useful comments and suggestions. Though the book has changed considerably since then I would also like to thank Farah Mendlesohn and Tory Young who were very helpful in the earliest stages of this project. Aga Jedrzejczyk-Drenda, Meg MacDonald, and Jen Willoughby were excellent cheerleaders. And lastly, but certainly not least, to Pat McKillip, whose rich books I could never quite do justice. Thank you, one and all. I am so very, very lucky in my friends.

Table of Contents

Acknowledgments	viii
Preface	1
One: Worlds and World-Building	7
Two: Fantasy Conventions	33
Three: Characters	61
Four: Legends	87
Five: Pastoral Landscapes	114
Six: Cities	138
Reflections	164
Chapter Notes	169
Works Cited	170
Index	177

Preface

It could be said that this book began when I was about thirteen years old, and picked up a Patricia A. McKillip novel, *The Forgotten Beasts of Eld*, for the first time. That story, and the lyrical prose in which it was written, stayed with me so strongly that over ten years later, when casting about for a suitable project, the novel, even its position on my shelf at home, re-emerged and demanded to be taken notice of. What astonished me was how McKillip's book remained in my thoughts, luminous, for so many years after first reading it. That so little academic work had been done on her writing seemed incredible, and so this study was born.

Patricia A. McKillip

Patricia A. McKillip ought to need no introduction. After all, she has won the Mythopoeic Award several times, the World Fantasy Award twice, and has been nominated for and won dozens of other prizes in her time. Until now, however, there has been no book-length examination of her works. The following seeks to address this omission while critically examining what her worlds can tell us about world-building in fantasy literature, a similarly under-studied topic.

McKillip is an American author who won the first World Fantasy Award in 1975 and who continues to work at the time this book was written (2016). In spite of her critical acclaim and large fan base, McKillip has not yet received the critical attention her works deserve. In 2005, introducing one of the biggest collections of critical work on McKillip's writing, a *Journal of the Fantastic in the Arts* special issue

(16.3), Christine Mains noted that up to that point, there had been little work done on McKillip. Even now, over ten years later, very little more work has been done on her novels. And yet, critic John Clute calls her *In the Forests of Serre* "one of a series of brilliant fantasy novels that Patricia A. McKillip has been writing for the past thirty years" ("Canary" 6) and author Stephen R. Donaldson is quoted on the cover of *Kingfisher* as saying "[t]here are no better writers than Patricia A. McKillip." Sites like *Goodreads* too are full of praise from readers. McKillip unites critics, fellow authors, and fans in respect for her craft.

If surprisingly little work has been done on McKillip's fiction, none of it is expressly about world-building. Some scholars have taken a feminist-informed approach, exploring McKillip's use of female characters as heroes and wizards; for instance, Mains discusses the depiction of Raederle as an equal to Morgon in "Having it All: The Female Hero's Quest for Love and Power in Patricia McKillip's *The Riddle-Master Trilogy*," while Ann F. Howey's "Changing Self, Changing Other: Patricia McKillip's *The Changeling Sea* as Feminist Fairy Tale" examines the Young Adult (YA) novel *The Changeling Sea*, in particular McKillip's portrayal of the main character, Peri, whose growth into adulthood is not dependent on traditional gender expectations. Faye Ringel's "Women Fantasists: In the Shadow of the Ring" examines McKillip, along with Rosemary Edgehill, Delia Sherman, and Greer Ilene Gilman, and the Tolkienian influence they all work with. The female heroes in McKillip, and the complications that arise from these heroes are looked at in "The Use, Misuse, and Abuse of Power: The Wizards of Patricia A. McKillip," also by Mains, and Sharon Emmerichs, "Straddling Genres: McKillip and the Landscape of the Female Hero-Identity," which comes to a different, less positive conclusion than Mains' work, especially "Having," which sees the possibility of a duomyth (a male and female partnership quest arc) in the structure of McKillip's heroic quests. McKillip's use of story is quizzed in Helen Pilinovsky's "The Mother of all Witches: Baba Yaga and Brume in Patricia McKillip's *In the Forests of Serre*," a comparison of the Baba Yaga figure of Russian folktale with Brume of *In the Forests of Serre* and Mains' "Bridging World and Story: Patricia McKillip's Reluctant Heroes," which also explores layers of story. Clute discusses *In the Forests of Serre* in terms of how it brings story to life in his essays "Canary in the Coal Mine" and "Pardon This Intrusion," and is generally complimentary of McKillip's work in the online version of the *Encyclopedia of Science Fiction*. Martha Hixon's "'The Lady of Shalott' as Paradigm in Patricia McKillip's *The Tower at Stony Wood*," also looks at story in McKillip, this time taking Tennyson's poem and working out how it shapes the narrative of *The Tower at Stony Wood*. Cultural elements of McKillip's worlds, in the form of how the riddles work in *The Riddle-Master* trilogy, are explored in "'I will play no games with you': Riddlery, Narrative and Ethics in 'The Riddle-Master's Game'" by Kerry Le Lievre. Ringel examines McKillip's love of, and appreciation for, music in "The Art of Patricia McKillip: Music and Magic," which explores how elements of music and its practice and performance have been conflated with magic in many of McKillip's works. Gary K. Wolfe discusses some of McKillip's magical creatures as metaphor in "The Encounter with Fantasy." Lastly, power, its use, abuse, and its outburst in violence, is examined in Mains' "For Love or for Money: The Concept of Loyalty in the Works of Patricia A. McKillip." Although these authors all take different approaches to McKillip, none truly examines her world-building as being essential to her fiction.

No books have studied world-building in McKillip (or McKillip exclusively, for that matter), though elements of her world-building are extant in a few of those books that do mention her. For example, when Stefan Ekman explores *Ombria in Shadow* through the nature/culture divide he naturally examines an aspect of its world (12). In *A Short History of Fantasy*, Farah Mendlesohn and Edward James reference the world of *The Riddle-Master* trilogy as Celtic-influenced (98), and note the "medievalist" setting of the world of the *Cygnet* duology (147), but these are only mentions. Charlotte Spivack looks at *The Forgotten Beasts of Eld* and *The Riddle-Master* trilogy as part of an overview of female fantasy authors, and she mentions a couple of the parameters of McKillip's worlds; for instance, when she argues that women in McKillip's work avoid the roles found in the "primary worlds medieval romances" (165). Brian Attebery references McKillip briefly as part of larger projects in a number of his books, examining her characterization in *Strategies of Fantasy* (74–75), and other (non–world-building aspects) of her books in *Stories about Stories*.

The comparative scarcity of critical work on McKillip is surprising considering her twenty-six novels, her short story collections, her recognition through awards, and the general acclaim for her work. This study attempts to go some way towards rectifying this situation, with a comprehensive examination of one large section of McKillip's oeuvre; that is, her secondary-world fantasies (nineteen books in total), through the critical lens of world-building.

Texts

The McKillip texts that I examine are classic fantasy texts. Defining fantasy as a genre is notoriously difficult, so much so that the battle to find a single definition has inevitably given way to the acceptance of multiple classifications (fantasy has numerous definitions, an excellent summary of which can be found on pp. 4–5 of Mendlesohn and James's *A Short History of Fantasy*). Therefore, I will not be making an argument about what fantasy is; I will only place McKillip within the fantasy genre by applying Attebery's "fuzzy set" from *Strategies of Fantasy*. Attebery describes his "fuzzy set" thus: "[g]enres may be approached as 'fuzzy sets,' meaning that they are defined not by boundaries but by a center" (*Strategies* 12). Attebery's definition depends on a clearly defined center, so the books linked to that center in some way are part of that same genre. If I take J.R.R. Tolkien's *The Lord of the Rings* as a touchstone text, McKillip's fantasy books fit easily into the "fuzzy set" alongside it.

Each chapter will contain a set of core texts that I feel demonstrate the chapter's theme particularly well. Additional texts will be used to add evidence as necessary, and to show the breadth of McKillip's worlds. Due to the nature of this project some books do not get the concentrated attention that others receive, nor do I examine any of her short stories. There is more work left for the future.

The nineteen books I include in my examination are:

The Throme of the Erril of Sherril (1973)
The Riddle-Master trilogy (*The Riddle-Master of Hed* [1976], *Heir of Sea and Fire* [1977], *Harpist in the Wind* [1979])[1]
The Forgotten Beasts of Eld (1974)
The *Cygnet* duology (*The Sorceress and the Cygnet* [1991], *The Cygnet and the Firebird* [1993])[2]
The Book of Atrix Wolfe (1995)
Winter Rose (1996)

Song for the Basilisk (1998)
The Tower at Stony Wood (2000)
Ombria in Shadow (2002)
In the Forests of Serre (2003)
The Changeling Sea (2003)
Alphabet of Thorn (2004)
Od Magic (2005)
The Bell at Sealey Head (2008)
The Bards of Bone Plain (2010)
Kingfisher (2016)

This array of books, containing both fantasy and secondary worlds, will enable me to narrow down McKillip's oeuvre to manageable proportions. These parameters allow me to analyze a set of books that are similar, but in which McKillip approaches world-building in a variety of ways. Each chapter scrutinizes a selection of books that contain specific features of world-building, with the end goal of showing how McKillip's worlds are rich, interrelated constructions.

ONE

Worlds and World-Building

This is a book about critical world-building. While the following chapters contain examples of how to carry out analyses of various aspects of world-building, this chapter provides a background to world-building in general, as well as more specifically in fantasy literature, before moving on to examples from McKillip's work in subsequent chapters. Any discussion of something as complex as how to build imaginary worlds requires a certain amount of terminology, and this is where I begin, with an exploration of what I mean by a critical use of world-building, and then a discussion of some of the ways that world-building will be examined in the subsequent pages.

World

The most basic term I work with is "world." By this I mean a contained space together with all its people and features. Ekman's characterization of "world" provides some scope, defining it as

> a universe or space in which all positions are, at least in theory, accessible to a person (fictive or otherwise) by means of (nonmagical) travel: by foot, boat, or spaceship, travelers should be able to make their way from one place to another even if it would take them millennia or more [9].

This definition is useful because it constrains "world" into an imaginable space, one that can be worked with both from an authorial perspective, as well as that of the critic and reader. I mean something slightly larger than this, however. Like Mark J.P. Wolf (25) I consider the world as a physical space as well as everything it contains, whether that is corporeal (plants, animals, characters) or not (myths, legends, time, history). The world of a book, and the story the book contains, are two separate entities. Wolf says "while the telling of a story inevitably also tells us about the world in which the story takes place, storytelling and world-building are different processes that can sometimes come into conflict" (29), but each is necessary to the book as a whole. As Wolf notes "story and world usually work together, enriching each other..." (29). A story must have some sort of world to take place in, just as a world must have a story to be a novel, in order to be larger than just a world.[1] A story is an account of events that take place in one (or several) world(s). Worlds can exist without stories, but we generally create them with the potential for stories. In other words, a story acts out what takes place in the world, and the world is a place where stories happen. In literary studies, David Herman describes the concept of storyworlds as "mental models of who did what to and with whom, when, where, why, and in what fashion in the world to which recipients relocate" (*Story* 5). It is key that Herman thinks of storyworlds as "mental models," pertaining to a nexus of effects that create a world. The world of a book is just as important to the meaning of a book as its plot, characters, narration, or any of the more traditional areas for critical scrutiny.

Two further terms of importance to worlds in fantasy literature as a whole, and this book in particular, are *primary* and *secondary* world. The definitions of both are somewhat controversial. I adapt and narrow Tolkien's definition of both, as expounded in his essay "On Fairy-Stories." Tolkien says that certain stories were created by man as a "sub-creation." That is, the author

> makes a Secondary World which your mind can enter. Inside it, what he relates is "true": it accords with the laws of that world. You therefore believe it, while you are, as it were, inside. The moment disbelief arises, the spell is broken; the magic, or rather art, has failed. You are then out in the Primary World again, looking at the little abortive Secondary World from outside [37].

Tolkien's definition includes our Earth as the primary world, and the secondary world as the world of story, one in which truth is subjective to the laws of the story and not the outside real world. Although Wolf sees a range of separation between various primary and secondary worlds, and puts them on a scale according to how different from our

One. Worlds and World-Building

reality they are (25), I leave this distinction behind to make it clear that by primary world I refer to our planet Earth, our recognizable world. By secondary world I mean an invented world that the author has created, one that is fundamentally different from the primary world in some way.

McKillip largely uses secondary worlds, and this is what I focus on in this book. This gives me a workable collection of texts, but I have also chosen McKillip's secondary-world books because this is where her world-building skill is most consistently displayed. McKillip rarely seems to go back to worlds previously explored.[2] This presents opportunities not only for new characters and stories but also for different landscapes, legends, and cities, all, as far as we currently know, completely separate from previous works. This allows for completely new possibilities, ones that the very nature of different worlds gives to new stories.

The McKillip texts that I study are secondary-world novels: those fantasy texts that concern imagined worlds, and thus primary-world defaults cannot always be assumed. The fantastic elements of a text must blend seamlessly with those parts that are real in order to make the whole world seem plausible. I have chosen those books of McKillip's (a list of which can be found in the Preface) that could be presumed to take place in secondary worlds because this displays a clear sense of worlds being built, ones in which primary-world concerns or laws cannot always be taken for granted.

Aside from wanting to examine an under-studied author, I have also used McKillip because so many of her books are single entities, and even those that are not, like *The Riddle-Master* trilogy, can usually be treated as one text. Wolf specifically targets media franchises in his book (7), examining them for a whole range of effects and details related to world-building. Wolf quotes Henry Jenkins, who contends that: "More and more, storytelling has become the art of world-building, as artists create compelling environments that cannot be fully explored or exhausted within a single work or even a single medium" (10). I would argue, however, that a single book can create a "compelling environment," even one that cannot be "fully explored" within a single text, and that McKillip is one of the best at this. Her books encompass whole worlds, richly realized, within a few hundred pages, and her world-building economy, in this sense, is of interest to me.

Elements

Worlds are often treated as just setting, or landscape, but they are constructed from a number of different kinds of building-blocks, structures, and relationships, and I refer to these as the "elements" of a world. Elements are "the many varied building blocks that constitute imaginary worlds, and comprise anything from geographical and topographical details, to flora, fauna, and ecologies, to social groupings and behaviours, political factions and ideologies, and cultural traditions and mores" (Ekman and Taylor 9). Elements will be used to indicate the various building-blocks of world-building that I examine, both by scrutinizing them individually and looking for connections from one element to another.

In *Basic Elements of Narrative* Herman stresses that the term "storyworlds" encompasses both the implicit and the explicit (107); that is, what is outright said and done and what is assumed or implied are equally important in evoking a whole world. Wolf too examines more than setting in his conception of world, though from a different perspective than Herman as his focus is largely on media. Wolf examines all of a world, noting "[t]he term 'world,' as it is being used here, is not simply geographical but *experiential*; that is, everything that is experienced by the characters involved, the elements enfolding someone's life..." (25).

The same is applicable to world-building as I use it. In the next chapters I will explore how implicit assumptions about gender, tropes, and types of landscape may all be played with and subverted, just as explicit content like setting and city structures will be probed to determine not only the process by which those assumptions are shown, but their effect.

The fantastic elements of the world are not all that build a fantasy novel, but they often take precedence because they are considered unique to it. Wolfe suggests that examining works of speculative fiction takes more than simply noting the factors that make them speculative. Instead, he proposes, "[t]o account for such works, we must move beyond the simple criterion of cognitive impossibility and examine such elements as tone and setting—elements that help to construct what we might call the affective sense of the impossible" ("Encountering" 72). This "affective sense of the impossible" that Wolfe privileges over impossibility is constructed, I would argue, by the various elements that also help to build the world. World-building, used as a critical tool, can help to examine these elements.

Setting

"World-building" has often been used as a shorthand for setting, and nothing more. For example, in *Writing Fantasy and Science Fiction*, author Lisa Tuttle begins her chapter on "world building" with a rumination on landscape, indicating that landscape is so important to a text that it can be considered a main character (30). This does emphasize the important nature of setting to fantastic fiction, but it seems to indicate that the world of a book is nothing *but* landscape. I am interested in looking beyond landscape (though this is naturally a prominent part of world-building) to see what setting combined with other factors and elements can tell us.

A world is more than setting, just as I argue that world-building encompasses more than location. I want to emphasize that though the term world-building might cause the reader of this book to focus on the world, and as a result, setting, I am looking at a broader parameter than that. When Michael Moorcock proposes in *Wizardry and Wild Romance: A Study of Epic Fantasy* that

> [a]n intrinsic part of the epic fantasy is exotic landscape. This dream scenery is fundamental to the success of any romantic work from Walpole to Ballard; it is often the substance of such work, and no matter how well drawn their characters or good their language writers will appeal to the dedicated reader of romance according to the skill by which they evoke settings, whether natural or invented [43].

Moorcock too leans heavily on the term "landscape," and instead seems to intend something broader. After all, there are certainly epic-fantasies whose actual settings are fairly prosaic (the desert landscape in *Sword Dancer* by Jennifer Roberson is a perfectly ordinary sand-and-sun desert, for example). I also think the term "dream scenery" is misleading. "Dream" implies imagination, yes, but of the type used by the absurd; that is, nonsensical, or of a type too heavily tied in with Freud and ideas of the unconscious. This seems to take reality out of the equation, which is a mistake. But I also take issue with the word "scenery." Certainly, some works only contain scenery; that is, set pieces that stand in for greater landscape or depth, but there are authors, McKillip among them, whose landscapes and, more importantly, worlds, are more than this. McKillip's worlds are rich constructions, with ideas, plot, narrative, characters and other elements all interacting in varying and engaging ways.

It is, however, often the case that more general discussions of setting are useful within world-building criticism. For example, Ekman's *Here Be Dragons* focuses on settings in fantasy literature but many of his arguments and points about setting as a whole are easily transferable to world-building. On the very first page he notes that, "[s]omehow, the stories seemed to revolve around these places, weaving in and out of them rather than just using them as backdrops for the action onstage" (1). That is, Ekman begins with an acknowledgment that setting in fantasy literature is much more than "backdrop": it is crucial to the stories being told as a whole. I want to develop a holistic approach to looking at world-building: because it is more commonly associated just with setting, I want to argue that examining it from all angles, setting included, could be a useful way of approaching a text critically. Ekman and I argue that "[t]hrough its composite perspective, critical world-building allows for a potentially limitless analysis of a world. Elements are interrelated in a complex structure of implications that extend the world and affect the understanding of other elements and their relations" (15). It is these implications and the way that elements interrelate that I want to emphasize. This is one of the reasons for a thematic view of the various elements of world-building that McKillip uses, rather than a book-by-book examination of her worlds. There are certain elements common to McKillip's very different worlds; highlighting these can lead to useful interpretations. Although each chapter stands alone they all speak to each other, and all the elements play into all of her worlds.

As I will argue in the next few chapters McKillip's worlds are more than an "intriguing artistic location," or any of the other things commonly cited as the be-all or end-all of world-building; rather, they are composed of all of the various attributes that contribute to the world, how they are put together, combined with the surprises that are sprung, that allow the critic to perceive more in the works of fiction than simply a "new world."

World-Building as a General Concept

World-building as a whole is not a new concept, nor is it a concept restricted to literature. Alison B. Kavey proposes in her introduction to *World-Building and the Early Modern Imagination* that "[f]rom rebuilding Haiti after its devastating earthquake to the digital wonderworlds on cinema screens, the twenty-first century imagination is obsessed with fixing old worlds and conjuring new ones" (1). As she points out, world-building is both a literal occupation in the real world as well as an imaginative construction. She goes on to argue that this is in no way a new preoccupation, but that in the past it largely focused on scientific and religious doctrine. People were trying to "fill in the gaps" and link their world together, just as readers must do with fictional texts now.

In cognitive terms humans "world-build" every day. We construct meaning from what we see, smell, hear, and more, turning this into internal monologues and narratives that shape our lives. Wolf expands this element of human perception (explored in gestalt psychology more generally) to include "narrative gestalt," (51) where we fill in narratives of movies or books just as we do in real life. He then develops this to include "world gestalten," where various elements are combined to create the illusion of a full world (52). I would extend this argument to suggest that in speculative fiction this is naturally an even more in-depth process, because a speculative fictional world is constructed, without the same attempt to remain mimetic and, as such, is more clearly a world built rather than perceived.

World-Building in Fiction

I have chosen the term "world-building" rather than worldbuilding or world building because I want there to be a clear connection between the "world" the book is shaped of, and what it is built with. But I also want it to be clear that they are distinct entities; thus, I have separated them out of a single word. The world of a story, and how it is built, are not the same thing but they do impact on one another, which is why I have linked them with a hyphen. A hyphen indicates that there is a connection between the terms, that there is a combined meaning and association between the words. I want it to be clear that there is a relationship between world and building, and that combined they take on a slightly different meaning than each component part. I intend for the words to be used together, as I am looking at both the world, and the building of it. One way of thinking of world-building is to think of it as world-architecture, that is, the world as building, and to investigate it as such. But the other way is to consider it as an activity, as something being built.

I work with books in part because they are what I know best, and what I am trained to analyze, but also because it is specifically McKillip's worlds that have fascinated me. I will not be examining media franchises, fan studies, or media other than books, but I would point out that they have been explored in terms of world-building, often in more detail than books. Wolf claims that "Media Studies, which acknowledges and accounts for the windows through which imaginary worlds are so often seen, provides the best basis for examining them as entities in and of themselves..." (6). While I naturally do not entirely agree, Wolf's *Building Imaginary Worlds: The Theory and History of Subcreation* is an excellent source for those interested.

World-Building in Speculative Fiction

I would argue that all forms of fiction world-build, though as I focus on McKillip's work, fantastic world-building is naturally my focus. Non-fiction texts are able to take reality for granted in a way that fictional texts must re-construct, and this is even more true with speculative texts, whose world changes mean that even less can be assumed. Mendlesohn points out this construction of reality in a chapter on immersive fantasy in *Rhetorics of Fantasy*. She claims that when done well, immersive world-building "at its most effective, is an ironic construction of the mimesis that we take for granted when we enter the strange world of the literary novel—*Pride and Prejudice,* for example" (101). In other words, the author of a fantasy novel recreates what we take for granted in a literary novel, those details that make it seem real. This can be expanded to most speculative fiction, not just immersive fantasy.

What makes world-building unique within speculative fiction is, perhaps, the "cognitive impossibility" which makes it speculative literature; however, it is not entirely what makes a speculative fictional world, and is thus not entirely what it is built of. It is impossible to be or represent anything truly unreal, as Wolf argues that "[a]ll invention that occurs in a world must remain analogous, in some way, to the Primary World in order to be comprehensible..." (37). For example, in science fiction, were you to have an alien that is actually alien; that is, completely divorced from any human understanding or language, it would be nearly impossible to write, and even more impossible to read. As Kathryn Hume explores in *Fantasy and Mimesis* and Attebery points out in *Strategies of Fantasy* "[t]hough they are contrasting modes, mimesis and fantasy are not opposites. They can and do coexist within any given work.... Fantasy without mimesis would be a purely artificial invention" (3). There is a certain level of the real that must be present in any text: speculative fictions are able to play with this reality in ways more mimetic literature does not, but this means that to balance that they must provide a grounding in some type of reality, some type of recognizable experience.

Wolfe contends that "a deeper belief in the fundamental reality that this world expresses" ("Encountering" 78) is necessary to successful speculative fiction. Thus, some measure of reality, of truth, is necessary. As William A. Senior states, "fantasy does not extend an absolute license regardless of its unreal or surreal elements" (135). Fantasy is sometimes considered complete fancy, an entirely imaginative exercise without recourse to the real world (Amie Doughty explores this aspect of fantasy's reception in *"Throw the book away": Reading versus Experience in Children's Fantasy* [16–17]), especially by those outside of and unfamiliar with the genre. This is usually a fallacy. An absolute license to use the unreal, or surreal, would result in something closer to the absurd, not the often carefully crafted stories and worlds of the fantasy genre. As a result, my examination includes both speculative elements and also more realistic aspects of the text, those elements that help to build the world in its entirety, not just those features (like dragons or magic) that make the books fantasies.

When we begin to look for the elements that build the worlds of speculative fiction we find that many have a familiar feel. Wolfe suggests

> [s]cience fiction, like many forms of popular literature, boasts a repertoire of recurring images that are emblematic of the major concerns and anxieties of

the genre. The most familiar of these icons ... gain power from their peculiar property of both revealing knowledge and withholding it; they are familiar, while at the same time they remain estranged from us in some significant aspect ["Encountering" 83].

Wolfe claims this for science fiction but the same could be said of fantasy. Fantasy too has a "repertoire of recurring images," some of which will be considered in Chapter Two. This familiarity mixed with estrangement is vital to the effect the genre can have.

World-Building in Science Fiction

Worlds, as creations, are important to speculative fiction. Science-fictional worlds are often set up as linked to, and often extended from, our Earth in some way. Consequently, world-building, and worlds more generally, have naturally been of importance to science fiction as it is one of the speculative genres that extrapolates from the mimetic most closely. Carl D. Malmgren argues repeatedly in his *Worlds Apart: Narratology of Science Fiction* that what makes science fiction, science fiction is its world or worlds. "The genre of science fiction must be defined by its unique fictional world or worlds.... SF can be defined by its peculiarly 'science-fictional' worlds" (1–2). While I want to escape from this notion that speculative worlds are wholly unique (and wholly composed of speculative elements) the importance of the world to science fiction (and, equally, fantasy and other speculative literatures) cannot be overemphasized. I would only broaden "world"'s importance to include all fiction.

World-Building in Fantasy

Fantasy as a genre is intimately connected with world-building in ways that other more realistic fiction is often not. Fantasy extrapolates less obviously from the mimetic, and so the world-building requires, at times, different parameters. Attebery notes that the reader of more mimetic fiction "does a lot of the hard work of bringing a story to life" (*Strategies* 131) but this is not always possible, or wanted, within a fantasy text. Because it is less related to the mimetic, fantasy requires a different understanding, as Attebery again comments: "the principle of extension ceases to operate" (132). For example, in McKillip's *The Bell at Sealey Head* the titular bell has rung "as always" on page 3. The reality of the bell is unquestioned, until page 6 when it is linked with magic. The bell's reality, or not, must be explicitly stated. A bell ringing in the primary world would indicate that there is a bell to ring. In the secondary world of McKillip's the possibility of magic is introduced, and thus a bell tolling every night does not have to have a bell with which to toll in the real world of that story.

Perhaps it is a reflection of world-building's very ubiquity that scarcely a book or article about fantasy goes by without mentioning world-building, or its attributes or lack thereof, in some fashion. As far back as 1983 John H. Timmerman claims that "the third trait characterizing fantasy literature is the evocation of another world. This trait has received by far the most attention in critical circles" (49). Perhaps this is true in pointing out that fantasies have different worlds, but in terms of critically analyzing those worlds as *built* worlds, I would argue that this was not, and is not, the case. Often, the world of a fantasy is explored in relation to one element, such as landscape, or else the world is ignored entirely in favor of more traditional critical areas of exploration, like narrative and characterization.

While there are copious creative writing guides on world-building, one of the curious gaps in fantasy scholarship is that there is no one, decisive definition of world-building within fantasy literature. Similarly, at times a critic may study world-building without mentioning the fact; for example, William Senior's in-depth examination of the world and makings of Stephen R. Donaldson's Thomas Covenant series. Diana Wynne Jones' spoof *A Tough Guide to Fantasyland* is also without a doubt entirely concerned with world-building while not once mentioning the fact. She concentrates on the sort of fantasy Clute calls "templated" in his essay "Notes on the Geography of Bad Art in Fantasy"; that is, a fantasy story "told again by another writer, reduced to a template other writers exploit" (112), but it is an investigation of the elements of a particular type of world's world-building nonetheless. It is curious that world-building as a concept is so rarely pinned down.

Similarly, none of the major dictionaries of science fiction or fantasy (including David Pringle's *The Ultimate Encyclopedia of Fantasy*, John Clute and Peter Nicholls' *Encyclopedia of Science Fiction*, and

Gary Westfahl's *The Greenwood Encyclopedia of Science Fiction and Fantasy: Themes, Works, and Wonders*) defines the term "world-building," though they occasionally use the term. Even John Clute and John Grant's *Encyclopedia of Fantasy* does not define the term, although Clute developed a definition for fantasy for it that is centered on the importance of "world" to fantasy:

> A fantasy text is a self-coherent narrative. When set in this world, it tells a story which is impossible in the world as we perceive it; when set in an otherworld, that otherworld will be impossible, though stories set there may be possible in its terms.

In his essay, "Notes on the Geography of Bad Art in Fantasy" he reiterates the definition with this sentence: "We were left with a definition of fantasy as being comprised of stories set in worlds which are impossible *but which the story believes*" (114). Even though Clute and Grant's *Encyclopedia of Fantasy* itself does not contain the entry world (or world-building), it is still clear that "world" is essential to fantasy, so essential that it makes up one of only thirteen words (and only one of two nouns, "world" and "story") Clute uses to encompass it as a genre. This definition prioritizes "world" above many of the features that are typically used to define fantasy (most having to do with its invented creations, or magic). It could be surmised, then, that Clute recognizes the importance of the world to fantasy fiction generally, even though its definition is conspicuously absent from the *Encyclopedia of Fantasy* itself.

World-Building as Process

Whether or not the term world-building is used, whether the built worlds being analyzed are mimetic or fantastic, critics who have explored the subject tend to confuse who is doing the building. Some focus more on the author, the work that the author must do in order to build the world; others on the reader(s), on the work of interpreting the words on the page in order to construct a world to explore, and all tend to muddle these together with critical understandings, which is why Ekman and I began to piece together a definition for world-building in the article "Notes Toward a Critical Approach to Worlds and World-Building." This article theorizes that when the wide variety of ways in which the term world-building (or its variants) are probed there are at least three types of world-building. Readerly world-building is how the reader builds the text and its world in their own mind, which is Herman's focus. Authorial world-building is how the author builds the world of the text (studied in relation to creative writing texts). Critical world-building is the way in which the critic both puts together the world and analyzes this construction. I would note here (as was done in the article) that though we have defined them as separate entities, human beings bring different levels of all of them to their reading. A critic is also a reader, and could even be an author, and vice versa. This is especially true with a "fan" reader; someone whose minute interest in a text goes beyond what is usually afforded by the reader. This confusion is one of the reasons I leave "fan readers" out of the discussion, and focus on a critical reading instead. What the article did not do was use this critical approach on extended text examples, as I will be doing throughout this book.

World-Building from the Authors' Perspective

World-building has received a great deal of attention from the authorial viewpoint as aspiring writers naturally want to know how to build a world effectively, one which will hold the stories they wish to tell. As a result, there are a number of creative writing texts that focus on world-building to some degree. Some of the many are *How to Write Science Fiction and Fantasy* by Orson Scott Card, Tuttle's *Writing Fantasy and Science Fiction*, and *Imaginary Worlds: The Art of Fantasy* by Lin Carter, to name but a few.

There is also an inordinate number of websites and articles devoted to world-building, and, occasionally, to warning authors away from the term (M. John Harrison's now infamous blog post "Very afraid" is but one example). Authorial world-building can also be studied critically, as in Catherine Butler's essay "Tolkien and Worldbuilding" which focuses on Tolkien as a builder of worlds, and his writings and interviews on the subject, though I will attempt to stay away from this type of criticism.

Consistency and realism are two aspects often brought up in relation to "good" authorial world-building. Mark J.P. Wolf, for example, has three criteria for what he believes to be effective world-building, a "high degree of invention, completeness, and consistency" (33). These authorial world-building criteria have been espoused by others as well. As early as 1893 George McDonald was advocating for the application of laws to invented worlds in his introduction to *The Light Princess and Other Fairy Tales*. Brian Sibley also contends that Tolkien "firmly believed that if the fantasy writer approached his subject with the same degree of reason as would be expected of the non-fiction writer, the better the resulting fantasy would be" (9). Tolkien's "reason" could be the completeness and consistency that Wolf speaks of. Consistency is often cited as a key to world-building, especially in fantasy literature, but I leave its examination to Wolf, and those interested in authorial world-building.

World-Building from the Reader's Perspective

Readerly world-building is primarily what is used, or focused on, in much of current literary criticism. Narratology, for example, is expressly interested in how a reader puts together the narrative of a story, and by extension how a world is constructed in their head. Herman, for instance, argues that his storyworlds encompass a wide range of things that influence the reader into creating the story as a full object in their minds, and that allow them to move from their everyday world to the world of the story.

Herman investigates what the reader must do, and which pointers must be in the text, in order for the world to form in a reader's head. As Wolfgang Iser has argued in reader-response theory, when someone reads a work of fiction they "fill in" gaps with their own knowledge. Mark J.P. Wolf, too, is interested in the reader, or viewer, of a world and how they make sense of it. In his third chapter he puts together a number of entities he calls "secondary world infrastructures." These include: nature, culture, language and mythology (155). He indicates that these are the way that readers frame, and keep track of, what they are reading.

Samuel Delany makes a slightly different point.[3] He contends that

> Words in a narrative generate tones of voice, syntactic expectations, memories of other words, and pictures. But rather than a fixed chronological relation,

they sit in numerous inter- and overweaving relations. The process as we move our eyes from word to word is corrective and revisionary rather than progressive. Each new word revises the complex picture we had moments before [4].

His argument is that from the very first word a book is almost entirely spent in revising the impression the reader receives; in his understanding of the reading process order is of the most importance. This can be translated into critical world-building, where it can be just as important to note what element is included when, as well as what the elements themselves are. Another key to Delany's theory is that it is "inter- and overweaving relations" that are important, and this focus on interaction and relationships is one I too share, even if the reader and their reactions is not my priority.

World-Building from the Critic's Perspective

What is often not considered fully enough is the difference between the processes followed by a casual or even fan reader, and the process followed by a critic. Critics come to a text differently from authors and readers in two main ways. The primary is that they come equipped with scholarly tools. They have been specially trained to use lenses such as ecocriticism, feminism, psychoanalysis and the like, which influence how the world of a text is considered, and what facets are focused on. Looking at a complete world from all conceivable angles is virtually impossible for a critic with limited space, so lenses are naturally used to restrict the scope of critical inquiry to certain perspectives. For example, critics using a Marxist approach would be interested in the power dynamics displayed within a world, thus focusing their gaze on particular elements of that world.

The second difference is that a critic will naturally be more interested in particular details (often details of importance to whatever lens they are using) as they do a close reading. Critics are trained to read more closely than the average reader, and as a result, certain details will be marked, and perhaps given more importance than by a less formally trained reader going over the same passage. This also means that the order of what is presented, and when, will be noted to a degree unlikely to be marked by a casual reader.

In this book I will primarily use "dynamic interplay"; that "takes into account the entirety of the world constructed, including the interplay between all its elements and the possible interpretations available to the critic who analyses it" (Ekman and Taylor 14). I devised this style specifically to enable a full investigation of McKillip's worlds. The major part of this book will be examining McKillip's world-building from the critical perspective. That is, not only will the elements of McKillip's worlds be examined, but the order in which they appear to the reader will be noted, and, most importantly for my approach, how they all work together to build the worlds of McKillip will be studied.

For example, signs that this is a fantastical world can come from anywhere in McKillip's work, but I have chosen several examples from the first few pages of *Kingfisher*, which begins prosaically enough, with one of the main characters, Pierce, catching crabs, before beginning to widen into a fantastic world. A group of strangers arrives and says: "Sorry to interrupt your work there, but could you tell us where in Severn's name we are?" (4) The invocation of "Severn," a god familiar to those of the world, but whose name has not been mentioned previously in the text, could, perhaps, just be an unfamiliar curse. McKillip's text, however, quickly invalidates this notion in the next few lines; "The shadow stretching out from the boots on the dock seemed to have grown wings. They expanded darkly across the wood, rising to catch the wind. The boots under Pierce's transfixed gaze refused to levitate, ignoring the wings" (4). That this is clearly unusual to Pierce must be taken into account, as must the wry humor in "refused to levitate, ignoring the wings," which provides a moment of humor to mark the strangeness. This subtle beginning is much of what the bulk of world-building consists of. We are introduced to a world at least nominally like our earth in that fishing for crabs is a usual activity. But the name Severn, used in the portion of a sentence where a curse or exclamation are likely, indicates that we are somewhere un-familiar.

This example is instructive too because it is the *order* in which the details of the world are rolled out that are important, as well as the elements themselves. Wolf points out that "how world information is doled out to the audience is an important part of world-building and design," (155) and that the "doling out" of information; the order, context, and style of presentation of world elements, is a central factor in how a world is understood. Thus it is not only the elements of world-building that will be considered, but how and when they are included.

Dynamic interplay is an approach in which a large number of world elements are probed in order to see what they say about the world as a whole. They are also, crucially, examined in terms of each other, and how each part impacts on the others. Dynamic interplay can be seen as a type of hermeneutic lens. I move from the micro level of details out to the macro of the world and book, considering what the details say about the whole, then return to see what that whole says about the details.

A reader sees a text as an organism, using their own eyes. Their view is both limited, in the sense that they have not been trained to use lenses, and, because they are unlikely to be interested in the sorts of micro or macro details that I am as a critic. My critical approach is akin to using a microscope to examine the pieces of a cell working together, before using a telescope to see the organism as a whole and how it interacts with a greater universe. Both include information that links to each other, and both impact on each other. Each also requires specific tools, and a particular type of training to both use those tools and interpret the information they convey. In dynamic interplay the pieces of a world are studied, but most importantly, how these pieces work together to build a "whole" world is examined. Thus, they are dynamic in relation to each other. Ultimately, "the entire web of implications that is an imaginary world can be approached as a dynamic system of interplaying elements and relationships" (Ekman and Taylor 15). Although each of the following chapters tracks one theme, together they examine how various elements interact to form the world, and ideas about what the world contains.

The elements that fill a built fictional world, and how they interact, are of primary importance to my approach. To give an example of the critical approach to world-building, versus what the reader or author might see, I take a passage from McKillip's *Kingfisher* which follows the characters Pierce and Carrie respectively as they work to build lives outside of their powerful parents' legacies, and to untangle the mystery of the failing inn of Chimera Bay. A part of the inn is described:

> [h]uge windows overlooked the water, each framed with stained-glass panels depicting wild waves, cormorants and albatrosses, the frolicking whales and mermaids of the deep. The old glass was bubbled and wavery; passing boats and birds grew distorted in it. Sometimes, Carrie glimpsed odd things in the shipping channel through those windows: small ships with rounded hulls and

too many sails, or leaner vessels with ribbed sails that raked at an angle that might have crossed over from exotic seas where fish flew and wales had horns like unicorns just to visit Chimera Bay [29].

An authorial reading of the passage could involve an interview by McKillip (one that does not, at present, exist), or asking her intentions outright. Perhaps what I have described below is not what she intended, for the reader or critic, but it is one interpretation and thus of more importance, for this book, than an author's recollection. There is also the possibility that McKillip would have no memory of writing the particular passage mentioned, or that she would remember incorrectly, or have had no conscious thought other than of connecting one piece of writing to another. I chose this passage in *Kingfisher* because it is of no great significance to the plot or narrative of the story. *Kingfisher* would have been the same book without it, but it is in small moments like these that the fullness of the world is accomplished, and the expansion of the world can be usefully examined by the critic.

From the critical perspective, the world of *Kingfisher* is, like the glass, "wavery." What is real or not is purposely obtruded, and that is apparent in this small passage. In this quote primary world birds like cormorants are listed alongside more fantastical creatures like mermaids, as though they both could be equally real in that world (and in fact, one of the interesting things about the world of *Kingfisher* is that they might be, but neither the characters nor reader is sure of this at this point in the book). The glass has seen better days; it is "bubbled and wavery," which indicates that it is quite old, but the size and detail of the stained-glass indicate it was also costly. This implies that at some point there was wealth to be spent. Lastly, the things Carrie "glimpses" through the glass—are they real? Or not?

Critical world-building takes into account the entire novel in the analysis, including information about what the character and the location are like. Carrie is one of the most prosaic characters in the novel so it is unlikely she has let her imagination run away with her. A casual reader may not pay attention to the phrasing in a way that a critic, trained to pay attention to word choice and syntax and close reading, will. A reader could be led by the phrasing to think that it is a certainty that Carrie sees these ships through the windows. However, the critic, with their wider knowledge of the rest of the text, and their eye for detail, knows that Chimera Bay is both a backwater and a failing one at that, perhaps the bay would indeed have seen such far travelling ships, but it is unlikely that Carrie "sees" what is really there now. There are indications throughout the text that the Inn in which these windows are placed occasionally "remembers" how it once was, and windows do not always look into or out onto the current reality. A critic familiar with other work of McKillip's, or conversant with fantasy, is more likely to take note of these indicators. As a result, it is possible to conjecture that despite Carrie's prosaic personality, what she sees through the windows is likely to not actually be there. These exotic ships also demonstrate Carrie's knowledge of, or familiarity with, the sea; one of the ships has "too many" sails, something someone unfamiliar with ships would be unlikely to notice. It also tells you what sort of culture Carrie is a part of, one that is at least loosely western European-based. The junk as exotic indicates that these are not the usual ships found in Chimera Bay. The reader of fantastic literature will be even more likely than the reader of mimetic literature to "pass over" such words without notice, as part of the background flavor of the fantastic: exotic or odd is not unusual in fantasy. But, as a critic trained to pay close attention to words, I grasp the word "exotic" and put it into this context and think about what it might mean to the world. "It is the links, and the ways in which elements of the world interact or form by implication to build that world, that create fodder for the critic" (Ekman and Taylor 12), and all of these details can be ascertained by the critic but are unlikely to be flagged by the reader, someone who is reading for the description but without the sort of minute examination I have just subjected the passage to as a critic.

This is an examination of the passage through the lens of the dynamic interplay that I will use throughout the rest of the book, but there are other critical approaches that are available, and will sometimes be utilized as well. For example, a Marxist reading could focus on the signs of wealth displayed by the window, and the trade presumed by the presence of the ships. A critic focused on the mythic could look at the same passage and would likely be interested in the mermaid being listed with more ordinary primary-world creatures, and would be absorbed by the fact that "where wales had horns like unicorns" indicates that it is perhaps more unusual in this world for there to be horned wales than for unicorns to exist.

I have focused on many of the minutiae of the passage because an important aspect of the critical process, especially within fantasy, is a focus on detail. Wolfe indicates that "the objects, events, and beings that we encounter in this fantastic world—however impossible—must exist in a fullness of affect that enables us to respond to them as though they were real" ("Encountering" 75). This "fullness of affect" can be accomplished within fantastic world-building in a number of ways but I argue that detail is particularly important. The devil is in the details and, I would argue, at times so is the reality. One of McKillip's key strengths as a writer lies in how the details of her worlds shore up those worlds. Some of the many reviews of her work note, "McKillip creates a wonderful world ... magical yet realistic..." (*Las Vegas Review-Journal*), "her tale rings as true as if it were being told from memory" (*Kirkus Reviews*). Her worlds read as "true." In each chapter I will examine instances when the smallest of words or phrasings builds the reality of the world. These details are important to critical world-building just as much as to the texts themselves, because "[e]ach detail enters the context of previous details, implying things about them and having things implied about it in turn, thus forming, by implication" (Ekman and Taylor 14), the world as a whole and "connections and interactions ... determine how implications extend and change the world" (15). Details provide more than background to the critic; they are a vital part of the world, how it is constructed, and so how it can be interpreted.

Similarly, "implications" are important, and it is not just the instance of detail that must be noted, but what is left out as well. Steve Walker indicates that the worlds of Tolkien "tend always toward expansion of the possibilities of his world rather than toward reduction, raising more questions than they resolve" (10). That is, the reader can imagine a world opening up, without definitive knowledge of each aspect always being provided. Tolkien, like McKillip, uses small moments, small details, to shore the reality of the world without overburdening it with explanation. Many examples could come from McKillip's *The Throme of the Erril of Sherril*, in which McKillip does not go into detail about any of the legends presented. In this, the earliest of her secondary-world fantasies, there are no drawn-out descriptions of what any of the legends are. They simply exist, as is often the case in the primary world, where fairy-tales, for example, are often a shortcut for meaning. *The Throme of the Erril of Sherril* is the story of Caerles, sent on an impossible quest to find a legendary book in order to marry Damsen, daughter of the king. Legends are given in short form, as in this brief moment; "The seven spears rose, flashing like birds. 'We are the Seven Watchers of the child Elfwyth of the Erle Merle'" (27). The child Elfwyth has been introduced into the story as an ordinary child; it is therefore a surprise to the reader as well as the main character, the Cnite Caerles, that she has such importance. Very little else is said of her; we are not told why she must have Watchers, or why she is so important, but this small detail gives breadth to an otherwise quite short novel, and a sense of more world, with a past and culture all its own, even if it is one the reader does not see. *The Throme of the Erril of Sherril*, in spite of its length, still presents us with the depth and lyricism that is a feature of McKillip's works and it does so in a way that allows the world to "expand" outwards from what is, and is not, said.

I find "depth" useful in terms of world-building because it labels the feeling of more world that I argue McKillip does so well. If a world has depth it is, as Mendlesohn and James argue of Tolkien, as if when "you turn a corner in Middle-earth, you know that there will be more world there" (44). This assumption that there is more world beyond the written page can be an important part of effective world-building, in the sense of creating a complete fantasy world. I use depth rather than "width" or some other term because McKillip's worlds are rich in terms of their history, past, and archeology as well as their present action and settings.

Tolkien was extremely good at this sort of detail, and so is often cited as an example. In his essay "Tolkien, Lewis and the Explosion of Genre Fantasy" James suggests of Tolkien's remarkable attention to details, and his reader's clear appreciation of it, that "it is a crucial insight into what is needed to make a 'full' fantasy world, as complex and intriguing, and hence as believable, as our own" (66). This credibility is especially important to secondary worlds as otherwise there is little to anchor them in the primary world. That is not to say that all readers (or critics, for that matter) are convinced of the excellence of detail, or its importance to stories generally. Sibley notes that,

> Some people simply can't get to grips with an author who goes to such elaborate lengths in creating an entire history, geography, literature and language as background to a work of fiction. Ironically, it is just this feature of *The Lord of the Rings* that others find most appealing [8].

It is interesting that Sibley does not specify what sorts of people are likely to feel like this. In fact, it is likely to be a specific subset; either people who are not used to reading fantasy, and who would therefore consider the extra detail unnecessary made-up history, or people reading more casually, who would want the action to resume.[4] The critic familiar with fantasy and in particular secondary world fantasy knows that such a level of detail is important to this kind of world-building. I depart in a couple ways from Wolf, however, when he contends that "[f]or works in which world-building occurs, there may be a wealth of details and events (or mere mentions of them) which do not advance the story but which provide background richness and verisimilitude to the imaginary world" (2). My initial point of contention is that all fiction contains world-building, whether an intentional focus, secondary world, mimetic or not. Secondly, although I agree a "wealth of details and events" provides "background richness and verisimilitude" I would argue that these do advance the narrative to an extent, whether this is overt or not. As argued above details are an integral part of world-building, and the minutest of happenings might not overtly refer to the plot but could be (and often is, especially in an author like McKillip) part of presenting clues, inferences, or other small instances of story progression, even if not actively marked by the reader.

Critical World-Building

My approach to world-building, one of it being a holistic network of connections that interact with each other, is especially useful with McKillip, whose texts' very density means that picking apart threads, one from the other, is often both difficult and too simplistic. Her writing rewards a critical reading. Reviewers call her works "intricate" (*Chicago Sun-Times*), "complex" (*Booklist*), and many critics (Attebery, Clute, Mains, Ringel, among them) and other authors have noted the same. McKillip largely avoids or subverts typical plot, characters, and other hallmarks of templated fantasy. There is always more to explore, to detect, and to puzzle over in her works. Imaginative worlds are one of the hallmarks of her works, and as a result, their examination as interconnected entities of different themes is important. A critical examination of world-building in fantasy, however, involves not just the speculative elements of a world; it is wider than setting, or characters, or any other single element. It includes the glass-domed house of Sybel in the *Forgotten Beasts of Eld*, her lover, Coren, and how he knows her creatures without having seen them before. It includes the legends that surround the beasts, and more besides. Thus, it includes landscape, the characters that populate it and how they interact with and are expected to interact with the world, and the mythologies that pin the world together. It includes all these things, and more, and, perhaps most importantly, how they all tie together to create the illusion of a separate world, one that, in Tolkien's terms, the reader can enter into.

Having scrutinized world-building closely each chapter takes a thematic look at those elements of McKillip's world-building that I deem most important. There are, of course, a number of other ways in which McKillip's worlds might be critically approached, but these are four components to the worlds that I believe warrant a closer inspection, and most of the chapters consider at least one (with the last two chapters splitting one theme). While I do not use the framework outlined by Wolf (154), he does touch on the necessary infrastructure for building fantasy worlds so I adapted some of his terms and concepts to use in my analysis of McKillip's work. I have moved away from Wolf's more temporal focus to try and show how the various worlds of McKillip interact, in Wolf's terms; for instance, the setting might be Natural, but in McKillip's work it also has elements of the mythic and temporal, complicating Wolf's framework. I also escape from Wolf's framework with the second chapter, on expectations. This seems to be outside of Wolf's conception of a world, but is important to how a world is conceived, created, and experienced, especially in a genre like fantasy, where readers tend to be familiar with certain characteristics. As Ekman and I note, "[t]he critic ... brings to the building of a world a familiarity with other worlds in terms of structures and tropes, clichés and traditions [thus constructing] the world in a wider context, seeing parallels with other worlds within and outside of the genre" (12), so this familiarity is important to consider.

I discuss aspects of the Material world (things like landscapes, vegetation, creatures), the Social world (characters, their creations and their relations, i.e., their social systems), the Temporal world (history, the world's past), and the Mythological world (legends, stories, gods, mythoi). Each group carries distinct characteristics, but an author like McKillip, whose works entwine in so many different ways, inevitably works with more than one at once, thus I do not attempt to keep them strictly separate. This examination of several groupings is particularly relevant, however, because there is a tendency to mistake the Material group for all there is to a world, or even just parts of it (landscapes, for instance) but in my analysis I take all four, and sometimes more, into account.[5]

These major groups of elements, interrelated and ultimately inseparable, come with some clear differences. I start from those general frames that impact on how McKillip's world has been set up; the expectations that we bring to a work with regards to genre, and the gender and age of characters. These expectations shape both how the worlds are moved through, and how or whether a reader might be surprised by their construction. I then move towards the more specific aspects of McKillip's work, such as the legends she includes (and why they are important specifically to McKillip's world-building) and her settings. This enables a discussion of several of the elements that comprise McKillip's worlds, moving from the pervasive structures to the more specific aspects of those worlds.

In the next chapter I continue to consider expectations specific to fantasy literature in order to study how genre staples are used to build the world. I review how I use tropes, before moving on to survey common expectations of fantasy world-building and their associated fantasy tropes. Stereotypical and expected tropes are often played with in McKillip's texts, allowing for rich, imaginative new worlds. Lastly, I look at how McKillip's worlds need a more literal interpretation than is sometimes required. This is all considered in the light of the kind of worlds that predominate in fantasy literature, and how McKillip's worlds negotiate and challenge these parameters.

In Chapter Three I investigate the Social world, with a look at how characters function as a part of world-building. As Wolf notes, "defining 'world' in an experiential sense requires someone to be the recipient of experiences" (154). Characters can thus be said to inhabit the world while constituting part of it. Characters are constrained in many ways in fantasy (just as people are in the real world) but in McKillip age and gender are central. Gender norms and stereotypes are well researched both in literature and the primary world and I scrutinize some of these and how McKillip's characters move beyond these usual expectations to create richer, more dynamic worlds. Age too constrains characters and people, and this is analyzed both separately and with gender. An exploration of how age and gender work in the primary world and within fiction allows a further examination of how McKillip's worlds are made more realistic and balanced.

In Chapter Four I focus on the legends that reside within the Mythological world as well as the Temporal and Cultural world frames. McKillip's worlds are distinguished by their richness and one of the main techniques that contribute to this depth is the use of legends, as they add a sense of age, overt history, and the texture of a foreign culture to her stories. McKillip's legends are therefore part of both the Temporal and Mythological worlds. Her legends are scrutinized in light of the worlds that contain them and how these legends both function in, and are crucial to, her invented worlds.

Although I argue that world-building is more than setting, setting is important and is investigated in chapters Five and Six, as part of the Material world. Each of these sections looks at setting but is far more than an examination of place within McKillip. The way in which each type of setting impacts on the worlds, or vice versa, is my focus.

Texts I have termed "pastoral" are studied in Chapter Five. Although the Material world is naturally of importance to a chapter on setting, so too is the Temporal and even the Social and Mythological worlds in McKillip. In this chapter I discuss whether McKillip is a pastoral writer; if she is, what does this tell us about her use of setting and also about how she sees man/woman's role in nature; and those human-made habitats, cities, and even politics and power? In other words, how does the landscape inform her worlds and her works as a whole? I investigate how McKillip's worlds use the conventions of the genre while opening up the typical city/country dualism. Pastoral elements set up McKillip's varied worlds, not only in terms of landscape but also values and attitudes towards nature.

In Chapter Six I move on to the argument that although McKillip is largely a pastoral writer, her cities provide a useful glimpse of how her worlds are built. In McKillip's cities the Historical, Material, and the Mythological all intertwine. These cities have various eras layered on top of one another, to create places with complex histories and featuring intricate political machinations, all of which offers a richer world. While there is a great deal of advice on how to build a fantastic city, and a plethora of books on how cities in the real world function, there is very little examination of how cities function in a world-building sense within a text, and this chapter rectifies this lack in small part by investigating the cities of McKillip's worlds.

The core theoretical argument of this book is that world-building is a useful critical lens. McKillip is used as an example both because she is generally understudied, but more importantly, because she creates new worlds that always give the impression that there is more world around the corner. In the following chapters I use world-building as a critical lens, but I also use what I find to grind the unfinished lens of world-building itself. The components of McKillip's secondary worlds will be examined: landscape, characters, stories, but interwoven with that is a study of tone, values, and choices, all of which come together to form McKillip's built secondary worlds.

Two

Fantasy Conventions

Critical world-building involves more than simply examining physical attributes like setting; it also encompasses elusive elements like expectations. This chapter contains an investigation of tropes, fantasy expectations and literalization. I consider these not strictly from an author's or reader's perspective, but within the frame of world-building, and consider how McKillip uses, and sometimes discards, tropes and other fantasy expectations in order to either subvert or uphold a reader's expectations of a fantasy world.

It is important to note that in this chapter when I say "reader" I mean an implied, perhaps ideal, reader, one who is aware of the fantasy genre and most of its common tropes and typical story types. This is within the parameters of critical world-building. As Ekman and I explain, a critical examination of world building:

> takes into account the hermeneutical building of a world that is performed by a reader, but the reader in question is generally a function in the text, an "implied" reader ... or simply an ideal reader who understands and reacts to information in the text as we, the critics, would have them do [11].

The implied reader, in this case, is familiar with common elements of fantasy literature. Many of McKillip's texts require some knowledge of the genre. As Howey argues for *The Changeling Sea*, "the novel depends, to a certain extent, on readers' recognition of such motifs and the expectations they create" (42). The examination of tropes and other typical elements of fantasy are integral to world-building because it gives an idea of the assumptions the reader might make, and how these expectations are either fulfilled or subverted within the world. These tropes and expectations are also important because they allow an author to "fill-in" a world without a great deal of description.

Tropes

Fantasy, especially a particular type of fantasy, has been accused of having rote formulas and simplistic fictions, but like all literature it has its good and bad examples. Attebery begins *Strategies of Fantasy* with two definitions of fantasy, one of which reads "[f]antasy is a form of popular escapist literature that combines stock characters and devices—wizards, dragons, magic swords, and the like—into a predictable plot in which the perennially understaffed forces of good triumph over a monolithic evil" (1). He goes on to contend that fantasy literature contains this and offers a second definition encompassing "a sophisticated mode of storytelling." I would push this point a step farther: not only is fantasy a literature of both "formula and mode" but it is one in which the same author can use both. McKillip is one such author using many of the "stock characters and devices" which I have grouped here as tropes, but in a way that allows her worlds to be rich, not merely formulaic, places. Tropes represent one of the main ways that authors of speculative fiction can summarize world elements quickly, but authors can also create surprising worlds by overturning tropes or using them in unexpected ways. Ringel proposes that the authors of fantasy, "[l]ike other postmodernists, [] depend on readers' familiarity with their tropes—in this case the tropes shaped by Tolkien" ("Women" 163; Howey makes a similar argument 42), and I expand this to include fantasy tropes more generally (though many have descended from Tolkien's work, as will be discussed).

Expectations are one of the building blocks of a world, and tropes are integral to this in a genre like fantasy, one which is full of "the cauldron of story" (Tolkien). World-building is expanded beyond more traditionally considered elements such as location, by Wolf, as well as myself, who notes that "[t]he term 'world,' as it is being used here, is not simply geographical but *experiential*; that is, everything that is experienced by the characters involved" (25). In McKillip's work this results, from the critic's perspective, in an examination of both how these expectations are upheld, and where what are likely to be surprises to the reader are presented. These surprises are one of the ways that McKillip keeps her worlds fresh and varied.

In literature the trope is usually defined as being rhetorical figures of speech such as metaphor and irony (Chandler and Munday) but it has also come to have the meaning of cliché in common parlance; that is, a negative term for something that has been overused (McArthur). It is this second meaning that I focus on when discussing "tropes" in fantasy literature. When I use the term "trope" I mean it as a shortcut for the common sorts of stories or characters found in fairy-tale, fantasy, and sometimes pop-culture at large. This form of trope is occasionally discussed as "archetype," and while I explore my reasons for using "trope" below, archetype has been used in relation to McKillip's work. Mains, for example, explains "[t]he realm of Faerie, as another archetypal symbol, carries with it certain connotations, qualities ascribed to it in its many incarnations in works of fantasy and in the fairy tales and legends that are their source" ("Having" 107). These "connotations" are what I, too, examine, though I have chosen to do so through the frame of tropes, rather than seeing them as archetypes. Part of world-building is expectation, and tropes, similar to archetypes, are a collection of expectations held by readers, and worked with by authors, built up over a period of time and occasionally added to, and thus one of many elements that build a world.

Trope and archetype are occasionally used interchangeably, and while a useful distinction should sometimes be made, many of the stock characteristics of archetype are applicable to trope as well. Joseph Campbell's famous *The Hero with a Thousand Faces* explores many of the common story or character types prevalent in cultures around the world—the hero, of course, being of particular interest to Campbell (the male hero, it must be clarified. Campbell provided few examples of women archetypes or stories, as explored by Mains and others, and this is tackled further in Chapter Three). In examining the character of the "tyrant-monster" Campbell gives a general definition for his other character types as well, "[t]he figure of the tyrant-monster is known to the mythologies, folk traditions, legends, and even nightmares of the world; and his characteristics are everywhere essentially the same" (15). This definition is similar to popular descriptions of both tropes and archetypes, as things universal and knowable in many forms and cultures, as part of the "furniture of the mind." Archetypes, according to Carl Jung, are repeated motifs (449). Tropes do, in some ways, act as archetypes. They provide broader meaning to a story, and can serve as a shortcut to significance. Tropes, like archetypes, are also widespread. They are often transferable. Lists of archetypes could easily be renamed "tropes" in fantasy, for example: "Examples of archetypes include the wise old woman, the witch, the divine child, the young hero (or heroine) sent on a quest, helpful animals, a walled castle, the wasteland, the dying king, shape-shifting, tricksters, dragons and unicorns" (Tuttle 22). Each of these can and has been treated as a trope as well as archetype.

Although I have chosen to use some of the research connected with archetype, I have also chosen not to use the term itself. This is because archetype has a weightier meaning than I intend. Although some psychology will be viewed in relation to tropes, I do not want my discussion to be derailed into examinations of myth or the human unconscious. A certain weight of historical baggage is another reason to avoid archetype, and other phrases associated with Jung, Freud, and Campbell, in spite of their redemptive helpfulness. Their ideas, especially Campbell's, were generally only universal to a white, western world, or as interpreted by such. Bettina L. Knapp contends that "[a]rchetypal analysis takes the literary work out of its individual and conventional context and relates it to humankind in general" (x). This definition of archetypal analysis is handy because it is this type of examination that I am *not* doing. I am, in fact, doing the opposite. That is, it is not just the close association with Jungian psychology that I want to avoid, and all that entails, but it is also that I am taking general conventions and examining their particular uses. Although many of the tropes that I look at can also be scrutinized as archetypes, I will refer to them as tropes, and treat them as such. This is not to contend that conversations about archetypes in fantasy are not useful, they are simply not what I focus on here.

It is advantageous to keep in mind that archetype itself has become a more rigid term than Jung originally intended. Susan Rowland maintains that "[t]he archetype as such, as a potential structure, contains numerous possibilities within itself" (30). This idea of archetype as potential structure, rather than definite object or image, is useful when considering tropes and other common derivatives of story as well. This more flexible interpretation is helpful when analyzing authors like McKillip. I use trope advisedly, but find that lists of "archetypes" can often be good examples of tropes as well.

Tropes have a negative reputation because they imply copying and little originality, but they also serve a purpose. Susan Sellers looks at myth and fairy-tale, but it equally works for tropes when she notes that stories give us an important way to talk to and understand other people (vii). Tropes play a similar role but in a more compact form. Their use provides a shortcut for meaning, and a way of connecting readers quickly to familiar material.

Elizabeth Barry argues for cliché, but it works similarly for the term "trope" as I use it, that, "[i]n the wake of the demise of classical authority certain assumptions persist through habit alone, repeated but unexamined" (1). This is where trope, like cliché, can become perilous. When tropes are repeated but not probed they then become a formula that is difficult to escape. They naturalize assumptions and make it seem as though this is the way the world is, and will always be. Tropes can be dangerous in that they can cement a certain type of story or ending as fact. Caroline Webb presents us with a case for escapism, but it works equally well for trope, that

> [t]his version of escapism involves the reader mistaking what is said in the book: believing that it is true. To fall into this trap need not involve accepting the story as literal truth, although that is a possibility. Rather, the reader may be misled by the pattern of the story, especially by reading stories with similar patterns, into believing that certain solutions to problems are inevitable [2].

This is relevant not just to whole stories, but to parts of stories, or even so small a part of a story as a trope can be, but it also extends to the world at large. The world in which a trope plays out can either challenge, or embrace, a trope. In McKillip, for example, Ringel, using the term "archetype," points out that the main character of *Winter Rose* "[i]n an archetypal reversal, [] is the quest hero who saves the enchanted Prince" ("Women" 169). McKillip's worlds allow these reversals to be possible. Much has been written on the problem of archetypes such as "the wise old woman," and this is addressed in Chapter Three. However, the same issues can be seen within certain tropes. The damsel-in-distress trope will be reviewed in detail below, for example, and many of the books that use this trope indicate that there is no way the damsel can effect her own escape.

Authors like McKillip can take tropes and twist them, which would not be possible without the expectations provided by the tropes as characteristic patterns. Many of the "typical" tropes of fantasy literature emerged from their inclusion in *The Lord of the Rings* and its subsequent imitators. This does not mean that they are included in every work of fantasy (or even every derivative work of fantasy). McKillip, for example, does not use dwarves or elves, both fantasy staples, even in her most Tolkienesque series, *The Riddle-Master* trilogy. She does have fairies, and here she stays with the trope of the wise, frightening and otherworldly fay in the character of the fairy queen in *The Book of Atrix Wolfe*. It is this, that McKillip does include typical fantasy tropes, that allows her diversions to be so powerful.

A demonstration of McKillip's use, and abuse, of trope and what this does for the world might be beneficial at this point. A trope of fantasy (and folklore) is the selkie who has been trapped and prevented from returning to their seal shape. In McKillip's *The Tower at Stony Wood* the character that is gradually revealed to be a selkie has willingly come to land, and has willingly stayed there, but this has created complications within her psyche, arising from the fact that she does long for her original home, is homesick, but has willingly stayed on land and as a human for her human daughters. *The Tower at Stony Wood* as a whole follows the noble but impoverished knight of Yves, Cyan Dag, on a quest to save his king from what he thinks is marriage to a monstrous sorceress (whose double is locked away in a tower, Lady-of-Shalott style). Along the way he encounters Sel the baker (the selkie trapped in a human life), her wild daughter Melanthos, and enemy of Gloinmere, Thayne Ysse, of the subjugated land of Ysse, all of whom get their own chapters throughout the book. The character Sel will be investigated in more depth in Chapter Five, but what is significant here is that a fairly clichéd character type has been broadened, giving it, and the character it defines, greater psychological depth. This in turn expands McKillip's world.

What is important too from a world-building perspective is that Sel has a past beneath the sea that is intimated but not explored in depth. Sel is introduced as human, and only as the story moves forward, and the world opens up, do flashes of her former life begin to come out. This affects two things in particular. One is that Sel seems ordinary, at least initially. But too, Sel's own burgeoning longing for home is emphasized by pieces of her past life surfacing to haunt her. There are only flashes of Sel's memory, as when she remembers her magic: "all the magic flowed like tide into her, catching light, dark tumbling within it, nameless creatures and unimaginably beautiful treasures" (166) which means that there is an intimation of more world without the details. This memory gives the briefest glimpse of what Sel's magic, and former home, must be like, and they are mixed up together; the magic is "like tide." That the seas of McKillip's world are just as magical and full of life as the rest of her world can then be inferred but without taking up story space with what is, in the end, irrelevant to the main plot. Sel is presented fairly prosaically: "the baker lumbered her slow, implacable way down the cobbled street between bakery and the tavern" (85), and yet, there are hints that she is not quite so ordinary a baker as she seems: "[h]er eyes, wide set like a fish's, were kelp dark, hiding thoughts and stray flecks of color deep in them" (86). The "wide set" of her fish-like eyes, "kelp," even the color that does not quite show itself are all reminiscent of the sea, and of seals. Sel is presented with uncertainty, someone clearly caught between the sea and the land but in a richer way than is typical of selkies found in folklore or the trope of the selkie trying to return home. Sel is undecided about returning and as a result her very looks are ambivalent, human but faintly other, with distinct references to the sea. Her husband has been taken in a fishing accident, presumably releasing her back to her seal-life, and yet, it is far more complicated than that. Sel ruminates on how she first found herself beached both metaphorically and literally in her now human body, "Sel, wanting to be as human as Joed, wanting to be loved, kept her secrets. She had not understood then, that Joed might leave her stranded, beached, alone in the world while he himself escaped into the sea" (202). The story, while remaining the same in its basics, has been changed. It is Sel who is left alone and forsaken on land, not the typical grieving husband, and she is kept on land not by magic, chiefly, but by the complications of love and being human. Hixon argues that Sel is ambivalent because she does not want to commit fully to the love and loss ubiquitous to human identity (197). But I would contend that it is the human aspects of loving and not wanting to lose someone that keep Sel human, and that prevent her from returning to her seal form. Not only is Sel-as-a-selkie turned into a more complex story through the interweaving of different aspects of the world, but the effect that she has on others is interrogated as well. Her grown children discuss the ramifications of their mother's increasingly puzzling behavior: "'She's fey' ... 'You say that. But you never really mean it.... Besides, what does it mean, exactly?' 'Magic.' 'I mean what does it mean to us if she is?'" (*Tower* 182) Neither daughter can really answer, but it poses the question to the trope as a whole as well. Beyond the trope, and the story, what is the effect of this particular kind of homesickness? In Chapter Five some of the ramifications of homesickness will be explored, but it is relevant here too as it is the consequence of the unseen parts of stories. Different parts of the world tie together and influence each other, creating both a richer story, and a lusher world.

Stories from the primary world are sometimes brought into the secondary world and given life there (by which I mean they are made factual in the secondary world). Occasionally this follows the expected patterns and behaviors, sometimes it does not, just as in the primary world expectations are not always met. T.E. Little claims that "[w]riters often make real in their Secondary World the legends of Primary existence" (107). While I will study legend in more depth in Chapter Four this holds true of tropes (and as such—archetypes as well). Tennyson's poem "The Lady of Shalott," for example, has become a trope in its own right: the woman trapped in a tower, waiting to be set free. In McKillip this trope is twisted in *The Tower at Stony Wood* (for a discussion on the poem itself and how this shapes the narrative, see "The Lady of Shalott as Paradigm in Patricia McKillip's *The Tower at Stony Wood*" by Hixon). As Hixon notes, "McKillip draws on this emblematic nature of the trapped Lady in her tower to examine those same issues from a twentieth-century lens" (195) and this "emblematic" nature means that a reader familiar with the key features of the poem, a woman trapped in a tower, will expect a similar lack of escape for the lady in McKillip's work. In *The Tower at Stony Wood*, for much of the story the lady trapped in the tower is, as usual, voiceless, watched by other characters through a mirror but without a story or voice of her own. The woman in the tower's viewpoint or story is not revealed until much later in the book and all that can be initially surmised is based on expectations of story, of the princess waiting to be rescued, in a tower specifically, something the characters as well as the reader are obviously aware of. Melanthos and Sel, watching the woman grow more and more impatient in subtle ways, at last bring the story to the fore. Melanthos remarks, "[s]he'd get rescued in the tale. That's how they end" (164). But, as usual, this is not a flat, traditional retelling, and McKillip's worlds are more complicated than this could imply. Sel responds to Melanthos' wondering if the woman is real, in a tale, or both, by saying, "[m]aybe ... she's gotten tired of waiting" (164). Towards the end of the

Two. Fantasy Conventions

book the woman in the tower at last changes her pattern of behavior from aimlessly embroidering what she sees out her window to embroidering words, and her inaction becomes action. Melanthos responds, "[w]ell, think about it. If you're caught in a web and can't move—if every line trapping you is a magic not your own—how could you spin magic out of yourself?" (164). The characters puzzle through the story of the Lady of Shalott, giving the woman a voice and alternatives when she does not seem to have any beyond passive rescue. Melanthos sees the transformation from story into reality, and it is marked, she is:

> compelled not by the woman's burning image but by her face, no longer a beautiful, nameless, thoughtless face out of story, but the face of a desperate woman threading her needle with hope, trying to work magic into her stitches, to transform the world that trapped her [177].

Melanthos has seen the woman behind the story, and in the end the woman is able to free herself. "She's made a picture of herself for the mirror to see, something that will sit and embroider forever and never leave" (216). The woman in the tower has not only rescued herself, she has left behind in the story the literal version of what she is meant to be, silent, unable to leave, occupied with the "womanish" craft of embroidery. Not only has the story come to life, but its ending has taken on a new life as well, while, crucially, remaining the same. The world has allowed for a feminist retelling to be constructed around an old and chauvinistic tale. The woman in the tower is allowed a voice, but her would-be rescuer is also given dimensions beyond the ordinary heroics required of the rescuer. Cyan does the expected; he crashes through walls and brings down a door to get to her, but, more importantly, in the eyes of the woman trapped in the tower:

> You looked at me.... They knew I was here.... Knights pointed to my window, told one another about me.... I was cursed, they guessed; I would die if I looked past the mirror.... I was some magical, fey being, fit to tell stories about to pass the time of day, to wonder about and pity.... You were the only one who ever saw that I was real, and came to help me [252].

By bringing the story to life, and filling it and the world that contains it with details, the story is questioned, the boundaries that keep women silent, presumably waiting to be rescued, unable to rescue themselves are interrogated. The story is a feminist revision but importantly it transforms the male rescuer's role as well within the traditional trope. The lady in the tower says to Cyan, "[i]f I looked at the world I would die. If the world looked at me, saw me with courage and compassion, and reached out to help me—how could I not live? How could that not make me free?" (252–253). It takes more than Cyan's brute strength or even courage; he must have compassion as well, thus also freeing him from the typical trope of rescuer. The world of *The Tower at Stony Wood* is instrumental in allowing this subversion of a common trope. It is a world constructed to allow women their own agency, but also one in which men too have more options than is usual.

The reworking of tropes is shown in other ways as well. Sarah LeFanu suggests, "[i]n literature, it seems to me, an act of revolution can be achieved only through a subversion of the narrative structure that holds the protagonist in place: a gender reversal is not enough" (35). Both this gender reversal and subversion of narrative structure is accomplished with the representation of wizards in McKillip's worlds. In Brian Stableford's *Historical Dictionary of Fantasy Literature*, the entry for "wizard" states: "A practitioner of magic, usually a male of considerable academic attainment and social status (unlike witches)." The female wizards of *The Forgotten Beasts of Eld* and the *Cygnet* duology begin as stereotypical wizards, cold and completely academic, like their male counterparts, but, crucially, they are able to grow and change, whereas many of their male counterparts within their stories cannot (for a further discussion of this see Mains' "Having"). At the beginning of *The Forgotten Beasts of Eld* Sybel, the main character, lives alone, surrounded by legendary creatures that her father collected and some that she has subsequently caught. Content with searching for more creatures and knowledge, Sybel's life is disrupted by the arrival of a knight, Coren, who brings her a kinswoman's baby to rear. As the boy grows, the outside world begins to invade Sybel's space until she is forced to enter the world of men and politics. Sybel is presented through descriptions that intimate both great beauty and also coldness: "ivory" hair and "black eyes" (6). Her first actions, as she prepares to have a stranger thrown off a mountainside without a word because he has interrupted her studies, too, intimate an emotional coldness. Her pure search for knowledge is all that is important to her and this is made clear immediately. We meet Nyx in *The Sorceress and the Cygnet* (part of the *Cygnet* duology) in an even more terrible fashion: her pursuit of knowledge has led her to taking bird wings and tongues (44), and seeing through the eyes of the dead, in a distinctly creepy beginning.

That the women wizards are able to defeat the male wizards in McKillip's books is key, but so too is how they are able to do so. In "Having It All: The Female Hero's Quest for Love and Power in Patricia McKillip's *The Riddle-Master* Trilogy" Christine Mains notes that even their presence is unusual (24). "Womanly" traits of caring are shown not as their downfall, as is so often the case. Rather, these traits broaden them and their experiences so that when they do go against the stereotypical wizards they are able to expose them for the cold men they are, and defeat them in their own milieu. The texts present the wizards as female, but they have also been expanded, their narratives changed and widened, so that they are free from the typical constraints that hold their male counterparts. They interact with, and are influenced by, the worlds around them in varying ways, leading to different endings and characters than might be expected. For instance, Nyx is influenced both by other characters for whom she comes to care, but also by the landscapes she explores. The Luxour desert of *The Cygnet and the Firebird* intrigues her, challenges her, and forces her to fight for her own, but also, crucially, for others' survival.

A trope that Nyx encounters, that changes her, are the dragons of the Luxour. Dragons are a common fantasy trope, but several of McKillip's texts play with expectations of them. Barry argues for Samuel Beckett's use of cliché but her comments can be usefully applied to McKillip's tropes, her dragons, in that they are: "repetition with a difference, the familiar phrase in a newly engineered form or an unexpected context, that works both to critique and to rejuvenate the medium of language" (2). Portrayals of fantasy tropes, are presented "with a difference," either in how the dragons (or other tropes) are dealt with or presented, but, crucially, enough of the trope is kept to enable them to be recognized *as* a trope. The "unexpected context" is also important as it is often how the tropes interact or are influenced by the world around them that lifts them out of their traditional form. Like Beckett, McKillip has not done away with "tired" language altogether; she has rejuvenated it, and the stories and worlds that contain it. The dragons, on the surface, do appear to be the fire-breathing horrors of traditional fantasies. What lies within the seemingly ordinary dragon skin, however, is very different. Nor are dragons treated in the same way across all of McKillip's books. For example, the dragons in *The Cygnet and the Firebird* are very different to the dragons that appear in *The Tower at Stony Wood*.

Each reflects other aspects of the story and the worlds in which they appear, rather than relying on traditional motifs to flesh them out. The dragon in *The Tower at Stony Wood* echoes the twisting, uncertain nature of the narrative as a whole; even which country it appears in is not made quite clear. In spite of being described in piecemeal fashion it appears a typical fantasy dragon, both beautiful and dangerous:

> Thayne Ysse saw himself reflected in the dragon's eye. The eye itself was enormous, a pool of liquid gold circled by dry, rough ridges of scale and skin. A very thin, pointed oval of dark slit the gold from top to bottom; paler streaks of gold rayed away from it. Thayne was a splinter of something human within the dark [105].

The descriptors, especially the repetition of gold, are typical of a dragon, while its dry, cracked skin is reminiscent of the deserts it is meant to haunt. In the end, the dragon is discovered to be nothing but the tool of a witch. Here the characters first begin to realize that all is not what it seems: "Some impulse from the dragon made him turn.... Sel felt it, too, as she lingered in the queen's gentle grasp: the glance of a dark eye out of the dragon's mind" (281). The witch has turned herself into a dragon in order to expedite the healing of two of the lands and their characters. But it is because the dragon is such a common fantasy trope, so fully realized in the book in a myriad of ways, that it comes as a great surprise to all that the dragon has been a person in disguise. There is nothing human about the dragon, it is presented as undoubtedly a dragon, an alien fantastical being. However, it is significant that near the beginning of his quest Cyan comments of the witch's (in)convenient absence, "[o]f course not.... Like your dragons, she vanishes every time I look for her" (69). The dragons are all of a piece and all, in a sense, part of the same tale, though they do not seem so to Cyan (and thus the reader) for most of the book. Having seen the dragon he has imagined brought to "life" embroidered onto a piece of cloth,

> Cyan blinked, suddenly remembering Thayne Ysse's dragon. But that was another tale, he decided tiredly, another tower ... he might have entered Skye, but Cyan guessed that even the smoldering Lord of Ysse, with all his dangerous intentions, would have trouble riding onto a plain made of thread [68].

As will be discussed below McKillip's worlds are often literal in their interpretations. As a result Cyan really ought to be worried, as Thayne Ysse does, in fact, manage to ride onto the plain of embroidery (as

Cyan too is able to in the end). The dragon changes from something embroidered (both onto cloth and into a story) as well as something imagined into something real, and then into an illusion once again at the end. Thayne, searching as literally for dragons as he is able, "scented for sulfur on the wind, for charred earth and bone, for gold" (75). However, when he dreams of the dragon it is a vaguer thing than he has consciously looked for: "The dragon possessed his dreams that night: a bright, sinuous, deadly thing that tore out his heart with the flick of one claw and swallowed it" (78). Here the dragon is undoubtedly made of tropes; both deadly and mysterious, but also tied into the landscape from which it comes, and the lore of the land it appears out of.

The dragons in *The Cygnet and the Firebird* reflect the mysterious nature of the land that Nyx and her cousin Meguet find themselves in. *The Cygnet and the Firebird* concerns a sorcerer who comes looking for an object he thinks is kept at Ro Holding (to which Nyx is the heir); he has not expected any resistance so is surprised at Nyx's power and Meguet's seemingly non-magical resistance to his spells. Nyx's curiosity eventually results in Meguet being transported back to the sorcerer's country, and Nyx having to follow them. Nyx then becomes entangled in the problems of the sorcerer's country and this results in Meguet having to follow and try to protect her, out of a timeless sense of duty. The world of the Luxour in *The Cygnet and the Firebird* is presented as one entire; the creatures it births are undoubtedly of that land, intimating an entire ecology that the reader does not need to see to appreciate. The dragons are seen through the eyes of the characters, and nothing is properly explained, just as the characters themselves lack full understanding. It is left to the reader and critic, and the characters whose eyes they use, to decide how much is reality and how much desert illusion. When Meguet is first magicked into the Luxour desert:

> Above her, a shadow blocked the sun. She looked up. The sun had vanished; an odd mass of air had swallowed a piece of sky overhead. She could not see what hovered; it was nothing, of no substance, but it cast a shadow all around her. She forced her eyes down finally, not wanting to look, but seeing it, black and clean-lined in the light: the shape of the little white-winged dragon of thread, but huge enough to swallow the sun [274].

At this moment Meguet is too worried about her own survival to comment on what she has just seen, to analyze it as truth or not, and so the reader too is left uncertain. The passage is full of contradictions.

"It was nothing," "of no substance," "could not see," all indicate something that is not there. Black and yet invisible, little but also huge. Megeut could be merely suffering from sunstroke, and therefore be bewildered. After all, even when she looks down she sees it as though she is imagining it. And yet, the text does not allow it to be mere allusion, or for there to be an assumption that Meguet is out of her mind (her next, practical, actions belie this).

Meguet and Nyx are presented with pieces of dragons, illusions of dragons, but it is only towards the end of the book that they are definitively shown a dragon. Even then, all is not what it seems. The dragon is evidently a mage of great power, and as such is able to shapeshift into a human that can be talked to and, almost, reasoned with but, like the dragon from *The Tower at Stony Wood*, it is also beyond human thought, clearly a fantastical being. Even Nyx, powerful sorceress though she is, has trouble making it comprehend how "human names, human dreams" could mean everything to her, even if they are "[a] dust storm. A random shift of rock" (*Firebird* 372) to the dragon.

The almost-dragons reflect the confusing nature of the land Nyx and Meguet find themselves in, and are reflective of the mirage qualities of a desert in turn. A woman Meguet stumbles upon in the desert compares the dragons and the land itself. "It lies. It says: *Once I was this, search me, find who built me.* So you search ... oh they're like the dragons, these old stones. They never say yes or no, but always maybe" (313). To people who have lived in mostly wet environments the desert is an alien, inhospitable place, and the text reflects this in Meguet's thought of it as an "exuberant, deadly place" (275). Even the book's descriptions do not clearly point to one thing or another, to dragons or their landscape. For instance:

> The next day [Meguet] walked into the dragon's heart. It was vast, golden, seething with hidden fires that blazed within stone, sand, shadow. Plumes of steam blurred the landscape, were snatched up and shredded by winds that blasted from the dragon's mouth. Mud bubbled and belched; the ground hissed [314].

It is not clear until the last sentence that Meguet has metaphorically walked into the dragon's heart, but the world of the Luxour does not allow even that to be clear. With the carefully chosen descriptors of "golden," "seething," "fires that blazed," "plumes," "shredded," "hissed," the text has intimated a literal dragon. Because the landscape and the dragon are confused it is not possible to be absolutely sure that Meguet has not, in fact, walked into a dragon's heart. After all, it does not say that Meguet walked into something like a dragon's heart, or that it appeared that way, and by this point in the novel we know that Meguet is a very astute young woman. Her vision, her descriptions, would not be vague because she has not noticed details but rather because she has. She knows the irregularities of the Luxour, knows that there is a possibility it is full of dragons, or is a dragon in and of itself. As discussed below, it is dangerous to assume literal descriptions are metaphor or allegory in McKillip's texts. The Luxour is a complicated place, and the dragons that might or might not inhabit it are complicated as well. In this way, typical fantasy tropes, dragons, become a rich way of fleshing out the world.

In the above examples the texts have used trope in their traditional form, while allowing them to reflect and comment on the rest of the narratives and worlds as a whole. The entry on the Dragon in Jones' *The Tough Guide to Fantasyland* (which often features a dragon on the cover, so ubiquitous are they in fantasy) has many of the fundamentals of the dragons in McKillip's books: "Dragons are very large scaly beings with wings and long spiky tails, capable of breathing fire through their mouths.... They are always very old.... They are very wise and can do MAGIC of a type not known to other MAGIC USERS. But they do not have human emotions" (79–80). McKillip's dragons are decidedly dragon-like but they also serve a wider purpose in the stories in which they appear. From a world-building perspective they work both as tropes, and something more. The fact that they are traditional tropes allows the reader to build certain expectations. Some of these expectations are met—the dragons look as they ought, for example—but others come as a surprise, such as the shape-shifting of the dragons.

Fantasy Expectations

Expectations of a genre allow readers familiar with that genre to fill in the gaps of their own accord (Wolf 50–51). In fantasy, if you mention a dragon it is assumed it will be a large beast that perhaps breathes fire. These expectations allow the reader to provide world-building outside of the text. If they expect something they are able to fill in other details around it without the author having to explicitly say so. This works to provide a more solid world with fewer words, but can also be exploited by the author.

For example, a story about a young king fighting for his throne could be expected to be about that young king. Instead, in *Ombria in Shadow*, we find several other characters are the focus, with the young king himself almost an afterthought in the story. *Ombria in Shadow* takes place in the failing city of Ombria where the old prince has just died, his son is a child, and the regent is his power-mad great (perhaps great-great-great) aunt, Domina Pearl. The old prince's mistress, Lydea, and bastard nephew, Ducon Greve, must try to save the young Prince Kyel as well as themselves and the city of Ombria. Complicating matters is Faey, an ancient sorceress who lives beneath the city, and her assistant, called variously "the waxling" or Mag. Though Lydea calls the young prince the "heart of Ombria" he only appears in a few scenes, and he is not the center of the important ones. *Ombria in Shadow* pushes the expectations of a fantasy story, and creates new expectations, ones that allow mistresses and bastards to have the spotlight. Lauren J. Lacey claims that:

> Recognizing the power of stories means coming to terms with how they both create and limit the possibilities we see for ourselves. Seeing the potential for stories to expand the parameters of our expectations is easier to do when the stories involved stretch the boundaries of our imaginations [1].

Ombria in Shadow, like many of McKillip's texts, "expands the parameters" of what fantasy can be. As argued in the preface McKillip is definitively a fantasy author, but within this framework she plays with typical expectations and this creates different types of worlds.

One of the many ways which McKillip's texts do this is through the confusion of good and evil, which complicates the moral framework of her worlds. In his entry on DUALISM in the *Historical Dictionary of Fantasy Literature* Stableford states that "much fantasy literature adopts a tacitly dualistic position," (119) but there are authors, like McKillip, who do not allow things to be this simple. Spivack calls this a "depolarization of values" (13) and attributes it more generally to women writers of fantasy. I will not investigate this broader argument but the worlds of McKillip certainly play with this expectation of dualism. They have very few evil characters; most are simply cold, or misunderstood. Brume, for example, from *In the Forests of Serre* (largely taken from the Russian folktale of Baba Yaga) is presented as the evil witch with fairly clear markers. Her house is made of bones, she curses a prince within the first few pages, and her appearance is anything but benign. In *Deconstructing the Hero: Literary Theory and Children's Literature*, Margery Hourihan contends that in the context of children's literature "[t]hose who are ugly are, without exception, evil embodiments of cruelty and malice or of smothering destructiveness" (156). This assumption is often made in fantasy literature as well, which means that McKillip's texts are able to disrupt it. Brume, with feet like chicken-claws, animal-pointed teeth, enormous lenses, and ugly features is a grotesque exaggeration of an ugly woman. Her looks identify her instantly as monstrous. And yet, in the end, all that she does is shake the prince of *In the Forests of Serre* from the lethargy he has allowed himself to fall into. She is continually threatening to put people in her cook-pot and eat them but never does so; her "evil" is merely appearance and the expectation that a woman as ugly as that will be evil. Brume, in her own way, is helpful, allowing the story to draw to its traditional conclusion (as will be explored further in the next section).

Maria Tatar notes that often "characters are defined solely by their relationship to the protagonist, each belonging unambiguously to the camp of good or evil" (61). In McKillip's texts this is largely ignored, especially in books such as *The Tower at Stony Wood*, where the same character hinders and helps the hero for the "greater good," or texts like *Alphabet of Thorn* that study complicated interpersonal dynamics (as explored further in Chapter Three), making good and evil difficult to judge, not least from the viewpoint of the main character. These complications mean McKillip's worlds are complicated as well, they are worlds of grey as well as black and white and this widens the actions that characters can take.

For example, in *Song for the Basilisk*, which follows Caladrius, an orphan raised by Bards, who has a mysterious past, Caladrius eventually remembers that he is the oldest child of the Tormalyne family, who in a bloody coup were (almost) all killed by the Pelliors, their rival House in the city of Berylon. Head of the Pellior family is the ruthless Basilisk, Arioso Pellior, whose daughter Luna shows a similar propensity for magic. The evil ruler is quite clearly Arioso Pellior, who slaughtered his opponents and their children in cold blood and has no compunction about murder throughout the story. What changes this from being a clear-cut good versus evil story, however, is Arioso's daughter, Luna. Presented as the mirror to her father, she is continually described as cold, calculating, and in league with her father. Because there is an expectation of dualism, Luna is quite casually grouped with her evil father. Her own brother asks, "[a]re you really something he conjured up in secret? ... I wasn't paying attention when you were born.... For all I know, he might have made you" (150). Even someone who ought to know has subscribed to the rumors, asking Luna outright if she was not born but made. At the end, however, Luna surprises her father into a deathly apoplexy, and the readers and the characters in the book, by granting a reprieve to her father's bitterest enemy, and then declaring peace for the city (as Mains also explores in "Loyalty" [226]). This ending is particularly powerful because Luna has been set up as such a coldly conniving character. There is no great expectation that she will be merciful, and certainly all expectations within the book (plot, characterization) and without the book (expectations of evil vs. good) point to her being evil. The world of *Song for the Basilisk* is more nuanced than this, however. There are moments of humanity within Luna and when probed more closely they provide the (easily missed) clues to her more complicated personality. For example, she "mistakenly" transforms a paramour of her brother's whom she has been ordered to kill into an old woman instead. In the book it is treated as an accident, Luna is vague when questioned by her father, but with the ending providing a clue to her true character it is possible to see this incident (and several others) as moments of mercy completely out of character for one assumed to be evil. It is the combination of the expectation of dualism, with the more complicated morals of the world of *Song for the Basilisk* that allows for the surprising ending.

Another similarly mispresented character is Faey in *Ombria in Shadow*, who balances out Domina Pearl. Both women will be discussed at length in later chapters but what is important here is that Domina Pearl is primarily cold and pragmatic, rather than evil in the classic sense, and Faey, who is presented as being at least a wicked sorceress, is far more complicated than that. This is reflected in both their domains, and the politics of the world they inhabit, explored further in Chapter Six. McKillip's texts take expectations of dualism, and work with them to imply things about characters that turn out to be false. This builds a richer, more realistic world, as primary-world life does not often come in neat shades of black and white. While playing with the expected good/evil didactic, McKillip's books do not behave as is expected of the story. Astrid Schmid claims that "[i]n the character of the double, the 'other' manifests itself as the non-accepted, the feared, the un-lived" (13). But, in McKillip's *Ombria in Shadow*, who is to be feared is complicated. Certainly, Domina Pearl is monstrous but she is at least human, with human motivations. Faey is Other. Faey is shown with ever-changing looks stolen from her paintings, and at one point is described as "so deeply immersed in her spell that the gypsy's face had smudged slightly. One eye was higher than the other; her nose had slid askew" (100). Faey slips on the forms and faces of the paintings that line her walls so that her true form is questionable. The bodies she chooses are beautiful but made grotesque by this costuming, as well as by Faey's disinclination to bother with their details: letting an ear or an eye slide exaggerates her monstrous attributes. Faey is presented as monstrous, yet in the end it is her love of a human (and thus her humanity) that saves the city of Ombria. Domina Pearl, the authority within the city, has brought Ombria to ruin, and killed many of its citizens along the way. The expected actions are reversed. Within Ombria who is good and who is evil is complicated, as well as who holds power. Authority, official authority, rests with Domina Pearl. She may be unscrupulous but she is the Regent, and therefore the true authority within the city. Faey has no official role whatever to play within Ombria. And yet, it is Faey who has complete mastery of the underground, and, in the end, the city of Ombria itself. Faey, the grotesque Other lurking beneath the city is the savior because she has learned to love a human child, and when Domina Pearl threatens her, Faey acts. Expected parameters are breached, actions reversed, and it takes the disorder of rebellion to save the city. It is when the characters are examined in relation to not only each other, but also their environments and the expectations that surround them, that the true, complicated dynamic that surrounds them and their world is highlighted.

From a readerly perspective, McKillip's novels play with a reader's expectations of how a fantasy story ought to go. Sometimes, she does this by subverting those expectations, but as often she does this by framing something as a typical fantasy contrivance, and then slowly destroying the "known" quantities, thus enriching the world and the reader's experience of it by filling in details but also causing the reader to question what they have automatically assumed. In *The Role of the Reader* Umberto Eco discusses "ghost chapters,"[1] those sections of a text where readers make their own assumptions, sometimes correctly but also, often, incorrectly. He contends that "every text is made of two components: the information provided by the author and that added by the Model Reader, the latter being determined by the former—with various rates of freedom and necessity" (206). These expectations, that can be upheld, or discarded, are an important way in which the author can play with a text, a genre, and therefore, a world.

Characters are what they appear to be, but, they are also more than this in McKillip's worlds. McKillip's texts present and use expectations, but they do not just subvert them (though they do this too), they open them to possibilities. What if a damsel in distress is, in fact, in distress, what if someone were to try to rescue her? What does she do, what are her possibilities beyond but encompassed by the traditional? In *In the Forests of Serre* the world is set up to explore this problem. *In the Forests of Serre* primarily follows the bewitched Prince Ronan (ensnared in the forest of Serre by the witch Brume) and the Princess Sidonie and her retinue as she travels from her country, Dacia, to marry him. The Princess Sidonie, introduced with appropriate princess-like beauty as well as distress: "seemed, in the drenching light, to be made of gold, honey, cornsilk…. She covered her face with her hands, shook her head violently. Drops of gold fell between her fingers" (25). Sidonie is being sent off to marry an unknown prince in a storied realm under difficult circumstances. One of her would-be rescuers, Gyre, is described in Chapter Three, but it is Sidonie herself who is relevant here. Although it is clear Sidonie has a mind of her own, she allows herself to be sent off (for the good of her country and family, threatened by a war they cannot win if she does not), travels fairly passively to her betrothed's lands, and is shocked into quiescence when she arrives there to find her groom gone and his ogre of a father furious. However, within this frame of passive damsel in distress, Sidonie's mind is always working on escapes or ways to make her life better, regardless of what her body seems to be doing in its obedience. Were she truly a typical damsel in distress she would be rescued by Gyre, or even by the young scribe who pictures himself doing just that:

> After climbing the highest mountains, crossing the interminable forests, scaling the steepest cliffs, battling witches and ogres, he would appear to the

Two. Fantasy Conventions

princess as marvelous and unexpected as any magic in Serre. Her violet eyes, drenched with the hopeless tears of many weeks, would turn to him as flowers to the sun [170].

The young scribe is practical about it; he does have money, access to a horse and maps, but he, subverting the expected male role of rescuer, remains as nurse instead, "[t]he scribe who was at that moment riding so bravely alone over the mountains looked back at the scribe standing at the sickbed of an aged, weakened wizard, wondering dubiously how to interest him a mouthful of soggy vegetables" (171). In the end Sidonie rescues herself and the Prince without really leaving her traditional role. When the Prince goes to rescue her as he knows he is meant to do, he ends up getting in her way instead. Having almost freed herself he appears and they are tangled back into Brume's grasp. "'I was nearly out the door! You got in my way.' 'I'm sorry.' 'We both would have been free!' 'Yes. I didn't know you would deal so easily with Brume. I couldn't'" (276). Sidonie is distraught, she weeps, but, in the end, she gets things done. She remarks about her own worth, "I couldn't think of anything. I'm worth heirs to you, and power to Ferus, and peace to my father, but I couldn't think of anything else. So I attacked her with the scissors instead" (278). Having found herself in the middle of a traditional tale, Sidonie takes matters into her own hands, and finds her own worth as a fighter in her own right. In what is key to the world of Serre, Sidonie remains within her fairytale, plays along until she is able to disrupt it and free herself. Her understanding of her necessary role is key to this, as are her personal characteristics and how she deals with the lands of Serre and its inhabitants. The world of Serre is thus expressed and moved through by Sidonie; it is far more than a backdrop.

There is also the damsel (called, appropriately enough, Damsen) in *The Throme of the Erril of Sherril*. Locked into a tower and waiting on her testy father Damsen is the typical damsel in distress, waiting passively, crying, for her knight love to save her. She is not even described in relation to herself, but rather in relation to her father; "He had a daughter who sat with him and wept and embroidered pictures of the green world beyond" (6). And for her sake the knight does try to fulfill his quest, going on a journey that leads him seemingly around the whole of his world. In the end he must fake the gift required to set Damsen free, and when discovered he resigns himself to going off in search once more of what cannot be found. "Then I will go back and look again, forever if I must, and Damsen, if it pleases her, will wait here for me" (106). This, however, is when Damsen becomes more than her story usually allows, and is a fully-fleshed-out character, living in a world with more depth and possibilities than meets the eye. All along she has been a singularly passive character, the perfect damsel in distress, but at the end she decides that she has had enough. "I will not wither here in these stones.... I do not care about your throne. I want this moon-haired, barefoot Cnite and I will have him" (106). When she makes this statement, and then follows up on it, she moves out of the role that has been assigned her by her father, and even her lover, and makes her own decision. LeFanu remarks that Jenny Wolmark "suggests that such stories—in which certain stereotypes are undermined within a traditional science fiction narrative—prompt in the reader more of a sense of dislocation than stories in which the narrative conventions are rewritten from a feminist viewpoint" (88). This, I would argue, is just as relevant in fantasy, where there is a similar use of stereotypes (often tropes) and traditional narratives. Stories like Damsen's allow for a more destabilizing ending because the narrative has followed a traditional quest pattern, and Damsen has been a stereotypical distressed maiden. She frees herself in the end but she does so from firmly inside a traditional tale. As a result it might be suggested that this has more impact than it would if Damsen's story entire had been framed in feminist terms (with her working outside of her traditional role from the beginning). This is one instance in which the world seems to be countenancing only one sort of story, while allowing the opposite. Like the character of Damsen, the world as a whole supports what seems to be a typical quest, but clues are presented throughout the text indicating that all is not what it seems (like the Cnite losing all his Knightly accouterments). From a readerly perspective, only by paying attention to this can the reader anticipate the non-traditional ending.

Literalization

Along with allowing or disenchanting expectations McKillip's worlds often literalize actions. This means that action can be tied intimately to the world from which it emerges. It is often dangerous to

Two. Fantasy Conventions

assume McKillip uses metaphor, or other figurative language. Tolkien, Clute, and others have argued that fantasy is often different from mimetic fictions in that it does not lie. What they mean is that it does not present something as one thing, when in actuality it is another. Thus, it is not allegory, but rather a more literal construction. What I have called "literalization" could also be seen as meta-fantasy at times, but I use literalization advisedly because it is not just fantasy recognizing it is fantasy, and drawing in outside fiction, though that happens, but because this process also changes how McKillip's worlds must be read; a reading strategy that deprioritizes metaphorical readings in favor of literal ones is required.[2]

Tolkien "cordially disliked" (34) allegory, but Tom Shippey, in attempting to prove that Tolkien used it in spite of himself, gives an argument for why Tolkien felt fantasy should not be reduced to *only* allegory. "One can go on making these equations, and one is *supposed* to; the essence of an allegory, Tolkien thought, was that it should be 'just,' i.e. that all the bits should fit exactly together, compelling assent (and amusement) by their nearness" (34). This fitting exactly means that allegory can be too easily invoked to equate one for one, and in doing so, alternate possibilities are limited and often excluded altogether. One of the things fantasy does is open possibilities, and allegory too often closes them. Others since Tolkien have argued against fantasy's use simply as allegory. For example, Irene Eynat-Confino contends,

> [f]or the fantastic to exist, it requires the reader or spectator's willingness to accept it as an integral part of human experience and not merely as an ephemeral flight of fancy. An allegorical interpretation of the fantastic ... obliterates the multiple import and significations of the fantastic and limits its function and effects to that of a rhetorical device [112].

While I take issue with Eynat-Confino's dismissal of fancy (fancy is just as necessary to human nature as any other aspect of our minds), the second point is well made. Fantasy is much wider, and has more uses than the simple one-to-one which allegory generally allows. Clute contends that fantasy does not use allegory; it does not say that something is like something else, it *is* something else. His example is particularly clear, which is why I quote it in its entirety here:

> Words mean what they say here, as Samuel R Delany argued years ago, distinguishing between the fantastic and what he called the mundane literatures. In fantastika a cigar is what the story says it is. Sometimes it is only a cigar.

> But if something that resembles a cigar opens its mouth for us, we have entered a Portal, not a dream which suggests psychotherapy; if we drown in contaminants, as the Congo nearly drowns Marlow in Joseph Conrad's *Heart of Darkness*, we have been swallowed by Cloaca, not by the spent cigars of imperialism. The Congo is the thing itself. It is not primarily an extractable image for darkness—*it is the darkness* ["Canary" 7].

That is, if the heart of the world is broken, as Clute says is true for *In the Forests of Serre* (6), then the world is actually broken. In *In the Forests of Serre* there is even a comment to this effect: "Never underestimate the power of a tale. What you put aside as fantasy in one land can kill you in the next" (24). McKillip's books overtly tell us how we must treat their worlds, as things full of elements that are true, features that are things in themselves and not to be treated as only figures of speech.

In McKillip's worlds what is said to be happening, actually is. This enables a slightly different type of world in that the effect of action is tightly woven to the world. For example, when the fairy queen's daughter is stolen into the mortal realm in *The Book of Atrix Wolfe*, the world itself revolts: "In the Queen's wood, seasons fought: Snow swirled across the torn boundaries of the world, clung to grass, oak boughs, the Queen's bright hair" (12). The disruption in the natural order of things is made clear through the snow out of season and the sudden wind, the connection between fairy queen and landscape is emphasized, through a physical, and not just psychological, reaction.

McKillip's texts use story, and its expectations, and these combine to shape the world the characters inhabit in more overt ways than is typical. The characters are regularly aware of Story, and as a result their actions are frequently less oblivious of traditional patterns than is sometimes the case. *In the Forests of Serre* contains Prince and Princess but it also holds Brume, a creation who could be straight out of fairy-tale (as Pilinovsky notes, Brume is a very close approximation of the Russian fairytale Baba Yaga character). Clute scrutinizes a moment when the witch Brume is confronted with the stereotypical situation of a wily hero unwilling to get into her cooking pot. When the moment comes for her to be "tricked" into climbing in herself, she is aware of what is happening and goes forward anyway. "Brume's 'long, opaque look' is the look of a sage refusing to break up her lines to modernise—or to post-modernise—herself" ("Canary" 9). Clute notes that at this moment Brume knows what is to happen, and continues anyway. She is honest to the story in which she appears. As he goes on to note, "[i]n fantastika, when we say X is really Y, we do not mean X is really like Y" (7). This ties in with the notion that fantasy should not be read, or at least, should not *only* be read as allegory, especially with authors like McKillip. Brume is tied into her own story, but also to the world that includes Serre, where fairytales exist both as tales, and as actualities that need to be navigated (Mains takes a different slant on this in "Bridging" 37).

Wholeheartedly believing the "truths" presented in the fantasy is not necessary for enjoyment, or for the world as a whole to work, however. For example, Wolfe is unconvinced of the efficacy of the Blammor and the Liralen of *The Forgotten Beasts of Eld* being one and the same.

> In Patricia A. McKillip's *The Forgotten Beasts of Eld* (1974), we can accept the final transformation of the hideous monster Blammor into the beautiful Liralen bird without necessarily agreeing with the identity of creativity and destructive passions that such a metaphor implies ["Encounter" 1].

It is a fair point, though I take issue with Wolfe's general argument: I think the Liralen and Blammor, and the book as a whole, are more nuanced than this gives them credit for. Wolfe describes the Blammor as "hideous" when the Blammor is styled more as a panther in the text; beautiful, compelling, and utterly dangerous. The Liralen we see much less of, crucially, because its very elusiveness, its beauty and freedom, are its key qualities. Thus, the metaphor is subtler than Wolfe allows, but, nonetheless, the belief in what these animals are meant to "represent" is not necessary. Indeed, they do not even have to be read as metaphor; they are largely treated as characters in their own right, as mysterious and majestic as the other magical creatures in the book. "Metaphors," and allegory, in McKillip can always be read as something greater, more intimately tied into the worlds they appear in.

Names, as indicated by Damsen in an earlier example, are significant in McKillip's texts, and are part of the literalization. I will not spend a significant amount of time on this because it is, in some ways, too obvious (others have also looked at names in McKillip, for example, Mains in "Having" 50–52, and 73–74). But a section on literalization would not be complete without at least a mention of this. Often, the characters themselves are aware of the significance of their names—in *The Riddle-Master* trilogy Morgon notes upon meeting the harper

Deth, "'I remember your name.... My father used to say Deth played at his wedding.' He stopped, listening to his words; a shudder weltered out of him unexpectedly. 'I'm sorry. He thought it was funny'" (16). *The Riddle-Master* trilogy follows Morgon, and later his love, Raederle, as they learn of their destinies in their chaotic world, one where ancient, god-like beings battle against one of their own, The High One, to use, and as a result, destroy the power of the world. It is a world fraught with death. The shudder from Morgon is because his parents have died prematurely, and thus death has indeed performed in their lives.

Action, names, story, character are all woven together in McKillip's worlds. In *Song for the Basilisk* Caladrius has his name chosen for him when his own is too dangerous to wear in the world, but it also charts his destiny, to overthrow a ruler. As Luna, the daughter of his enemy, astutely notes, "I will listen to you as well ... on my father's birthday, Master Caladrius. Unlike my sister, I know your name. The caladrius is a beautiful bird, is it not, who sings at the deathbed of a king?" (227). As one of the few characters to point this out in the story Luna is subtly presented as both perceptive, and aware of Caladrius's true nature and purpose in a way not otherwise shown for most of the story. Thus, names give hints (sometimes more than hints) to a person's character or place in the story, and must be paid attention to. There are dozens of other examples in each book; Clute notes that in *In the Forests of Serre* Gyre, "who is accompanied, therefore by spiraling winds" ("Canary" 7), has a personality as well as a psychic reality that reflects his name. He is described thus: "The wizard Gyre, who had a startling ability to change shape, had found their way through the mountains with an eagle's eyes" (44). And, even more pointedly, "the wizard dipped on outspread wings down an angle of sweet twilight breeze, landed at Sidonie's feet, and turned into himself" (44). Here he is not only the embodiment of movement, but he is literally coming down on a gyre, and as a bird of prey at that, perhaps an allusion to the widening gyre of William Butler Yeats's "The Second Coming." Whether an intentional reference or not, the name and character are clearly associated with one another, and with characteristics of movement, and brash energy. Therefore, the names in the books are some of the many elements that play together to create an integrated world, one where everything, even names, matter.

Sometimes a character's true affinity and spirit are emphasized by

Two. Fantasy Conventions

their lyrical descriptions just as well as their names. What might otherwise be a pathetic fallacy in realistic fiction is often real in fantasy (or at least gives clues to the truth). For example, the prince of *The Changeling Sea*, at this point a mysterious stranger, is (though he does not know it) the son of the sea. A vivid passage comes alive because of its associations with nature (specifically the sea), a hint at his parentage, and the trouble it will soon cause to the watcher:

> The dark horseman from the sea gazed up at her, mounted at the foot of the cliff. She caught her breath, chilled, as if the sea itself had crept noiselessly across the beach to spill into her circle.... A wave boomed and broke behind him, flowing across half the beach, seeking, seeking, then dragged back slowly, powerfully, and, caught in the dark gaze of the rider, his eyes all the twilight colors of the sea, Peri felt as if the undertow had caught her [11–12].

What ought to be a simple description of a man on horseback, staring back at a girl, is turned into something rich and strange, illumining not only the character involved but the world he is a part of. He is explicitly linked with the sea "as if the sea itself," his eyes are described as "the twilight colors of the sea," and his gaze is given the power of the "undertow." The sea is also described as "seeking," and while this could be a simple description of its motion, the fact that powers in the sea are searching for the prince is evidenced without being directly stated. The horseman's power and his affinity with the sea are emphasized, and even his longing to return to it (and its desire for him to return) is intimated through description. This occurs with other characters, like Sel (who will be explored further in Chapter Five and whose name gives the clue to her original nature as selkie). In fact, several other examples are included in Chapter Five because it is in this closeness with the land, and the physical nature of the character's bonds to it, that the literalization of story is often showcased in McKillip's books.

McKillip's texts can be just as playful with their literalizations as with other aspects. At one point, Cyan of *The Tower at Stony Wood* is commanded by Sel to "take off your towers" (209). What she means is for him to take off the surcoat adorned with towers that he wears, but there is also a moment of humor where the reader (and a surprised Cyan) try to picture him lifting off the physical towers he has been searching for. Of course, this works in a figurative as well as a literal way. He is able to unburden himself to the canny (and older) Sel in a way he has been unable to with many others, and is able to lay aside the psychological burden of his quest for a moment while she repairs his clothing. But, it is the moment of hesitation, of not knowing which towers are being referred to, that brings both humor and a depth of understanding to this very small moment. Cyan's weariness is clear, but shown in an amusing way, one that would not have quite the same moment of hesitation in the story if the text had not previously literalized story in important ways.

Names, descriptions, actions, all create characters that are more than surface characterizations, are more than their traditional roles in stories. This means that McKillip's worlds can be taken as truth in a way not possible with some fiction that emphasizes allegory, or that uses the fantasy as descriptor.

Three

Characters

In Chapter Two I explored the expectations for fantasy literature and their implications for McKillip's worlds. This chapter will focus on the expectations laid on characters, specifically by age and gender, and how this shapes the Social world of McKillip's texts. Characters, in how they adapt to and are shaped by their environment, how they reflect their surroundings, and how they see what surrounds them, are integral to the world of a book and thus must be integral to the world-building as well. When Harrison argues against the use of world-building as a useful concept for fiction, he uses a fairly narrow definition, intimating that narrative, and thus largely character, are divorced from it ("Very afraid"). However, how do we see a world but through the characters we follow? Without characters there is often no world, and vice versa in fiction. Thus, characters must be studied as part of the world in which they roam. This chapter addresses some of the subversions found in McKillip generally, followed by an exploration of age, and lastly, an inspection of gender and how these frames all work in her worlds.

Subversions

The Social world of the text is particularly important in that it is one of the ways that an author may comment on the primary world. Wolf contends that "[b]y changing the defaults of the Primary World, especially in playful ways that reveal and reverse audience expectations, secondary worlds can make strange the familiar by exploring alternatives to the ordinary" (33). This "making strange the familiar" is part of what McKillip's texts do in their world-building. As Mains notes "[t]he reader's relationship with fictional worlds is not only a matter of personal and individual growth, but also can lead to a change in the larger sociocultural world" ("Having" 119). Real-world issues can be explored afresh, or highlighted, through what the texts do with characters, and how they fit into their worlds. This chapter has sections from a more authorial perspective, as McKillip is clearly interested in gender, but it will also include a closer critical inspection of McKillip's characters, and how they interact with the worlds they live in.

The last chapter's examination of tropes included a number of archetypes, many of them having to do with the types of character found in texts. McKillip's worlds do much to disrupt not only these character archetypes and tropes but also expectations of gender and age found in the greater fictional world. As Ringel notes "McKillip has been quietly and persistently interrogating gender conventions in the genre since *The Forgotten Beasts of Eld*" ("Art" 179). This interrogation does not extend to just gender conventions, however, but encompasses a much wider milieu, aided by the way that her worlds are constructed. Gender and age restrictions are often part of archetypes, or tropes. In response to James Hillman's belief that archetype is something we believe "is basic, necessary, universal" Estella Lauter and Carol Schreier Rupprecht propose that "the trouble comes when we begin to believe that what we have valued is the essence of what is real" (10). Of course, for many years there have been questions about who is considering particular archetypes "basic, necessary, universal" (white, western, males, generally) but there is no doubt that these tropes and archetypes are prevalent. As Lauter and Rupprecht note, the real danger of archetypes and tropes is not that they exist or are examined, but rather that they are taken too seriously, as Truth, and the only truth available. As a result, authors have grappled with these archetypes (or tropes) in a number of ways, chiefly within the persons of characters. Authors like McKillip consider these assumptions from within and without the fantasy tradition. Sometimes this means showing where there are gaps in the typical characterizations, by fleshing characters and their worlds out. This can also mean taking these fictions and showing them to be false by making them hard to categorize, and thus bringing them closer to the reality of human complexity. Archetypes are taken as truths but as Demaris S. Wehr states, "[t]he central problem is this: Jung ontologises what is more accurately and more usefully seen as socially constructed reality" (23). Rowland and others have clarified that the ontology ascribed to Jung was usually the work of his successors; however, the point is still a good one. Treating archetypes (and thus tropes) as "socially constructed realities" allows authors like McKillip to explore the more complex depths of the characters, as well as the worlds they reside in, and to play with them in a way not possible if they are treated as Truth. Even Jung conceded that there was a difference between the true archetypes of the psyche and how they are used in myth, fairytale, and more. Jung acknowledged that biases, his own among them, prohibited these from being true archetypes, both because the human mind cannot truly examine itself without bias, and because the weight of history and multiple contacts with authors and cultures have removed these archetypes from what they might have been to begin with. He proposes that there is a large difference between the historical formula and the archetype from which it evolves (5). Thus archetypes in story, like tropes, have been changed and fossilized, becoming something that might not reflect actual reality. If a male hero is a socially accepted truth rather than an ontological one, what is possible? McKillip and others take up this challenge in regards to gender but also age, which is just as often biased in favor of a particular type of trope. Because archetype and tropes are such a well-entrenched concept, McKillip and others are able to surprise us with their subversion, and to build richer worlds through their examination.

In *Myth and Fairytale in Contemporary Women's Fiction*, Sellers notes that author Jenny Diski is one of many who do not see a way to turn traditional tales, and traditional structures, to truly feminist aims:

> Princesses may periodically question the regime that promises rescue, but they are too firmly stuck inside the story, Diski's tale implies, to even try the door. The pattern is too entrenched for an insurgent princess to be anything other than an exception which proves the rule [25].

As with the trope and general fantasy expectations investigated previously many of McKillip's characters fit within the typical expectations and tropes anticipated of fantasy characters but crucially, they also explode their boundaries. In their introduction to *Feminist Archetypal Theory* Lauter and Rupprecht contend that "[a]rchetypal images that Jung had described were frequently understood as absolutes. Instead of being explanations of reality experienced by females, archetypes of the feminine had become categories to contain women" (7).

Many of the structures and patterns that are studied in an academic sense (Vladimir Propp's emphasis on the male of action comes to mind as well) are related to a particular type of male, with females constrained into patterns it is difficult to break out of. That these "categories to contain" are prevalent has been widely suggested, but McKillip, and other creative writers tackle this problem away from psychology and academia in general. Rather than attempting to ignore these "absolutes" entirely, McKillip and others like Diana Wynne Jones break them open and examine them. And it is not just women who are constrained by their traditional roles in story, though they are rightfully the usual focus of such critiques. Gyre, for example, previously considered because of his whirlwind name, is a classic trickster character. And yet, he grows and learns, shows concern and develops wisdom outside of the boundaries his traditional role presumes. Part of his learning is an internal growth, but it is largely triggered by his external environment, the mysterious land of Serre, and the world that challenges him. He is described towards the beginning: "As far as Sidonie could tell, he viewed the world with a great deal of curiosity and no fear whatsoever" (44). His impetuosity, curiosity and lack of fear lead him through several adventures during the book; he is trapped by a dragon's heart, thrown out a window when his disguise is revealed, and almost eaten several times. Like the classic trickster he keeps playing tricks and does not seem to learn. The wizard who has rescued him from one of his scrapes muses, "[i]t never occurred to me that, having been trapped for days in the dark with a casket gnawing at his wrist, he would risk putting a hand back into it. But that was Gyre and that was his mistake" (77). Gyre makes several such mistakes, and his tricks escalate until he changes place with the Prince of Serre, in order to secure the Princess Sidonie but also (and more importantly to him) the magical land of Serre. He is not an unchanging Loki, however, though it is not an external force that changes him, or any fluke of the narrative. By the end of the book his own curiosity has got him into such trouble that no one can help him out. He must use his own wiles, his own trickster cunning but also, crucially, he must use love and compassion for others, traits usually alien to the trickster, that he has learned, in order to free himself. Only when he is willing to sacrifice himself, the most unlike his previously selfish self he could be, is he redeemed. "'If you cannot find your heart, take mine,' he whispered. 'But let the firebird live'" (267).

Three. Characters

In the end he is willing to sacrifice everything he is in order to save something outside of himself, and his own compassion allows him to be more than the trickster of the story. It is Gyre's emotional maturity, but also his interactions with the world around him and its inhabitants, that has allowed change. Coming to love the land and the firebird, and in some ways to understand them, allows for growth that even the other characters do not inspire. In the end the character of Gyre is allowed out of the constraints his typical character might otherwise require, and this in turn permits surprises within the narrative and within the world.

My principal argument for this chapter is that not only are characters an integral part of world-building as a whole, but that they are one of the many ways in which the texts allow for real-world critique within their worlds. McKillip's books have the princesses, the heroes, but also old women, young girls, young boys, old men, princesses who are interested in archaeology and heroes who are aging and creaky. McKillip, like other writers of speculative fiction, has found that it "offers a freedom to women writers, in terms of style as well as content, that is not available in mainstream fiction," (LeFanu 2) and when she takes this freedom and uses it to its fullest she builds a richer world, one that her characters not only inhabit but are also intrinsically connected to.

Age

McKillip's books have a range of characters, and the ages of those characters are similarly diverse. McKillip's worlds have young characters, old, in-between, and none are relegated solely to one role or another, one part of the world or another. They move between domestic and world spheres, serve a variety of functions and seem to live their lives beyond the borders of the books in which they reside.

Roderick Townley's novel *The Great Good Thing* does a charming job of literalizing a story book, where characters move from one part of their book to their next scene, in between the pages. McKillip's characters, like her worlds, feel more fleshed out than this. Even minor characters have details enabling them to be seen as people, and it is possible to imagine them all living their lives off-page, not just living in service to the plot. The worlds in which they reside are richer for their detail and variety. I will note here that McKillip does not have diversity in the sense of characters of color or different sexual modes; however, what she does do is fairly subversive in itself. I mean this not only in the larger sense of having female heroes for example, but also in the much smaller details. In *The Cygnet and the Firebird* there is a moment when "the Gatekeeper held her horse while the stable girls ran across the yard" (87). Stable *girls* rather than the ever-present stable boy. This moment is completely unimportant to the course of the book, not noted in any way by the other characters, but it is vital to building a richer, more real, and more inclusive world. Traditional gender roles are present throughout McKillip's books; a few examples were given previously, but they are almost always subverted in ways small and large. This is not true of age, where McKillip seems to largely ignore "real world" preoccupations with appropriate age roles. For example, the sorceress Vevay, discussed at length below, not once thinks of herself in terms of a grandmotherly role, nor do any of the other characters think of her in that light in any way.

Margery Hourihan claims that the hero (specifically in children's literature but also generally) is almost always an adolescent or young man, rational, active and violent (72). It is, she proposes, "[c]ommonplace that twentieth-century Western culture ... fetishises youth in a way that devalues the experience and wisdom of older people" (196). McKillip's worlds work to disrupt this commonplace in a number of ways. Primarily, this is done by revaluing wisdom and experience, and allowing older characters a place in the world, but it also means providing younger characters with flaws natural to their age. In this way there is a balance of expectations (some of McKillip's heroes are the traditional young men) with careful intrusions of reality. It must also be noted that in McKillip's novels, even when a young man is the heroic lead, there is just as often a woman by his side. Even when the typical male hero is present, he is not allowed center stage. The only exception to this is *The Throme of the Erril of Sherril*, already discussed at length and discussed further in later chapters. Even here, however, the young hero is often lonely, frightened, unsure of what to do next, weary, none of them attributes expected of a heroic ideal.

McKillip's worlds include a range of ages not generally allowed in realistic fiction, creating divergent scenarios for characters, which in turn allows for them to impact on their worlds in ways that can be unexpected. For example, several of McKillip's characters are, if not immortal, near immortal. The way that longer-lived characters fit into her stories indicate she is neither taking a realistic look at how long humans are actually capable of living, nor is she looking at the social consequences as a science fiction text might do. Stefanie Giebert asks in "A Place for the Silver Horde or No Country for Old Men? Age and Aging in Fantasy and Science Fiction":

> Being non-mimetic genres, SF/F are not bound by natural laws, such as the one that says that all lives must age and die at some time. Thus, anything is possible. How do writers use this freedom and what are the recipient's attitudes towards this? [187].

From an authorial perspective, McKillip seems interested in the personal consequences of mortality and the consequences for power, and this drives the plot of several of her novels. From a critical perspective, the age of her characters is tied into the narrative but also more broadly into the worlds in which they live. Part of her world-building with characters is not just about allowing all ages, but in extending age into something not possible in the primary world. In reality, longevity of the kind seen in McKillip's books is, if not impossible, improbable. Anthony Farrant notes that longer lifespans will be achieved gradually, and are unlikely to extend to hundreds of years (ix). Even if it were possible to live a vastly expanded lifespan, the socio-economic effects are worrying to the scientific community and to society as a whole. Overpopulation and the burden on the younger generations of older relatives who live past their expected lifespans, among other aspects, could be the focus of a science-fiction novel—and is the focus in most literature looking at longevity—but not for McKillip. The key for critical worldbuilding here is that McKillip has included longevity as a discussion of age, and power; the Temporal world bleeds into the Social and it is one of the ways McKillip builds a world like, but unlike, the primary world.

One of the less dramatic ways in which McKillip's texts disrupt typical age assumptions can be found in *Alphabet of Thorn*, which explores how age is felt and dealt with. The main character, Nepenthe (whose name, tellingly, means "drug of forgetfulness"), is the unknowing daughter and heir of a sorceress and her conqueror-king partner. Nepenthe has been left in the kingdom of Raine as an orphan (in what is to the sorceress and her king "the future"). Translating a book of stories that only she feels drawn to, Nepenthe unknowingly calls her sorceress mother, Kane, and conqueror father into her adoptive land from a distant land and time. Trying to stop the nebulous threat is the young queen Tessera and her advisor, the ancient mage, Vevay. In *Alphabet of Thorn* the wise mentor and the silly adolescent girl are transformed into detailed characters, linked with the world in which they live and crucial to its understanding.

Neither character is defined solely by their age, but it has impacted each. The past and experiences of the adolescent queen Tessera and her mentor are so different that time has made them strange to each other. The typical teen/advisor role is exacerbated by the addition of magic, however. Like Morgon in *The Riddle-Master* trilogy, explored below, Tessera's real age in *Alphabet of Thorn* is confused by her natural affinity with the environment and her ability to shape change, as when:

> Peace, layered in rings of wood rippling out from the word, was one of the dreams; she breathed it in, or swallowed it. Now she lumbered like a tree, heavy with time, her thoughts too slow for words, her outward body a small, unwieldy thing crusted with bark [199].

She becomes the tree, and it is not just the physical shape she takes on but the "thought" process, and its sense of time. Tessera is intimately connected to her world through her magic, and it influences how she acts and reacts. As someone able to change shape at will, her human concept of time is necessarily skewed. When her older mentor, Vevay, is frantically looking for Tessera only to find her staring out at the sea, Vevay's expectation for Tessera, of an ordinary mortal's sense of time (that is, a non-magical adult's sense of time), is disjointed. Tessera's father was evidently non-magical, as is her mother. There is no expectation of power or of a different mind-set, and this complicates their differences. Vevay says, "'I didn't remember.... What power is like when you're that young. If no one names it for you, how can you possibly know what it is? She had no way of telling me'" (231). Power and age conflate to provide even more misunderstandings than might ordinarily be expected. Alison Waller proposes that "[a]dolescence is always 'other' to the more mature stage of adulthood" (1). In the case of Vevay and Tessera, this "othering" is exacerbated by the presence of magic. In this way the parameters of the world; there is magic, and shape-changing, but not always where expected, interacts with character expectations to cause surprise.

Age affects how a character perceives their world, and how they interact with the other characters that fill it. Waller argues that adolescence is "other" from the viewpoint of the adult, but the reverse can be true as well. The disjunction between different life stages is felt on both sides. Vevay cannot understand the Queen, but neither can the Queen understand her. Tessera thinks, "[p]erhaps I must grow old and gray, Tessera thought, and learn to use a sword and even grow a mustache, and Vevay will finally grow fond of me" (*Alphabet* 129). Her adolescent mode of thought is focused on the physical; the mental stage that Vevay is experiencing is too distant and alien for Tessera to even be able to fathom attributes in common. Tessera does not wish for wisdom or even actual old age to be able to understand Vevay; she sees the divide as something mostly physical, as something that a "gray" "mustache" might fix. Age and their vastly different pasts have made them both Other from one another's viewpoint. The final resolution in the book is only possible once Vevay is able to remember some of her youth, and Tessera matures and is capable of putting into words the power she uses instinctively. This understanding, and maturation on both their parts, is crucial to their ability to work with one another. They need to understand each other and this understanding can only be reached when their very different ages and experiences are reconciled. It is a key to the equality of McKillip's worlds that both the old and the young must change in order to reach a resolution. The onus for change is not entirely on one character or the other; they must both modify how they perceive the world and each other in order to understand one another. Both characters have typical attributes; Vevay is creaky with age, Tessera is self-centered with adolescence. However, neither trait defines them; these are consequences of their ages but not the entirety of their beings. The world has worked on them over varying amounts of time, allowing differences in personality and wisdom, but it continues to work on them throughout the text as well. Eventually, Vevay ignores her old bones, Tessera becomes less selfish, and the understanding each gains of the other is crucial to the happy ending of the book.

Like Tessera, Morgon's ideas of time and age come into conflict with those around him. The world of *The Riddle-Master* trilogy is a cohesive world in that Morgon's internal circumstances are echoed and re-enforced by external forces. Even without involving his destiny, and the influence of the High One (a sort of God in his world), Morgon's own lifespan is complicated, and this is reflected in the world he occupies, and how it interacts with him. As a farmer his personal lifespan is linked with the seasons. Because *The Riddle-Master* trilogy follows a cyclical path of the turning seasons rather than the passing of minutes, hours, and years, it is not in conflict with the general structure of the book. However, Morgon's ability to shape-change affects how his age is perceived, and how he feels it, dramatically. Thus, Morgon's affinity with his world has consequences for not only his thoughts, but his physical being as well. The difference between his usual human age and the animal or plant he has become must also be considered. As a vesta (a reindeer-type mammal) Morgon runs through King Har's domain with no awareness of how much time has passed for humans. As a tree "[h]e dwindled back into his own shape on a rainy, blustery autumn day. He stood in the cold winds, blinking rain out of his eyes, trying to remember a long, wordless passage of time" (497). The passage of time is marked with a season, autumn, but Morgon has no other indication of how much time has passed other than a vague feeling that it has been a long time. All the time he is a tree others have been searching for him, but their frantic day-to-day movements mean nothing to him because he has hibernated as a tree and has passed, in some ways, beyond the human concept of time. These journeys in and out of non-human time give him the indifference to others that the immortals have; the moments when Morgon is outside the human conception of time are also the moments when he is not human. Morgon's becoming plants and animals means that he is tied into his world in sometimes literal ways. Although *The Riddle-Master* trilogy is fairly clearly a bildungsroman it is also more than that because of Morgon's shape-shifting, actual age (that is, the years he has occupied his world as a conscious being, which puts him, likely, in his early twenties), and his projected age (he learns in the course of the book that he is immortal, or nearly so) are all in conflict in some way. What ought to be a fairly straightforward projection of growth is anything but. Both Morgon's age and perception of it are intimately tied to the world he occupies. His understanding of other creatures, other ways of thinking, is crucial to his growth as a man and a character, and it is only through his careful connection to his world that this can be managed.

Three. Characters

In *The Riddle-Master* trilogy, Morgon's age and how he has experienced it is sometimes in conflict with how long he has actually been alive. This is because once he begins the process of being the High One's heir, even if unknowingly, the difference between how he perceives time and how others do can cause conflict or highlight differences and these variances are woven into the world in which they live. For instance, Morgon, who has slept after living out Har's memories, questions Raederle: "'How long–how long did I sleep?'" "'Har said over two thousand years.'" "'Is it day or night?'" "'It's noon. You've slept nearly two days'" (536). In this passage various kinds of time are mentioned. In his and Har's minds and experience Morgon has lived thousands of years. In the time that the other characters have experienced, it has been two days. He holds both the recognition of these two very different time spans, as well as the here-and-now time of noon in his head without much apparent difficulty. It is important to note also that Raederle knows without clarification which question he is asking at which point. Her own sense of time expands with his so that she is just as conversant with the different times as he is. (For a further exploration of Raederle and Morgon's relationship, see Mains's master's thesis "Quest"). Morgon, Har and Raederle are all in tune with their world to the extent that these giant leaps in time are not too much of a problem for them. In McKillip's world near-immortality is possible, and it is not simply a feature of the world but integral to it and how the characters (and even the landscapes) are shaped.

Like many of McKillip's books *The Riddle-Master* trilogy is full of a history sometimes only lightly sketched. What is slightly different in *The Riddle-Master* trilogy is that the land itself is steeped in time and past occurrences, with the various pasts occasionally coming into conflict. Raederle has discovered that she has an ancestry that has been hidden from her, and while it has thrown her off-balance (she is the product of her enemy but also likely immortal) to deal with the truth of her own lifespan, she must also deal with the consequences of others' ages, and thus their own sense of personal past. Her understanding of various types of time is useful not only with Morgon, but with others as well. The world of *The Riddle-Master* trilogy is one in which the past can interrupt the present in sometimes unexpected, and violent, ways. Raederle finds this out to her frustration when dealing with a ghost set on revenge:

> She wanted to scream at him suddenly that she had nothing to do with his feuds or his death, that he had been dead for centuries and his vengeance was a matter insignificant in the turmoil of events beyond An. But his brain was alive only in the past, and the long centuries must have seemed to him the passing of a single night over Hel [345].

However, though she is exasperated, Raederle is able to deal with the ghost when others have failed. She is capable of doing so because she makes an effort to understand his past, unlike others who have missed the importance of this understanding. Her sense of time has come into contact with his; her understanding of his age and sense of time allows her to understand him, perceive what he desires, and bargain with it. She, like Morgon, is tied into an understanding of the land she lives in, and as a result is able to manipulate and bargain with it in ways other, less astute, characters are not. Consequently, McKillip's world contains a hierarchy, but not one dependent on age. Morgon and Raederle are the same age as some of the other, less perceptive, characters. They accrue more power, and are more successful than these others because of their understanding, and their assimilation into the world around them, not their age, or gender.

Time as history but also process, and viewpoint is applied to people living as well as dead throughout McKillip's work. *The Bards of Bone Plain* deals with the characters Nairn and his son, Phelan. As a famous bard, Nairn was cursed to immortality in a competition near the beginning of his country's founding. Phelan writes a research paper on Nairn for his own (unwanted) Bardic mastery. The book is split between chapters of the research paper Phelan writes, time in the novel's present, and time in Nairn's past. Phelan's understanding is complicated by the fact that the man he knows as his father, the peculiar Jonah, and the man known in legends as Nairn the Deathless are one and the same.

At the very end of *The Bards of Bone Plain*, when he knows his father to be both Nairn and Jonah, there comes a moment when "Phelan gazed at him wordlessly, seeing again that strange double vision of his father: Nairn the Deathless, the Unforgiven, imposed over the father he had grown up with, history pleated endlessly across a moment in time" (299). This vision of his father as both ordinary father and extraordinary man out of a tale is possible only with the peculiarities of time constructed into the fabric of the world of *The Bards of Bone Plain*.

Nairn's experiences, stretched over untold years, give him a completely different perspective—one he is unable to share with his son, and this tension drives the entire book.

Different senses of time are tied into McKillip's worlds, both in terms of how the characters, and the land, have been influenced by it, but age also affects how people deal with one another and what they are able, or expected, to accomplish. Humans comprehend time to an extent, but we also move through it; that is, we age. McKillip's worlds work realistically upon the old, and it is one of the ways in which there are checks to those who should have tremendous power. Great age means that certain characters have accumulated great wisdom, yes, but they are not spry Merlins to jump around after young boys, like in the Disney movie *Sword in the Stone* (1963). They are old men and women who feel their pasts, they are tired of the world and its consequences, and they feel the weight of what they have done in their weary bones. From an authorial perspective their existence at all argues strongly for McKillip's predisposition towards inclusion. Betty Friedan states in *The Fountain of Age* that, "the *non-existence* of images that [are] not 'young' [is] dismaying" (36). McKillip provides a variety of older characters in many of her works; this range of ages adds to the richness of her worlds and provides a variety of perspectives and character motivations while also allowing McKillip to move outside of the expected.

Vevay, in *Alphabet of Thorn*, for example, is presented as having limitations. At Vevay's age patterns become routine, and when the new queen does not conform to expected patterns of behavior and thought Vevay feels too old to deal with her effectively. Having lived a long time often means that experiences begin to fall into patterns, and actions outside of these patterns are difficult to deal with. Vevay is ancient, with an extended life to give her great wisdom, but her age makes it so that she is tired and also overlooks some important details. She explains to her consort: "'I don't' Vevay said bleakly. 'I don't understand her at all.' 'What were you like at that age?' 'How should I know? I barely remember the last century.'" (42). In *Alphabet of Thorn*, the moody starts of a teenager are so distant from Vevay's current place in time and reality that she is unable to cope. As Phillida Salmon explains, "[r]evelations that time has worked changes in us can also arise out of relations with others" (12). Vevay has perhaps not recognized her great age until this point because a person's sense of age generally feels "natural" and is thus unquestioned. It is only when Vevay needs to understand the much younger Tessera that she feels her own age for what it is. This reflects how the world of *Alphabet of Thorn* is one where consequences are tied into the amount of time spent in the world. Time has put so much distance between Vevay's own adolescence and the queen's that she is unable to remember enough to effectively help, or even understand, the young queen. However, Vevay's presence at all is a strong argument for the feminist element of McKillip's worlds; as Baba Copper notes, "one of the primary definitions of patriarchy is the absence of old women of power" (15). Vevay might be realistically portrayed in her old age, but she is unquestionably present and undeniably powerful, both in terms of magic and political might as the monarch's chief mentor. In a tweet on November 21, 2014, the author Kate Elliott writes, "[w]hen I see a lack of older women characters I see girls being told they have no future to grow into even if they are the kickass heroine now." McKillip's texts have gone some way in addressing this problem, for heroes as well as heroines, with a range of character ages, occupied by a range of characters, all important to their worlds.

Characters, including Atrix Wolfe, are also given limitations by the realistic portrayal of age and the results of a body's prolonged contact with the world around it. *The Book of Atrix Wolfe* examines the aftermath of a magic-influenced war. The great mage Atrix intervenes in a battle that is in stalemate, but in doing so he unleashes a horror into the world that kills many members of both sides of the army. He puts his knowledge into a book and hides it, only for Talis, one of the sons of the king killed at the battle, to find it. A character such as Atrix, a mage of almost limitless power, needs some check in order to provide interest and conflict to the story; as Terry Eagleton states, "[i]f magic could resolve all human problems, there would be no narrative," (170) and age is one way to ensure conflict. The years that Atrix has existed in his world have given him immense power, but they have also taken their toll. Atrix is an extraordinarily powerful mage, but he is also old and tired. His great deeds are in the past, and he has to be dragged unwillingly back into the world of the active. Atrix has retired into wolf shape: "The mage was old, and lingered, every year, longer and longer in the mountains among the wolves. That year, he had forgotten it was winter and that he was human" (*Atrix* 2). Time has become meaningless to him as he loses his sense of humanness and of self, testament both to his great powers and to his advanced age; he is powerful enough to literally live as a wolf, but old enough to forget that he naturally takes a different form. Unciel, in *In the Forests of Serre*, is a character whose age is similarly a hindrance. He is enormously powerful, but also old. Euan the scribe's first impression of Unciel is telling: "The wizard, around whom legends swarmed and clung, each more fabulous than the last, seemed worn by the burden of them" (16). Unciel might be a legendary wizard with all the attendant power, but he is old and "worn," and the last battle he fought has weakened him considerably. Ordinarily, a great and wise wizard would be the focus of the action, battling the realm's foes, but, forced to lean on a younger wizard and helper, Unciel cannot do what is necessary to save the kingdom. He is powerful but also old and tired, able to see what needs doing but unable to do it. Unciel's choice of the younger wizard Gyre to take his battle-worn place is not itself without complications, meaning that youth alone is not presented as an answer. Gyre is impetuous, without fear or, in the beginning, compassion. Although powerful, he is young and lacks Unciel's wisdom and knowledge of self. In this way the plot is driven forward; Unciel's wisdom cannot be used to its best advantage because of his advanced age and frailty, and Gyre causes problems in spite of his youth, energy, and power because of his unacknowledged inexperience and brash naiveté. Gyre is not allowed to be the hero of the story in spite of his otherwise typical heroic attributes (youth, health, power). McKillip's worlds balance expectations with reality, leaving no character un-touched by the time they have spent in their worlds. From an authorial perspective McKillip's creation of a world where age has realistic consequences ensures plot conflict.

Time works on everyone, and it is not just the main characters that McKillip's texts treat realistically, creating a world where even the insignificant characters are believable. Minor characters such as Vevay's consort in *Alphabet of Thorn* are not exempt from the strictures of time: "Gavin, sighing over his stiff joints, rode among her guards, to ease Vevay's mind" (106). Gavin's lightly sketched background is one of power; he had "commanded armies," (36) and been a favored counselor of the old king. In his prime he could have been any number of brave young sword-wielding fantasy men, but McKillip's world treats him differently. He is respected at court, but his joints are stiff and he is tired. Old wounds scar him, and, most importantly, he is not the center of the story. Nor is the "shrewd and vigorous King" (38) whose death precipitates the action of *Alphabet of Thorn*. Instead, the teenage protagonists and their struggles with their still-forming identities are the focus of the story. I am not making an argument for *Alphabet of Thorn* as a young-adult book though it, and other of McKillip's books, certainly could be; rather, I am arguing that McKillip's texts treat all of their characters and their ages with a complexity that fights cliché, allowing both the old and young a chance to be central to story, and, in turn, their worlds.

Moments of age-related realism can be found in many of McKillip's books, and these small gestures can be just as important to character as they can be to the pastoral, for example, in building a richer world, one more realistic than the stereotyped fantasy sword-and-sorcery. A person's past affects his or her physical state, and these realistic touches are added to several of McKillip's characters. It is one of the ways that McKillip's worlds and their rules tie into characters; age has consequences in McKillip's worlds and even small details display this. For example, in *The Book of Atrix Wolfe*, Atrix has given another elderly mage shocking news: "He laid a hand over his heart ... [Atrix] knelt at Hendrix's feet, took his other hand, felt the shocked blood pounding through Hendrix, and the pain pushing against his heart" (68). It is not written that the news is unwelcome, or that it is singularly shocking; instead, the realities of age demonstrate this. These small moments can also be used for humor, as when "Atrix ... took his own shape, trembling with exhaustion. His own shape refused to do anything for a while but lie on the oak leaves" (127). The realities of his great age allow for this slightly humorous moment, as does Unciel's great frailty in *In the Forests of Serre*: "In the garden he could see Unciel digging so slowly to unearth the roots of weeds that they probably expired naturally before he got them out of the ground" (24). Both these trivial moments of humor are only possible through the accurate portrayals of old age. McKillip's texts normalize aging but also build a more complete world with these small, realistic touches. Neither old man is treated as comedic in and of himself, but humor is created by their circumstances. They are presented with realism but also with sympathy, and the effects of their strenuous pasts are not glossed over but rather are intimately connected to both the story and the world's realism as a whole.

Three. Characters

The older characters of McKillip's texts are realistic, but they are not weighted with the bias often seen in primary world life. McKillip's Vevay might not be able to understand Tessera until the end, but she is an unusual creation in that she exists at all. Copper maintains that the lack of older women in any sort of media is concerning (7). Vevay is wise, powerful, and has no children. She is none of the stereotypes Copper argues against: "The mythical prototypes of the Wicked Old Witch with unnatural powers, the old Bad Mother with neurotic power needs, and the Little Old Lady, ludicrously powerless" (14). Vevay has an important role to play that goes beyond definitions of her either as a woman, or as old, and although her age creates limitations it does not do so in an unrealistic or dismissive manner; Vevay is feared and respected throughout the book.

The limitations of age are expressed upon the young as well as the old in McKillip's worlds, and just as the old can be burdened by their pasts, the young are sometimes disadvantaged by their lack of past experience. Mendlesohn contends that "in children's and adult's fantastic fiction, all too frequently adulthood is reduced to a mere matter of power, disengaged from emotional maturity or complexity" (*Diana* 20). McKillip's worlds fight this tendency, creating complex power relations as well as complex characters, unique to their individual circumstances and upbringings as well as ages. The young queen of *Alphabet of Thorn* is not a precocious and poised young woman for example, prepared to rule a kingdom from the moment it is suddenly passed to her. She is naïve, restless, saddened, and a teenager. Moody and vacant by turns, Tessera frustrates her mentor with her inability to understand the obstacles that she faces. Vevay, muses: "[Tessera] had learned everything obediently, but with a distinct lack of interest, her mind occupied by other matters. What matters these were eluded Vevay completely" (38). To Tessera the danger outside is vague, and her interests are more self-focused. This causes conflict with Vevay, who is supposed to be her counselor but is so far from the queen in age and experience that they are unable to understand, or effectively deal with, one another. The dynamics of their different ages, and the magic that complicates this further, are elements of the world in which they reside. However, even though there is conflict they are both allowed places in their world; each is vital not just to the plot but the kingdom of Raine and its world.

Time works on the body and mind in a variety of ways, and the tying of this aspect of the Temporal world into characters as well as landscapes (as will be discussed in later chapters) allows for a more complete world. Talis, in *The Book of Atrix Wolfe*, is a prince whose age is given as twenty, but who acts as though he is in his mid-to-late adolescence and is sympathetically portrayed. From an authorial perspective, while McKillip is compared to the Romantics in Chapter Five, her portrayal of adolescence is one way in which she differs. As John Neubauer suggests in *The Fin de Siècle Culture of Adolescence*, the Romantics portrayed the child as innocence in contrast to the corrupt adult (77), but this does not leave room for those who are between these two stages. Talis is one of McKillip's many characters who fills this gap, and does so sympathetically. This means that Talis is able to act in spite of his not-yet-fully formed powers and lack of wisdom. A deficiency of wisdom is not something inherent to Talis' character, or to any of the adolescents in McKillip's books. They are not created as inferior adults. McKillip's worlds work against what Christine Overall proposes is "the unthinking assumption that adulthood is the apex of life, for which childhood is the preparation and from which old age is merely the decline and downward deterioration." (297) McKillip's characters are allowed to be more nuanced than that. Talis's "callings were complex and surprising" (*Atrix* 146). Talis' power is strong, unexpected, and he comes into his own, yet he is not presented as a miniature adult with all the wisdom that implies. For example, in classic teenage fashion, he is slightly petty with the faery queen he encounters and falls in love with her. His older brother sees the danger he is in, but Talis insists that: "It really wasn't like that at all. It was like nothing I have ever known," (90) a typically adolescent response. On the other hand, this naïveté is balanced with an awareness of the complexity of the world. When speaking of the battle that killed his father, Talis muses: "No ... it wouldn't have been. Anything that simple" (111). He offers more than the black-and-white understanding often expected of adolescence. Talis and Tessera are balanced in adolescence, where age and identity become interwoven and essential to a sense of self. They are important to the worlds in which they reside, and neither is entirely dismissed for their sometimes adolescent responses.

Alternatively, the great wizard Atrix's mind is as active as ever, but the extended time that his body has lived limits him: "He rose again, compelled by mysteries, though he wondered how long his weary human shape could bear the confusion and strain of them" (148). This strain on his "weary human shape," along with the formed pattern of Atrix's thoughts, means that the action is often left to Talis. When the faery queen needs Atrix, it is Talis she ensnares and sends to get him, because Atrix has been unable to make his own way. Thus, McKillip's characters are fully integrated into their worlds, with logical consequences to their ages. Like Vevay, Atrix's advanced age means his thoughts have been corralled into patterns, making it difficult to see what he does not expect or understand. However, McKillip's worlds do not allow for clear-cut dichotomies. Just as Talis is able to mature, Atrix is eventually able to make it into the faery kingdom by widening his view. His advanced age does not entirely prevent him from reaching the faery kingdom. It simply means it takes him longer to change how he has seen the world. Vevay, too, needs the younger Tessera, though in a slightly different way: "'I was remembering,' [Vevay] said. 'Things that I had forgotten long ago.... You reminded me that that they are still there, buried away underneath the years'" (*Alphabet* 205). Vevay needs Tessera's youth and fresh understanding, just as Tessera needs Vevay's extensive experience.

Age is used in another fashion as well, however. Heroes are an important part of most fantasy works, and McKillip's books are no different in this. Where her novels do diverge from many others is in their portrayal of heroes in various life stages, especially the middle-aged hero. Her worlds do not favor any particular epoch, nor are characters pushed "off stage" when they reach a certain age. Some of McKillip's heroes are aging and it takes far more encouragement to set them off on adventures because they know that adventures are dirty, painful, and perhaps life-ending experiences. Journeys are not things to be eagerly anticipated and embarked upon without thought or care. This is one of the major ways in which McKillip's texts subvert the usual fantasy quest narrative, using older characters who must be driven into action, and who cannot be lured with promises of wealth or other treasure.

An example of an aging hero in McKillip's worlds is Cyan in *The Tower at Stony Wood*. He is someone who has fought well in the past, has behaved as a knight should, but is a reluctant hero, with a beloved he is loath to leave. As an older man, the thought of glory is not enough to motivate him. In this quotation, in which Harold Bloom explains his favorite version of Falstaff from William Shakespeare's *Henry IV*, we see a similar character: "Richardson's Falstaff was neither an adorable roisterer nor a kind of counter-courtier, eager for possibilities of power. Rather, he was a veteran warrior who had seen through warfare, discarded its honor and glory as pernicious illusions" (2). McKillip's middle-aged characters are under no illusions, and this gives them a particular sort of power and awareness of how the worlds in which they reside work.

In the stereotypical sword and sorcery-type fantasies, heroes are men (or masculine women) who seem to exist in the prime of youth, perpetually strong. McKillip's books largely ignore this tendency. McKillip's books do have conventional young heroes, but they are generally impetuous and not the main characters. Riven of Kardeth, in *The Book of Atrix Wolfe*, is an example of this. His refusal to back down from an unwinnable fight begins the slaughter that will haunt both his land and those he tried to conquer. He is only given a few lines at the beginning, showing him to be the brash young man he is, and that is all the reader sees of him. Salmon contends, "[i]n our society, the politics of age render some life phases more rewarding, more powerful, more prestigious than others" (20). From an authorial angle McKillip has done what she can to reverse this by not only focusing on characters who are not within these privileged categories, but by also allowing them action and power within the worlds in which they reside.

Another of the ways McKillip's worlds disrupt this typical fantasy trope is through characters who are accurate to their chronological ages, and to the amount of time they have lived on their worlds. If they are old and wise, they feel their age in their bones. If middle-aged, they see no reason to go haring off on adventure for the sake of it, leaving attachments and formed lives behind. And if young, they are aware of only what would be logical for someone their age and experience to know, without being dismissed entirely.

The past of McKillip's characters changes how they act in the present. *Od Magic* follows the untrained Brenden as he goes to work in the magic gardens of the School of Magic in the city of Kelior. One of his mentors, Yar, has a past filled with hardship but also wonder that colors his present actions. As a middle-aged man trusted by his employers and comfortable in his personal habits, Yar should be the epitome of the status quo. However, his past flavors how he deals with the present. Yar's creativity is explored in Chapter Six in relation to the city of Kelior where he resides, but what is important here is that he has *not* forgotten his past, his beginnings, and that enables him to be an actant for change rather than the middle-aged static person that he might otherwise have been. Yar's actions are unexpected because he is not the staid character he ought to be; the world he resides in has worked on him in subtle, often hidden, ways, and as a result he proves a surprise to those around him.

Simply because a character is middle-aged, however, does not mean that they have experienced their worlds in the same way, or that they are the same, or that their treatment in the text is similar. McKillip's characters grow organically out of their worlds, environments, and personal pasts. Each character, whether sketched briefly or given main character status, is given the detail or care necessary so that they appear to be people, with backgrounds and lives outside the main action. Just as McKillip's worlds are richer for being built as though there is more waiting to be discovered in terms of landscape, so too are her characters a part of building a denser world. There are no stand-ins or cardboard cut-outs in most of McKillip's books; each character, no matter how unimportant, influences or is influenced by the world around them, making the works of fiction holistic in that there is a sense of a complete world, one where everything ties into everything else, just as in the primary world.

Gender in McKillip

Characters are an integral part of a world; they are what populate it. Therefore, a rich and authentic world must be full of characters from all walks of life, women as well as men. Joanna Russ claims of science fiction that "[t]here are plenty of images of women in science fiction. There are hardly any women" (57). This is perhaps less true in fantasy than in science fiction (in fantasy there has always been the princess character, at least) but it is generally true that novels like *The Lord of the Rings* trilogy have hardly any women at all, while novels like Terry Brooks' *The Sword of Shannara* have women characters that seem to be made of cardboard, as place-holders or trophies. McKillip's worlds are enriched by ignoring, or playing with, gender conventions and allowing both men and women important places in them.

The most obvious place to start in terms of gender in McKillip is with her heroes, and, with her most pointed reply to Tolkien, *The Riddle-Master* trilogy. Hourihan proposes that female heroes "in most retellings of their exploits they are little more than honorary men" (68). McKillip's female heroes are both heroic and definitely female, not simply male heroes with long hair. Similarly, LeFanu contends that, "[t]he problem with these role-reversal stories—as with role-reversal societies—is that they do not necessarily challenge the stereotypes that they have reversed" (35). By having a variety of ages, occupations, characters, the women in McKillip's worlds, and the men too, challenge the stereotypes in which they are usually immersed. This variety of heroes means that I must disagree with Emmerichs who contends that McKillip wants to entirely circumvent the male hero and his quest (206). As Mains and others have noted, McKillip still uses the quest structure but she often expands this to include women as well as men, as examined below (see also Mains' "Having," which chronicles this extensively).

Emmerichs goes on to argue that the female hero's "identity is scripted by both function and (hero) and gender (feminine), a combination that does not yet fit seamlessly into the genre" (208). What Emmerichs contends might be true of some works within the genre, but it is not true of McKillip's works and this is largely, I propose, because these heroes do fit seamlessly into McKillip's *worlds*. From the authorial perspective this is clearly of interest to McKillip. In a guest blog post, McKillip herself writes of *The Forgotten Beasts of Eld*:

> It seemed very natural to me to wonder why in the world a woman couldn't be a witch or a wizard, or why, if she did, she had to be virginal as well. Or why, if she was powerful and not a virgin, she was probably the evil force the male hero had to overcome. Such was my experience reading about women in fantasy, back then ["Women in SF&F Month"].

This wondering has affected all of her books, and all of her characters, men as well as women. Spivack speaks of a trend in feminist fantasy, that,

> just as major women characters are often both masculine and feminine in their abilities, both expert with swords and devoted to peace, so male characters are also complex, with their aggressive natures modified by sensitivity. At the same time, those traditionally male traits of pride, sexual prowess, and desire for domination are often subjected to negative scrutiny [8].

I would expand this further within McKillip's work, however. McKillip's men have not all got "aggressive natures," modified or no. And "male traits of pride, sexual prowess, and desire for domination" are often missing altogether. For example, at the end of *The Tower at Stony Wood*, one of the witches who has sent Cyan on his quest explains to Cyan why he had to be the one to create a lasting peace:

> "We needed you." ... "We needed you to help Sel, and Thayne Ysse and the North Islands. We wanted all your courage and your gentleness, your determination, your loyalty and your gift for seeing and for doing, as when you heard the young boy crying in the rain, what must be done" [288].

None of these characteristics (other than courage and perhaps determination) are particularly male, or typically heroic. Gentleness certainly is not, and neither is empathy. It is these moments, when McKillip allows *both* men and women to escape gender constraints, that her worlds come alive.

From an authorial angle this is clearly of interest to McKillip. In an early interview with Ringel, quoted in "Women Fantasists: In the Shadow of the Ring," McKillip says "'[e]ven in college I thought I should write at least one volume from a woman's point of view ... because there were no women *for me* in Tolkien'" (166). This interest in writing women characters clearly spread throughout her works. Mains has explored McKillip's widening of the typical monomyth into a duomyth in the characters of Raederle and Morgon in "Having it All: The Female Hero's Quest for Love and Power in Patricia McKillip's *The Riddle-Master* Trilogy." They are definitively equal in the books; Morgon is the famed Riddle-Master of the title, but is, at times, stubborn, rash, and Raederle tells him so. Raederle too, like Morgon, appears to be an ordinary human at the beginning of the books. Aside from her beauty she is not remarkable in any way (like many a would-be heroine in a fantasy cliché). But, when their pasts become clearer, their heritage more frightening, it is discovered that Raederle is just as powerful as Morgon, and is perhaps even more dangerous as the half-child of his enemies. Raederle and Morgon are equal, and do not allow the problem Hourihan sees in much heroic fiction: "Even if she is lively and has a mind of her own ... the hero's greater age, experience and strength means that he is inevitably dominant in their relationship" (196). Raederle is allowed to be equal in many dimensions. As the daughter of a land ruler she is just as conversant with politics as Morgon, sometimes even more so because while he comes from the tranquil island of Hed, she was reared in the restless land of An. They are similar ages, and their magical powers grant them equal strength. If anything, it is Raederle who holds the upper hand as it is she who repeatedly refuses to marry Morgon, in spite of his and her family's wishes. It is a reflection of the world that they are in that Raederle is "allowed" this freedom, and can be Morgon's equal without question throughout the text.

It is not only in the character of Raederle that McKillip's worlds subvert gender expectations, and allow characters to maneuver against what might be their destiny, however. Spivack claims McKillip avoids women's roles found in "primary worlds medieval romances" (165) but this is not entirely true, and I would argue that it is her subversion of many different roles that allows her work to be so powerful. In her very first secondary-world fantasy there are already hints of subversion, especially within the character of Damsen. What appears to be an ordinary tale about a damsel in distress (she is even named Damsen in the story, as noted in Chapter Two) being rescued by a questing knight (or, Cnite, as he is in the book) ends with Damsen refusing to be won, or given away, or kept prisoner when she chooses her own destiny, and chooses to walk out of her father's castle in spite of (or perhaps because of) the Cnite's failed quest. Damsen is a true "feminist heroine" in LeFanu's definition because she resides squarely within a typical fantasy tradition, and yet escapes it. LeFanu notes:

> [w]hile Alyx and Jaisel are heroines in terms of their representation as tough, clever and independent, it is their place within a particular literary tradition of sword-and-sorcery and their subversion of that tradition that makes them what I would call "feminist heroines" [36].

A key point concerning Damsen is that she is not given particularly tough, clever, independent characteristics through much of the novel (although, since we only see her weeping and not her inner thoughts it is possible she is all of those things), but this means that it is, if anything, more a subversion when she does break out of her traditional role, her expected story. *The Throme of the Erril of Sherril* is a very short book, and as a result has little room for the un-questing Damsen, and yet, she is the memorable part of the story, and the crux of it. Her decision, not a successful conquering, stops the knight's quest. The world of *The Throme of the Erril of Sherril* allows for this subversion, and though most of Damsen's thoughts are unvoiced and she is given little of the action, she is allowed the upper hand in the end, and makes her own choice. It must be noted too that the Cnite is a knight who does

Three. Characters

not fight, and rather than being robed with the accouterments of knighthood he slowly has them taken away so that at the end he wears a leaf cloak instead of chain mail, has a lantern instead of a sword, and so on. All the implements for making war are changed to something else, and throughout it is his mind and empathy he must use and not his brute strength.

There have been discussions of "strong female characters" and what this entails. The term is a problematic one, and the reason why is best explained by authors such as George R. R. Martin, who have replied to the question of why they write "strong female characters" with the answer that they are people (Salter). McKillip's characters are people, whether male cook or female general. There have certainly been fantasies looking to subvert the barbarian/knight hero wielding his sword by replacing the man with a woman but no other change. McKillip's texts are much subtler, and as a result, her worlds and her stories are richer. McKillip's books not only have strong female leads like Sybel in *The Forgotten Beasts of Eld*, Sel in *The Tower at Stony Wood*, and Nyx in the *Cygnet* duology, they also, and more importantly, create tiny moments of subversion. When two characters from *The Bell at Sealey Head* go to rescue a friend, there is no assumption that it will be the male of the pair doing the rescuing. The female, Gwyneth, states: "I'll help with the awkward parts, like getting us into the house; you can have the heroics. The ones I don't want, that is" (243), and her male counterpart, Judd, suggests another friend can have the heroics. There is no assumption that Judd will be the one doing the heroics, and in this moment of humor the world allows them to be equal, even though it is otherwise a book with traditional seeming gender roles.

The texts also have strong female characters with flaws, and crucially, flaws unrelated to their gender. Sybel must learn to love, and to be hurt, Melanthos must accept she is human, Nyx must learn to take care of those around her. Sybel, Nyx, and Raederle are all powerful sorceress-type women, and this is another potential trap that McKillip's worlds have avoided in characters like Melanthos of *The Tower at Stony Wood*, and in Peri of *The Changeling Sea*. Peri is young and lost and stubborn, and allowed her own story in what could have been a simple romance. Melanthos, without grand magical powers, is also allowed her own story and strength within a greater plot, and a larger world. It is in this richness of characters that McKillip's worlds come alive.

There are babies, and elders, and everyone in between. Sel, the baker in *The Tower at Stony Wood*, goes to the tavern to have a drink, Guilia, in *Song for the Basilisk*, goes to sing because it pleases her. Neither is the focus of a male-centered authorial or otherwise gaze, and it is easy, indeed, necessary, to imagine them each with their own lives outside of the curtain of the book.

Characters in McKillip function both as introductions to her worlds, and disruptors of typical fantasy clichés. The interactions between her characters and their worlds means that their surroundings are richer, and in turn, the characters have more depth, enabling a fuller and more complete vision of a more equal world.

Four

Legends

McKillip's secondary worlds are rich for many reasons, but perhaps one of the most distinctive things about her work is her use of legend to add age, depth, and the texture of culture to her stories. McKillip's legends are both stories, and a way of inspecting the books in which they reside as a whole. The way in which they entwine with their books and worlds means that "[t]he interrelations, whether by authorial intent or not, provide critical insights not only into the world and its structure, but into the stories that are told within the world" (Ekman and Taylor 12). Legends are the primary way in which "the stories" "are told" within the worlds of McKillip, but also how those stories are examined. The legends of McKillip's worlds are part of the Social, Temporal, and Mythological worlds of her books, meaning the interrelations between history, the past, how characters are treated, and the mythology of the word are all incorporated into them.

I will start with a brief definition of what I mean by legend, go on to explore how McKillip invents her own legends, and then investigate how they are used. The legends tend to be used in one of three ways: as backdrop to the main story, as will be explored in a discussion of *The Forgotten Beasts of Eld* and others; as the framework for the story, as found in *Alphabet of Thorn* and *The Bards of Bone Plain*; and as an exploration of truth and how it can change from history into legend. Her legends, however they are used, serve to highlight the authenticity of her worlds as they intertwine with the present-day of the story. McKillip's legends both tie her worlds together internally and provide a way of distancing them from the primary world. This chapter is, therefore, an examination of one of the principal ways that depth and a secondary nature are emphasized in McKillip's secondary world fantasies.

Legend: A Definition

Myth, legend, and fairy-tale (or folktale) are often used interchangeably. I seek to differentiate them, not because they are wholly and always separate, but because a useful definition can be obtained by pointing out what legend is not. This clarification also serves to define what I mean by McKillip's legends in this chapter, which are generally not myth, nor fairy-tale.

Legend has classically meant a story having to do with heroes that might have once been historical but which has been changed into something larger than reality. This definition of legend is still relevant, but there is a second modern meaning as well. Modern legends still concern themselves with heroics, but they are not necessarily based inside our primary world and past. They are, however, something grounded in the world, whether that is of the primary or secondary kind. Attebery comments on the world aspect of legend, as well as its truth, "[t]ales provide rationale and an outline, ballads suggest an appropriate diction and tone, but legends, because they are told as true, offer whole magical worlds saturated with belief. Legend settings are vivid, self-consistent realms already adapted to the presence of the marvelous" (*Fantasy Tradition* 33). Attebery means something slightly different from me; he is talking of legends from the primary world, but his comment works equally well when moved to secondary worlds. It is this aspect of truth, of a tale to be believed in, and of a "marvelous" world, that I work with below.

In the *Encyclopedia of Fantasy* legend is described as "[e]vents or stories which have grown to mythic proportions.... Legends are closely associated with folktales, but usually on a heroic scale.... A collection of legends related to a culture's foundations and HERO figures becomes a mythology." In these definitions, myth, legend, and even folktale, are confused. A legend can grow into myth, according to this iteration. I would contend that it is, in fact, the opposite, that a myth, by becoming more specific, and concentrated, becomes a legend further down in time, when applied to a specific character.

Myth is a creation tale; it is man explaining how life came to exist. It is also an explanation story, presenting the unknown as knowable. There is usually a sense of great age about myth. Wolfe criticizes the term "new mythology" as being:

> An oxymoron, perhaps too often used to characterize science fiction or fantasy's function or appeal. Such terms possibly arise out of a desire to find cultural significance in a field that has seldom gained the serious attention of the dominant literary culture ... characterized by some rather vague and unpersuasive claims [*Critical* 81].

Although I believe the term "new mythology" can occasionally be helpful, as it is with Tolkien's *The Lord of the Rings*, Wolfe's argument is accurate in another way. What is often problematic about the term "new mythology," I would propose, is the use of mythology. Mythology is usually a set of stories or parables either explaining the occurrence of natural phenomena or explaining the creation of the world. In a scientific and rational age, this is no longer common. Where many use the term "myth," what they mean is "legend." In *Strategies of Fantasy* Attebery explains that "*myth* is used to designate any collective story that encapsulates a world view and authorises belief" (2). When there is not a need to explain, legends can provide a similar sense of age and heroics. Legends are therefore a way to provide a history and culture to an invented world. I do not argue entirely against the utilization of the word myth in relation to fantasy. What I am suggesting is that there is a different something at work in various ways within some of McKillip's works, something that is connected to the past, like myth, but separate from it and more closely related to individuals and the epic. And that is legend.

Fairy-tale is another term often tangled with legend and myth that I will not work with here. It is defined in the *Encyclopedia of Fantasy* as "[a] narrative derived from oral tradition which relates a well understood and recognizable story" (359). Tatar also explains it as a limited form of literature (xvi). Fairy-tales are predominantly seen as stories relating to the folk (thus their conflation with "folktale") or lower classes, with a prescribed plot and type of character (as explored by Propp in *Morphology of the Folktale*). Fairy-tales serve a purpose in society, but it is not the same function as that performed by legends. Legends are grand and heroic. They tell of lives writ large by circumstance or fate. Fairy-tales usually explain the familiar and legends the epic.

From an authorial point of view, when authors began creating entirely separate secondary worlds, a need for new legends also arose. Because tales based in secondary worlds are separated from our primary world, the inclusion of our primary-world legends could break the disconnect. Secondary worlds are, by and large, full of heroics, legends give this stature and a familiar sense of form. Ekman notes that "[f]antasy is a genre where old tales, motifs, and characters are brought to life again, in ways which make them relevant once more to their contemporary readers" (7). Modern legends are a part of secondary world fantasy that serve this purpose "bringing to life" not just the characters in the legends, but the worlds that form them.

When Ursula K. Le Guin, McKillip, and others began to create autonomous secondary worlds in the 1960s and 1970s, they created stories with power outside of themselves as well as a need for new terminology to encompass what they did. Le Guin and Tolkien are considered mythic storytellers. They are often grouped together, but in fact, the basis of their worlds is different. Le Guin's Earthsea is entirely independent of Earth, and life in our primary world. In Middle-earth, however, Tolkien created a mythology for Earth; it was still connected to our world, albeit tenuously. Tolkien's tales are myth because he sought to create a backstory for England, a shared history of how man came to power on the earth. Alternatively, Le Guin and McKillip are creating their own separate worlds, with their own separate histories. They seek to explain life, but not through any real or forged mimesis. Thus a different terminology is needed.

The farther into the rational and scientific age humanity goes, the less need there is to re-tell traditional myths. As Attebery contends in *Stories About Stories*:

> the difference is not the ability to apply skeptical reason to magical motifs and supernatural beliefs; rather, it is the new awareness of myth as something belonging to others, to the past, to unfallen primitives. The advent of the scholarly study of myth marked the loss of myth [26].

Myth has changed from its historical antecedents, and I propose that this change has made it into something that McKillip is not doing in her fantasies; she is not looking (by and large) *to explain*. What she does do, is provide legends; stories about the heroic, connected in some way to truth. I will explore how this different iteration of story is used to enrich, and tie together, McKillip's worlds.

Legend Invention

Legends in McKillip's work are important from an authorial as well as critical perspective, so I will touch on that briefly. McKillip uses primary-world fairy-tales, such as the Russian fairytales found *In The Forests of Serre*, which Pilinovsky explores in her article "The Mother of All Witches: Baba Yaga and Brume in Patricia McKillip's *In the Forests of Serre*." McKillip is also frequently lauded for adding feminist twists to fairytales (see Ann F. Howey's "Changing Self, Changing Other: Patricia McKillip's *The Changeling Sea* as Feminist Fairy Tale"), but fairy-tales are not what I am focusing on here. Although she uses primary-world stories in some of her novels, such as *The Tower at Stony Wood* and *In the Forests of Serre*, (the Lady of Shalott and Russian fairytales respectively),[1] McKillip also invents her own legends. In the following pages I explore McKillip's invented legends, everything from the fabulous animals in *The Forgotten Beasts of Eld* to the aging but infamous mages in *In the Forests of Serre, The Book of Atrix Wolfe*, and *Alphabet of Thorn*, and argue from a critical perspective that this is one of the primary ways in which depth but also an alien, unfamiliar nature are added to McKillip's worlds.

Attebery proposes in *The Fantasy Tradition in American Literature: From Irving to Le Guin* that "[a] perceptive writer of fantasy can take hold of remembered legends and extract the truth that remains in them" (36). McKillip does this to a degree but using her own legends, her own inventions to "extract the truth." She accomplishes this by exploring how legends are formed, what happens to the people (or animals) who are in the legends, and by inventing her own secondary-world legends. Attebery goes on to contend that:

> Fantasy is not myth, which is generally held to be ancient, anonymous, and traditional, but it is one of the many endeavors we have undertaken to continue the process of mythmaking into a literate, individualistic age [166].

McKillip's invention of and use of legend is another way to "continue mythmaking" in the modern world, but in a way separate from traditional myth. The wavering line between good and evil, light and dark, is part of what differentiates modern legend from its classical (usually Judeo-Christian) forbearers. The broader the world becomes, the more obvious it is that evil is often simply difference or the unknown. The breaking of the world into absolutes is no longer as easy as it seemed in the past, and thus a new kind of legend as well as myth is needed. Ann Swinfen writes in *In Defense of Fantasy: A Study of the Genre in English and American Literature since 1945*, that "the modern writer of fantasy cannot start from a widely accepted basis of belief"

(2). A modern legend, therefore, does not begin with a familiar historical figure, as perhaps ancient primary world legends did, but rather with the familiar shape of one. A legend by traditional definition is filled with heroic characters, a grand tone, and a sense of historical importance. McKillip's legends, though invented, fulfill these qualifications. McKillip's stories are filled with heroes, both big and small. The importance of their tasks is never in doubt, even when the motivation is. McKillip's prose style is one of the most remarked-upon features of her writing; it is lyrical and old fashioned. Lastly, the past is thick in McKillip's works; her works (and worlds) have their own pasts, their own histories. The Temporal world is conflated with the Social and Mythological world; the heroes one is reading about become part of this tradition within the books themselves, like when Nyx's lifestyle as a swamp witch in *The Sorceress and the Cygnet* is treated as legendary by other denizens of her kingdom in *The Cygnet and the Firebird*, tying the legends and characters into the fabric of the worlds.

There are several reasons for the invention of legends. One is that this allows more freedom. There are no traditions to be satisfied, no endings or characterizations to be upheld or not when invented legends are used. For example, when McKillip rewrote the story of Tam Lin for *Winter Rose* deliberate choices were made about what parts of the traditional story to keep, and what to discard. By working with an already extant legend, McKillip had to make choices about where to stay with traditional ideas of the story, and where to break from them. By creating her own legends McKillip is free to use them as she wills. There are few expectations to negotiate with; those expectations that are present, which McKillip can play with, are those applicable to all legends. For example, McKillip has aging heroes in *Alphabet of Thorn* and *The Book of Atrix Wolfe* or women heroes as in *The Forgotten Beasts of Eld* and *Alphabet of Thorn*. Thus, McKillip can use the expectations provided by the form of the legend, without being constrained by specific primary-world legends and their attendant expectations.

From a critical perspective, as well as having fewer preconceived ideas to uphold or disrupt, the invention of legend keeps the secondary world intact and adds depth to it. To be sure, the change of names (Brume for Baba Yaga for example in *In the Forests of Serre*) helps with this disconnection, but the recognizable primary-world fairy-tale attributes are still there. The Baba Yaga story, for example, has certain familiar characteristics, giving the story specific expectations. The mix of primary world tale and an invented secondary world can also be done clumsily, as James remarks in his essay, "Tolkien, Lewis and the Explosion of Genre Fantasy": Tolkien's exclamation of "[i]t really won't do!" (71), probably alluded to Lewis's "apparently slapdash world-building" with its inclusion of Greek mythology, Father Christmas, and a host of other primary-world characters. Without allusion to outside fairy-tale, myth and legend, McKillip's texts are able to have the same effects of these forms, but without breaking the secondary world barrier. There can be warning stories, learning stories, and at times poetic stories within McKillip's worlds that act just as legends do in the primary world, but without overt reminders of them. Tristram Coffin in *The Female Hero in Folklore and Legend* defines the difference between folklore and legend as "there is an atmosphere of belief present when legends are told" (4). It is this sense of belief that is vital to secondary worlds. As Tolkien argued in his seminal essay, "On Fairy-Stories," full belief in the world created by fantasy is essential to its purpose; and by inventing legends, this belief is uninterrupted in McKillip's texts.

Legend is never given a definition in McKillip's work, though small clues are presented. For example, in *The Sorceress and the Cygnet* Calyx says: "Legend says that during a siege by the Delta armies, the house moved to the northern fields of Withy Hold." And her sister responds, "[l]egend.... It's a thousand year old tale" (147). Legend and tale are differentiated here; legend is something that could be true, and tale is not, is something that has been distorted with time. In the preface to the second edition of *Deutsche Mythologie* (1844) Jacob Grimm explains; "[t]he fairy-tale flies, the legend walks, knocks at your door; the one can draw freely out of the fullness of poetry, the other has almost the authority of history." Legend then is set apart from tale; it has the weight of history behind it and is therefore seen as something old, and changed, but at some point true, adding weight and authenticity to the secondary worlds that encompass it.

Some of the best examples of McKillip's created legends are found in *The Forgotten Beasts of Eld*. The legendary beasts of the title are vital to the story, and to creating a sense of a different, more luminous world than our primary world. Each is given a traditionally-phrased backstory. Cyrin the Boar, for example, is introduced thus: Sybel's father "caught like a salmon the red-eyed, white-tusked Boar Cyrin, who could sing ballads like a harpist, and who knew the answers to all riddles save one" (4). The lyricism of the lines lends to the atmosphere of legend, as does the syntax; "All riddles save one" is both an elegant phrase and one that adds scope to the description of Cyrin. The natural question, which riddle does he not know the answer to is brought to the fore, but in a deft way. Cyrin is introduced with appropriate aplomb, and even within those few short lines, is given a backstory suitable for a legend creating a vista opening out from the specific narrative being presented. There is the intimation that there is much more to Cyrin and his backstory, even if it is not directly presented in the text. This opening out is similar to Clute's *Encyclopedia of Fantasy* concept "time abyss,"[2] where there is an intimation of action and history having happened in the past of the world that is not necessarily made explicit in the story.

McKillip's texts trace the creation of legend in a number of ways, which adds to the sense of history and a past that grounds her worlds. In *The Forgotten Beasts of Eld* the animals are so legendary as to be assumed to be mere story. However, in McKillip's books legends are brought out of the past and story and in to the present and the world. Stories are not just stories in McKillip's work. (Mains in "Bridging" and Pilinovsky also examine the nature of story in McKillip's works.) The legendary creatures in *The Forgotten Beasts of Eld* have been out of recollection so long that even their legends are known by only a few. A woman who married one of Sybel's wizard ancestors, for example, "was of poor family, with tangled hair and muscled arms, and she saw in Myk's household things that others saw perhaps once in their lives in a line of old poetry or in a harpist's tale" (4–5). The animals that walk casually around Myk's, and then Sybel's, households are so legendary they only exist in fragments out in the greater world. The animals are presented not only as old, as legends, but things of beauty, incorporated into poetry and song, but also as things so ancient as to be lost, unreal to most of the denizens of the world. This assumption of unreality happens to the animals of *The Forgotten Beasts of Eld,* but in other of McKillip's works as well meaning that various stages of legend are presented and this is dependent on how they are treated within the world they inhabit.

In *The Sorceress and the Cygnet,* for example, the stories told as complete fiction are shown to be alive. *The Sorceress and the Cygnet* follows a young man, Corleu, on his quest to free his trapped love from the constellation sign that holds her captive. On his journey he meets a sorceress, Nyx, who agrees to help him out of curiosity. Nyx and Corleu discuss the reality of the legends they are encountering;

> "It is a banner, a constellation, an ancient war sign. A song. How could you walk into it?" [Nyx asks] "Who am I to know that?" [Corleu] asked her. "The likes of me? How did the Cygnet get into the sky? How did the Gold King's house get into a song? Maybe it was us put them there. Or maybe they're the ones whispered to us that they were there. Or something was there, hiding behind Cygnet, behind sun's face. Something dark and powerful and terrible, that we hung faces on to make them less terrible" [48].

In this quotation several reasons for the founding of legends are explored: that humans invented them, that the legends themselves influenced humans to "invent" them, or that nature was vast and terrible and given human stories to become more comprehensible. This variety intimates that the legends have grown organically out of the world in which they are placed, just as they do in the primary world. Different kinds of worlds create different stories, and the various ways in which McKillip's texts have legends form is in perfect keeping with this.

In one of McKillip's earliest books a clear interest in legend and how it evolves is already presented. *The Throme of the Erril of Sherril* is filled with moments of backstory and legend. The book as a whole is an adventure that charts the hero's progress from legend to legend, only to discover in the end that nothing is quite as it has appeared. The hero, Cnite Caerles asks: "But the Mirk-Well of Morg does not exist. It is a line in a song, a passage of a tale told to children by firelight. How can I go to a place that is not there?" (30). Yet he attempts to go to several places that are lines in songs, or tales; showing that within McKillip's worlds, story can be entered and changed. Meredith Veldman in *Fantasy, The Bomb, and the Greening of Britain* claims that

> A central theme in *The Lord of the Rings* is that legend and reality interweave in a seamless web.... Tolkien's characters discover that "the songs have come down among us out of strange places, and walk visible under the Sun" [81].

The same can be said of *The Cygnet and the Firebird*, but also *Alphabet of Thorn* and others of McKillip's books where ancient legends come to life. Legends are not left in the legendary past in McKillip's worlds; they are played with, brought to life, and treated with realistic consequences.

In *The Sorceress and the Cygnet* the exploration of story and in a way history, is done from inside the story itself; Corleu discovers this to his horror when he finds himself inside what he had thought of as a children's rhyme:

> It was a small folk rhyme, about a dark house falling, falling out of the sky, and how you must never enter it, for having entered you will never leave....
> He lay listening, his skin prickling with horror, because the door was open, he could have touched the dusty sill with his hand, but he could not move; he had leaped beyond the world into a child's song, into the story behind the song [31].

Corleu has become part of a rhyme, something used to entertain children, not just assumed but *known* to be unreal, until he lands in it, and must find his way out again. To find his way out he must go from story to story, and only by dealing with and acknowledging them as reality can he move on. The world of *The Sorceress and the Cygnet* is designed to show the truth behind song and legend, but in a different way to other books by McKillip. McKillip enhances the authenticity of her worlds by adding layers of story within story (Mains discusses a slightly different aspect of this in "Bridging"), creating worlds with depth to them. These stories mean that there is not just Material life to her worlds—there is a life of the mind, a Social world within the characters, who invent legends, or hear of them, or try to discover the veracity of them.

Woven into this exploration of story is the old superstition that fairies and other supernatural creatures need belief to stay "alive." In conversation with one of the constellations Corleu has been trapped by, in *The Sorceress and the Cygnet*, he is told;

> The Gold King is a moldy old shepherd's tale, one of those silly stories that get passed around the world like air, only if they were dreams and smoke they wouldn't be keeping such as the Gold King alive, would they, listening to his spoken name? [34].

Therefore, the need works both ways. The constellations are dependent on people's belief, but people need the stories as well. It is intimated that the stories attached to the constellations are ancient, and even when they are considered to be mere stories they are passed from generation to generation, implying that there is importance in them beyond being "just stories." This ties the stories to the fabric of the world and vice versa, as each is dependent on the other. Sellers contends that stories are an important way for people to connect and communicate (vii). In *The Sorceress and the Cygnet* and in others of her works, McKillip presents legends in ways that make clear their continued importance, both to their own secondary world and to the primary world.

The stories that McKillip has created, surrounding a group of constellations that she has invented, serve as the equivalent of secondary-world legend. They are not stories from the primary world, but they serve similar functions to those types of tales. Bruno Bettelheim emphasizes in *The Uses of Enchantment: The Meaning and Importance of Fairy Tales* that stories serve as fun, but also as warnings, and guidance. McKillip, by implanting her own stories, maintains the secondary-world immersion while allowing the stories to serve the roles they play in the primary world as well, further shoring up her secondary world.

By having their own, unique, sets of constellations and their attendant stories, the *Cygnet* duology is doing something different to many other stories that explore the same topic. Jones' *Dogsbody*, for example, tells the story of the star Sirius from our primary world constellations. *Cygnet*, however, in having its own constellations, keeps the secondary world intact. Having their own stories and legends in the secondary world intimates that they have their own culture and history as well. This layer upon layer of history and story creates a dense world in a short amount of writing, and ensures that the Material world is entangled with the Social, Temporal, and Mythological worlds. From the readerly perspective it would, perhaps, have been easier for the reader to follow had there been familiar constellations like the Big Dipper. However, the use of invented constellations means that the reader is in an alien land. Stars, which are familiar to everyone, take on new strangeness when their patterns are different to what we are used to. Thus the reader is thrust fully into a fantastic landscape, one with a different physical look as well as stories, and a past, all its own.

Just as the reader is encouraged to experience the songs and traditions of the secondary-world's past as actual things, stories that are both story and true happenings, so too are McKillip's characters in *The Sorceress and the Cygnet*. The concept is introduced subtly but quite early on in *The Sorceress and the Cygnet*. Boys listen to stories told by Corleu. "They were silent a little; the thick, blazing stars had edged closer, it seemed, to listen to Corleu's tales" (10). The clue is a small one: "stars had edged closer," but because this is a fantasy, and a McKillip fantasy at that, the stars have literally done so. The constellations that will come to life are indeed listening to Corleu and his tales. When Corleu asks why it is his life that has been interrupted, one of the star signs, the Gold King replies; "You were always saying our names, stargazing, never thinking who might be listening. Why did you go into my house? You knew what it was" (36). Corleu is somewhat like Coren in *The Forgotten Beasts of Eld*, someone close to the old legends, the old stories. However, Coren is different from Corleu in that Coren struggles against the disbelief of others, not himself. Coren argues with his brother Eorth: "A boar told you all that?" "He talks." "Oh, Coren, you have told us ridiculous things, but—" "It is not ridiculous. It is true. Eorth, you never could see farther than the sword in your hand—" (145). Coren is disbelieved by others, but he knows with certainty that the legends he perceives are real. Corleu, however, must struggle against his own disbelief. The sorceress Nyx chides him: "For someone who just came face to face with a story, you're far too ready to dismiss them" (*Sorceress* 56). In the fantastic, belief is imperative. Corleu has the constellation's stories, the knowledge of their meaning, but not, quite, the belief necessary to deal with them until the very end of the book and this encourages the reader, too, to invest fully in the veracity of McKillip's worlds.

This belief in story, in legends, is important to other novels of McKillip's besides *The Forgotten Beasts of Eld* and *The Sorceress and the Cygnet*. In *Alphabet of Thorn*, remembering legend, piecing together history and the past, is vital to the peaceful resolution of the story. The famed sorcerer Kane and her king have to be reconstructed, rediscovered in history and story before the land of Raine can be prepared for their invasion. "King and mage. Rulers of the entire known world. No one born who didn't learn their names. And where are they now? Vanished like rain" (35). This mystery is not just of historical importance in *Alphabet of Thorn*; it is vital to keeping the world as they know it intact. *Alphabet of Thorn* and *The Bards of Bone Plain* are structured differently, but the reconstruction of old stories and legends is just as important to the denizens of Raine as to Corleu in *The Sorceress and the Cygnet*.

All stages of legends are investigated in McKillip's work, implying that they have grown organically out of the worlds in which they exist.

Four. Legends

In *The Forgotten Beasts of Eld*, before the book has even ended there are further legends being created. To the reader, the lion Gules has become familiar, no longer a creature of legendary status but a lion, almost a pet of the sorceress Sybel. However, the legends that surround Gules are being continually remade, as the last glimpse of him makes clear: "There was a harpist-warrior who made a song already of the sight of Gules bounding before twenty unarmed warlords across the Slinoon river" (206). At the end of *The Forgotten Beasts of Eld* the beasts of Eld have been transformed back into the legends they had been, moving out of the real and back into story, making clear that acts of creation and dilution can work both ways.

The same transformation is shown at its beginning, taking shape around someone who is far from being legendary material. The young queen, Tessera, in *Alphabet of Thorn* is described as being quite plain, sullen, and a typical teenager in most respects. Vevay, however, has overheard others speaking of Tessera and muses: "Along with beauty, strength, and wisdom, [Tessera] had acquired magical powers. She would be the last to recognize herself" (108). The legends are shaping around the "rabbitty"-faced young Queen even before her reign is stable. The power of story has already begun to transform her into what history will remember. McKillip's books trace this path of reality to history (and therefore story, poetry, and more). In *Alphabet of Thorn*, the old warrior Gavin says, "[h]eroes die a hero's death. Always. In tales if not in truth" (36). With this, he notes that the reality of the past is easily changed, and turned into something more interesting, or perhaps just more beautiful than the truth. The awareness of legend and how it is shaped means that McKillip's characters are more conscious of stories than is sometimes typical. Though I will not go into a discussion of metafiction here, from an authorial perspective this is an aspect of how McKillip reminds her readers of story and its importance, and its probable influence in their own lives, in turn adding reality to the worlds she builds.

This looking at the end of legends, rather than their beginning, does not just apply to people in McKillip's novels. In *The Bards of Bone Plain*, the bardic school founded by the legendary Declan is described: "The school's reputation had spread far and wide, causing bardic schools to spring up everywhere to emulate it. It had become legendary, and as happens with legends, it was relegated mostly to the imagination"

(243). The school has become legendary, and in doing so it has passed beyond its prosaic purpose into story. The wry sense of humor in the comment also serves to highlight that being a legend is not always a positive. The text is not only speaking to the school's fate but also more broadly to that of the people who inspire the legends. They are treated as being just as mythical as the creatures of *The Forgotten Beasts of Eld*. It is their deeds that are remembered, but it is their reality that is shown, thus adding to the Social world, as well as the authenticity of McKillip's worlds.

Use of Legend

McKillip rarely seems to go back to lands she has already explored. The kingdoms in *The Forgotten Beasts of Eld* are explored once, for example, but not again. This limited space means that there is an impetus to create backstory, and a feel of history and past, succinctly. In describing the main sorceress Sybel for example, her lover Coren tells her "[a]nd you are beautiful, ivory and diamond-white, fire-white, with eyes as black as Drede's heart ... blacker ... black as the black trees in Mirknon Forest where the King's son Arn was lost three days and three nights and came out with pure white hair" (29). The line is beautiful; "ivory," "diamond-white," even "fire-white" all create a feel of sumptuousness and beauty in keeping with the lyrical tone, but the description of a lover's eyes as black as a cruel man's heart is also atypical and reflects on their relationship. From Coren, who knows the legends of the lands of *The Forgotten Beasts of Eld* better than anyone save wizards, this description is a compliment rather than insult. The legend itself can be used as a shortcut; to express unusual beauty, as well as the lover's relationship to each other and their relationship to the world in which they live. The insertion of a legend from within the world of *The Forgotten Beasts of Eld* works in keeping the mystique of the world intact. An explanation of who Arn was, or where the Mirknon Forest is, is unnecessary. All of this is created with a quick allusion to a legend that is not detailed.

These small sorts of details are important in other ways. The minor details given to the animals of legend in *The Forgotten Beasts of Eld* are an example of what Mendlesohn and James claim, in *A Short*

History of Fantasy, made Tolkien so popular, the feeling of more world (4). The same can be argued for McKillip's texts; there is more world intimated beyond what has been placed on the page, and it gives her books a depth and feeling of great age that they might not have had otherwise. A clear example of the type of detail that Tolkien was famous for can be found in McKillip's description of the Black Swan of Tirilith from *The Forgotten Beasts of Eld*: "the great-winged, golden-eyed bird that carried the third daughter of King Merroc on its back away from the stone tower where she was held captive" (4). Neither King Merroc nor his daughter are discussed at any other point in the book, but this bit of detail gives the Swan's backstory a richness that it might not have had otherwise. It places both the Swan, and the story, within a specific history, one grounded in a world. Furthermore, as Marek Oziewicz contends, "[t]he specificity of time and space is highly important and entails the need to construct a whole history of the secondary reality which is the background for the plot" (88). Invented legends are but one important way that McKillip's texts imbue secondary worlds with intricacy and detail. The invented legends give the books a feel of depth in terms of there being more world hidden away, but an awareness of time having passed is important as well; this is a clear expression of Clute's time abyss. Though the history intimated in the Swan's background is not detailed, it is there, and because of this the world of *The Forgotten Beasts of Eld* has an evident detailed past as well as the present-day that is presented, even if it is a past that is not viewed fully.

These small moments of legend and depth can be found in others of McKillip's novels, although not, perhaps, in quite the same way. For example, in *The Bards of Bone Plain*, "[t]he leaf was flying across the grass toward the great standing stones that circled the crown of the knoll above the river in a dance that had begun before Belden had a name" (10). At this point in the book the standing stones have not been explained, and their relationship with the land of Belden too is a mystery; this simple description provides the reader with several clues without being explicit. In *Alphabet of Thorn* the main character, Nepenthe, says to her lover, Bourne, that; "there is a legend—" and he responds: "There always are.... They gather on places of great antiquity like barnacles" (74). In establishing these "barnacles," in moments both large and small, McKillip's texts weave a tapestry of age and breadth throughout the worlds without overburdening them. By not always focusing on these "barnacles" there is a feeling that there is more to the world, and its past, than is visible in the book.

In several novels, including *Ombria in Shadow*, legends also serve as framing devices. The legend in *Ombria in Shadow* is presented as something not to be taken seriously. It begins with a tale told to the young prince, of a shadow Ombria: "A city rose behind Ombria, a wondrous confection of shadow that towered even over the palace" (40). The language is fanciful, ornate, and sweet; "confection," "wondrous," the story is told by a goose puppet to entertain a frightened young boy. The story is treated as just that, a story, but it takes on additional meaning as it winds through the background of *Ombria in Shadow*. The story's veracity is revealed, but only gradually. The ending of the book is framed by the same sense of unreality that began it. In the end, Ombria has shifted, the tale has come true, and we once again see the tale being told as just a story by those who have forgotten their previous adventures, meaning that the truth-as-tale begins and ends the book. Although the parallel Ombria and its legends can appear superfluous to the main story of the young prince Kyel, fighting to keep his throne, it is this different slant, this peculiar framing device, that allows *Ombria in Shadow* to be one of McKillip's most challenging, and most enjoyed, books. The threads of the tale of the parallel Ombria wind throughout the book, and its world, meaning that inconsequential oddities—a chimney beginning below a plot of sunflowers, for example—are important clues to the reality of the tale.

The story that shapes the plot is barely visible but of fundamental importance to the book itself as well as to the world of Ombria. Ombria's past incarnations and parallel shadow self are defining legends, but as none of the characters (or the reader) are sure of their veracity, they are left as a mysterious backdrop. Lydea tells the tale of Ombria's shadow other to the Prince Kyel at the beginning of the story;

> The shadow city of Ombria is as old as Ombria. Some say it is a different city completely, existing side by side with Ombria in a time so close to us that there are places-streets, gates, old houses-where one time fades into the other, one city becomes the other. Others say both cities exist in one time, this moment and you walk through both of them each day [4].

Ombria in Shadow begins with truth presented as fairytale, as false. At the end of *Ombria in Shadow*, Lydea is again telling a story to the Prince. The Prince asks if there is a sorceress who lives beneath the city, and Lydea "paused again, glimpsing a barely remembered tale. 'I think she does. Maybe even her own city beneath Ombria'" (290). The sorceress does exist, Lydea has even been to her ancient domain beneath Ombria, but it has been forgotten. The reality of Ombria has been forgotten, returned to legend. Legends start and end *Ombria in Shadow*, and in between their truth is explored. In this way, legend frames *Ombria in Shadow* as it does *Alphabet of Thorn* and *The Bards of Bone Plain*, but to a much subtler degree.

In *Alphabet of Thorn* and *The Bards of Bone Plain* legend and story are used as a framework but by a more obvious means. Both books are structured around a central legend which in the end is found to be true. In this way the Material world of characters; the world they live in, and the Mythological and Temporal world of tales and past, are all woven together inextricably. In *The Bards of Bone Plain*, the chapters alternate between a scholarly paper on the legends surrounding the bard Nairn and the modern day quest of his son for answers. In *Alphabet of Thorn*, a translator piecing together a legend's meaning in troubled times is alternated with chapters of the document itself. In *Alphabet of Thorn*, a bit of poetry or song is presented along with what happened. For example, "*Axis slew his father, / The good, the just. / The Serpent swallowed his bones, / And the bloody-handed child became king.* It was actually a tranquil afternoon beside the river" (46). The King is eaten by a crocodile while playing with his son, and this, in turn, is woven into the much more ruthless poem. This transformation gives flesh to the world and adds multiple layers to its structure.

In *The Bards of Bone Plain*, the tone of the intermittent "truth" chapters is scholarly. For example, Nairn's beginnings are given prosaically. "*He is first named in the records of the village of Hartshorn as the son of a farmer in the rugged wilds of the north Belden known then as the marche*" (14). From an authorial perspective McKillip does not go as far as some authors (like Jorge Luis Borges or Susanna Clarke), who construct fake footnotes to add a sense of authenticity, but there is still an attempt at a different type of language use. From a critical angle, in both novels the tone of the chapters dealing with the past of the legend is different from the story chapters. The chapters in the contemporary time of the book, where the reader follows the main characters, read more like the typical third-person story of other works by McKillip. Both books show their subjects as being real people instead of simply legends, who will interact (or who already interact in the case of *The Bards of Bone Plain*) with the modern characters. The introduction of the legendary people as real is done quite late in both books, though less so in *The Bards of Bone Plain.* This placement is perhaps because the terror of the unknown is what motivates the characters in *Alphabet of Thorn*, while for the contemporary characters in *The Bards of Bone Plain* it is only when they understand that the legends have "come to life" that they become truly frightened. Because the character Nairn is active within *The Bards of Bone Plain*, disguised as Jonah, clues to the legend are interwoven throughout the book. *Alphabet of Thorn* takes shape in retrospect when the identity of the legends is proven to be real. Even though slightly different takes are employed, both books use the frame of legend come to life to explore the legends, their protagonists, and the worlds from which they are formed.

In both books there are clues and hints about the legends that can prove to be both true and false. For example, in *Alphabet of Thorn* both the first ruler and the great sorceress Kane are presented as men in poems, story, and history. Both, however, were women. Characters in *Alphabet of Thorn* argue:

> "Legends change through time. They get tangled up with other legends, names change, events that have nothing whatsoever to do with the legend cling to them and change." "I know that. But sex is usually constant. Men don't change into women" [117].

And yet it has happened not once but twice, highlighting the mutability of story, and the fallibility of words. Several of McKillip's texts deal with this mutability of story, and though the politics of what is remembered and what is forgotten is not commented on (no one emphasizes that it is *women* of great power who have been changed into men), it is still important to the story and to the sense of progression the worlds contain. Alexandra Bolintineanu, in her essay "'On the Borders of Old Stories': Enacting the Past in *Beowulf* and *The Lord of the Rings*," proposes that: "Both [*Beowulf* and *The Lord of the Rings*] sometimes offer competing versions of past events (one authoritative, the other suspect), showing that the legendary past can be distorted in the telling, from conscious desire or ignorance" (265–266). In McKillip's books, the transmutation of fact into legend does not often seem to be deliberately distorted, but it is shown happening quite frequently.

This adds to the authenticity of the worlds, their legends are created and distorted just as legends are in the primary world.

One instance when this distortion is deliberate occurs in *Alphabet of Thorn*, when Kane's legendary status has been intentionally changed because she needs to remain a mystery. Her status as lover to the king must be disguised, as well as all the basic details about her; her gender, who she is, where she actually came from. This is one of the few times where history is shown being distorted purposefully, and there are clear reasons for doing so within the world:

> They had not yet become lovers, which is why legend was silent about their early relationship. Until she masked herself, Kane remained simply unseen. Until the cousin vanished, presumed lost in an unremarkable life between the lines of history, the magician, the lover, the Hooded One, could not exist [53].

This deliberate retelling is different from alterations when ignorance, or fancy, are involved. For example, when the old king is killed by accident, the child Kane who has witnessed it gives a credible account, and yet "while events were sorted in a haphazard fashion to a coherent conclusion, impressions lingered and turned, long past memory, into myth" (49). A simple, if sad, tale is transformed through time. "He wore a light shirt of metal scales and a gold sheath for his knife in his belt. These things were magnificently transformed later into elaborate armor and a sword that had drunk the blood of thousands" (46–47). Legend has taken the place of fact, has mutated the past into something fanciful. This transmutation is perhaps self-referential, much of fantasy is about the ordinary being made fantastic. It also means that each world of McKillip's is not a static one, built and then left changeless. Legends are one of the ways there is an intimation of movement, that builds a sense of a Temporal world, one that changes over time. Robert H. Boyer and Kenneth J. Zahorski contend in "The Secondary Worlds of High Fantasy," that, "[a]lthough of vital importance, verisimilitude is not enough. A secondary world must also create in the reader a feeling of 'arresting strangeness,' a feeling of awe and wonder" (57). Although McKillip's works themselves inspire both verisimilitude and moments of "awe and wonder," by creating her legends she includes the transformation of these moments within her texts as well. This feeling of "awe and wonder" is helped by the transmutation of the truth within story into grander legend. In the example from *Alphabet of Thorn* above, a man's accidental death, and what happened with the event, is shown mutating into a moment of blood and glory. Though not purposefully distorted, the tale takes on new shape through poetry and legend, and McKillip's books trace this change.

In McKillip's works empirical reality and legend and story are intertwined, creating a richer world in that it is one both real within the story, and fictionalized as in the primary world. Small moments where truth and story are questioned provide reminders of what Warren G. Rochelle contends: "Truth ultimately becomes a question of language, an issue of story" (1). The truth is not always given outright in McKillip; it is often woven into legend. An example can be found even in smaller moments, such as this description of how the mage school in *Alphabet of Thorn* came to be floating in a wood;

> [l]egend said that as the palace grew more complex through the centuries, the school broke free of it and floated away, searching for some peace and quiet in the wood. Another tale had it hidden away within the wood for safekeeping during a war. Yet another said that the wood was not a wood at all, but the cumulative magic of centuries spun around the school, and that the magic itself could take any shape it chose [16–17].

Various legends are given, but nothing is presented as certain. This uncertainty, this permutation of fact, suffuses McKillip's worlds. Even though the mage school is not of central importance to *Alphabet of Thorn*, it is still given its own small mystery in the series of legends, and its own stories, intimating a Mythological world beyond what is stated. That such a small part of the book should have such an ambiguous (and legendary) history lends the same air of depth and past to the world of *Alphabet of Thorn* that legends have in other of McKillip's works.

Wavering "truth," such as that found in *Alphabet of Thorn* and *The Bards of Bone Plain* (and even, to some extent, *Ombria in Shadow*), means the worlds of McKillip allow for an exploration within fantasy of what many postmodernists seek to do in their work. Peter Middleton and Tim Woods argue:

> Postmodern historical fiction is unconvinced that there is a single unitary truth of the past waiting to be recovered, and is more interested in who has or had the power to compose 'truths' about it, whereas historical realist fiction tends to assume that the literary narrative has a special power to present the past in a language of the present and give direct access to the thoughts, speech and of events of that other time without distorting their significance [21].

McKillip's texts are not historical fiction from the primary world. However, both *The Bards of Bone Plain* and *Alphabet of Thorn* set out to look at this transformation of what actually happened into history via songs, poetry, and stories. By doing so McKillip's novels bring several layers of story and truth into their worlds, giving a degree of depth to the world. An example can be found in a small moment from *Alphabet of Thorn*, and in the legend that is being transcribed from notes about a conquered country: "And doom it was for Gilyriad, after three days, or thirty days, or ninety days and ninety nights of constant battle, depending on which poet wrote of it" (212). Though Gilyriad's doom is certain, how it happened, with what force and for how long, is amplified in poetry. In McKillip's fantastic worlds there is a paradigm where the possibilities of the past and story can be explored by presenting both the events as they happened and their legendary after stories. It is intriguing that in *The Forgotten Beasts of Eld* the legends have been forgotten, but the veracity of the legends is not questioned. In later works McKillip's texts complicate this, as the legends are sometimes both forgotten and/or can also be wrong.

In *The Bards of Bone Plain* for example, the fragility of story is explored by layering stories into a secondary world and seeing what happens. Phelan explains to his class what likely became of the bard Nairn, and notices that a student's mind is: "Lost, it seems, along with Nairn in the mists of poetry." Phelan continues with his lecture, noting that Nairn has been lost: "Between the lines. He did exist once; that is a matter of documented history. But the exacting demands of storytelling, requiring a sacrifice, transformed him from history into poetry" (11). Phelan does not know that he speaks of his own immortal father when he talks of Nairn, doubling the mystery. Nairn indeed existed/ exists, but as Phelan observes, he has been lost first in history, then in poetry and song. This transformation, from actual past into an artistic representation is charted throughout the book, with the events as they happened being presented close to the representations (in stories, poetry, or scholarly treatise) of those actions. In the research paper that alternates with the story, the author is bewildered by this transformation:

> It's here, around the time of Declan's competition, that the boundaries of history begin to blur into the fluid realm of poetry, much as a well-delineated borderline might falter into and become overwhelmed by the marsh it

crosses. Where, the historian might ask bewilderedly, did the border go? Nothing but this soggy expanse of uncertain territory in front of us, where we were stringently following the clear and charted path of truth [160].

Part of the trouble is that as a fantasy *The Bards of Bone Plain* includes moments of magic. Declan's competition is one of those, and as such a prosaic scholar is not able to follow the truth because it is out of his/her experience. Historical truth, even without magic, is a difficult concept. In her article "Bending the Arrow of Time: The Continuing Postmodern Present," Alison Lee argues for a postmodern interpretation on this undertaking, but it works well within *The Bards of Bone Plain* or other works of fantasy that explore the veracity of history.

> One of the tasks of postmodernism is to examine the discourse of traditional history and to see the other journeys concealed within it, not just the physical journeys of those who are often excluded from historical narrative, but also the ideological journeys of the writers of history, and the taken-for-granted assumptions which remain unquestioned [219].

McKillip's texts contain both ideological and physical journeys, and though this is done within works of fantasy, they hold lessons that can be transmuted to the postmodern, of how story changes, and why. The first ruler of Raine being a woman and not a man as history has painted her, is (we must accept) unintentional, but Kane's disappearance from history is more deliberate: "It was assumed through the centuries, by anyone taking note of her disappearance, that it was brief, and that, during the blink of history's eye, an inadvertent glance away, she was found or chose to return home" (82). Kane has disappeared as the king's female cousin and reappeared as the sorcerer Kane. To do that, her own, personal, past has to be erased so that she may be recreated as a legend to be feared. There are layers of possibility within every interpretation of the past; mistakes can be made both on purpose and without meaning. The person writing the history will have their own skewed views, as will those who read it, and this is examined as an extension of the world in McKillip.

One person writing the history within the novel who has his own skewed view is Camas Erl, in *Ombria in Shadow*, one of the few characters to treat the legend of Ombria's shadow self as fact, as something that can be searched for and proven. Hints of the truth of the story of Ombria are also provided through the eyes of Ducon Greve, whose unique parentage means he can sometimes see the parallel Ombria. However, the majority of the characters (and presumably the townspeople who are only briefly mentioned) treat it as story, as un-true. The structure of Ombria, a city layered on ruins, is discussed in depth in a later chapter, but what is important to note is that these ruins are perhaps further evidence of the changed Ombria, the story Ombria. Like snakeskin sloughed off, these buildings had their uses and then were left to slide into obscurity when a new incarnation was needed. This means that the legend of Ombria, and its truth, is tied into the physicality of the world. In *Cognitive Poetics: An Introduction,* Peter Stockwell proposes that; "[t]he way that we divide the world up and name it to ourselves determines what we think the world is, and, even more importantly, how we think that we think at all" (27). How something is named, is presented, influences how it is thought of. Because the past of Ombria, and alternate Ombria, are thought of as a legend, they are treated as legend. They are initially offered as something fanciful. Most of the characters in the book treat the current incarnation of Ombria as the only one, because to them, it is: legend is not real to them. It is Camas Erl who sees the potential history behind the story. Although Michaela Baltasar is talking of Tolkien specifically in her essay "J.R.R. Tolkien: A Rediscovery of Myth" it is also applicable to McKillip and *Ombria in Shadow,* in that "[i]t portrays myth, in full function, as a means of experience, a continuous story changed by its progression, shifting according to those who became involved in it" (22). The story that is Ombria is both real and legend; the telling of the tale and its understanding are similarly mysterious in *Ombria in Shadow.* The truth cannot be seen through the story, but the story is affected by the characters acting it out in their reality. Thus, their independent actions are not, quite, so autonomous as they appear, and the Mythological as well as Material aspects of the world are tied into every other element.

    The progression from reality to story is not something limited to *Alphabet of Thorn, The Bards of Bone Plain,* and *Ombria in Shadow.* This thread is picked up in other of McKillip's books, though not in quite the same framework as those examples. In *The Sorceress and the Cygnet,* for instance, a young Corleu tells stories to his friends. "He told them the tale of the Rider in the Corn many different ways, always feeling his way closer to the truth of it, until one day they all stumbled into understanding" (8). Here, instead of the past mutating into legend, the story has illumined the past through continuous, though different, repetitions. *The Sorceress and the Cygnet* explores how story can elucidate truth, as well as the more explored reverse, and both entwine the characters with story, with the legends their world is familiar with, and with the legends developing around them. Legends in McKillip's worlds are not just stories; they are reality to the characters in those worlds.

Legendary Characters

Characters as part of McKillip's worlds have been discussed in an earlier chapter, but here I shall explore how characters are transformed from legends into people, and vice versa. The legendary figures of McKillip are presented not just as paragons of youth and vigor, but also as being past their prime, which is an unusual way to begin. As discussed in Chapter One the order in which elements of a world are presented is often important to world-building. Books about legendary figures usually either show them in their prime, doing tremendous deeds (like Conan the Barbarian) or show them growing into their legendary status. Rarely explored is what happens after legendary status is achieved.

McKillip's texts take a different tack. Story reversal provides a way for the worlds to be complete; heroes do not simply disappear at middle-age but are seen in "retirement," with the difficulties that this might present, no matter how heroic they were in youth. Atrix, in *The Book of Atrix Wolfe*, and Unciel, in *In the Forests of Serre*, are both portrayed as being past their prime, as discussed in the previous chapter. *The Book of Atrix Wolfe* examines the aftermath of a magic-influenced war. The great mage Atrix intervenes in a battle that is in stalemate, but in doing so he unleashes a horror into the world that kills many members of both sides of the army. *In The Forests of Serre* primarily follows the bewitched Prince Ronan (ensnared in the forest of Serre by the witch Brume) and the Princess Sidonie and her retinue as she travels from her country, Dacia, to marry him. But it also features the ancient mage Unciel, who has fought something very evil, and has come back to Dacia to recover. Not only are Atrix and Unciel shown as being old, but even Unciel's final battle is not given the glory it might otherwise be wreathed in. The scribe, Euan, notes:

> He had thought the wizard's last battle would be a tale of terror and courage, feats of unimaginable magic performed with heart-stopping skill and passion, good and evil as clearly defined as midnight and noon, a heroic battle for life and hope against the howling monster.... Instead he was trapped in the middle of something grisly, ugly, dreary [212].

The reality of a fight to the death is often "grisly, ugly, dreary," and by having the legendary character allow this truth into the world, via diary entries he has transcribed, *In the Forests of Serre* is showing this reality. Later Euan discusses the fight with someone else: "'It's a horrible tale...' 'Of course it would be. Look at what it did to him. Were you expecting poetry?' 'I suppose I was.' 'It will get turned into that soon enough'" (254). Euan has already distanced himself from the fight by calling it a "tale," and the person he is talking to notes that it will be distanced further as it is turned into poetry or song. The transformation from ugly fight to beautiful poetry is made visible. In this way, legends are explored from a different angle than is usual. Going back to front means *why* the characters are legendary is not necessarily even explored. There is an aura of past strength and legendary status to both old men. However, this is told, not shown, as is typical. The barest hints are given, for example, when Unciel is described as a series of rumors in *In the Forests of Serre*, "[h]e was the son and the grandson and the great-grandson of a long line of powerful sorcerers, and he had become the most powerful of all.... Another had him born in a land so old all but its name had been forgotten" (16). Or, when Atrix is described in a similar fashion in *The Book of Atrix Wolfe*, with deeds past: "The Shadow of the Wolf, the students called the mist. They climbed the mountain to look for the White Wolf, impelled by the legends of him, tales the mages told" (21). They are given legendary status, but with the slimmest descriptions. They are not presented as men in their prime in the midst of their great deeds. McKillip's texts seem interested in presenting them as people rather than as legends. This is also done in other books, though not to the same scale. In *The Sorceress and the Cygnet* for example, a legend is briefly mentioned: "The ancient mage Diu, a descendant of Chrisom's, was such a legendary figure it was difficult to conceive of him still alive and swapping spells" (241). The characters in the book, and the reader, are reminded that legends were and are alive in McKillip's worlds, they have not been allowed to remain in the legendary past but are brought forward into the present, and into reality.

Atrix and Unciel are considered differently to other legendary characters in McKillip as neither Atrix nor Unciel has a reason to hide their identities (unlike Kane and Nairn), and though powerful wizards, they are not, quite, fables in the same sense that the animals in *The Forgotten Beasts* are, or the constellations come to life in *The Sorceress and the Cygnet*. Their status within their worlds causes problems, as it is the very fact that they are legendary that causes characters to forget that they are wizards, but also people. They are both legendary men in terms of power and deeds, but they are also similar in how their reputations have overwhelmed them as fallible individuals. Neither is expected to be frail, or imperfect. Unciel is described: "The wizard, around whom legends swarmed and clung, each more fabulous than the last, seemed worn by the burden of them" (*Serre* 16). This first description presents him as a legend; he is not shown as a man but rather as a wizard, with legends swarming around him. However, he is also shown as "worn," indicating that this will not be a typical recitation of a legend. He is shown with a weakness and not at the height of his strength.

Both Atrix and Unciel are legendary but they are also proven to be fallible. They are given the status of legends, but without the usual infallibility. Both Unciel and Atrix make mistakes that are hidden almost too late because the other characters in their books see them first as legends and only much later as men capable of error. Ironically, because Atrix has been the one to make Pelucir wary of magic; the King of Pelucir tells Atrix that "[w]e may be suspicious of sorcery in Pelucir, but you have a name as ancient as gold" (*Atrix* 128). He is trusted because he is a legend. And yet, it is his sorcery which has caused the near-destruction of Pelucir, and made them wary of magic to begin with. This implicit trust in their legendary status is explored in both texts. Only when both Unciel and Atrix are understood to be human are their errors corrected, and not without help. Both Unciel and Atrix require the aid of younger characters. They are legends, yes, but this legendary status has come at a cost for both of them. It is only when their legendary status is acknowledged but then put aside that resolutions can be found. The characters are tied into their legends, as well as to how they are perceived in the world in which they live.

Four. Legends

This exploration of legend is carried out to a smaller degree in some of McKillip's other books. For example, in *Alphabet of Thorn* Vevay too is old and legendary. She is described: "Her blue-gray eyes, hooded with age, had once inspired poetry; her hands had inspired epics. Her deeds had inspired a great many passions; she had managed to survive them all" (36). Her description is more romantic than that of Unciel or Atrix, but she is still shown having had tremendous power. Like Atrix and Unciel, Vevay too needs younger insight into the problems in her land, but she is also shown as powerful, though old. An intimate look at characters who are often ignored at this stage in their lives is offered, again providing the worlds with a complete age range and a broad balance of power.

I have shown that legend, story and truth interweave in McKillip's books in ways that add depth and mystery and bring the past into the present, and the personal. McKillip's legends suffuse her books; the cities are full of history and stories, the characters are legendary, the land itself is full of legend (sometimes literally as is the case in *In the Forests of Serre* and *Alphabet of Thorn* where aspects of the landscape itself are legendary), and all of these facets combine to give a sense that the past is always present and that there is always more world, and more history, than is explicitly told of in McKillip's worlds.

Five

Pastoral Landscapes

Though not of sole importance, setting, and the landscapes from which the written world is shaped still require exploration as facets of the Material world. In the following two chapters I review two of McKillip's primary types of landscapes: the pastoral countryside and the city. McKillip is a pastoral writer in that many of her books—*In the Forests of Serre, The Forgotten Beasts of Eld*, and *The Riddle-Master* trilogy—show worlds that center on nature and pre-industrial values, but these are expressed alongside the sorts of complications found throughout her work. The pastoral in McKillip is much more than setting, and thus more than the Material, it is also part of the Social and Temporal world of many of her books. In this chapter, I consider the pastoral in relation to McKillip, followed by an exploration of the simplicity ascribed to the pastoral, and lastly I examine the manner in which the pastoral is complicated in McKillip, and given a positive slant.

Pastoralism

Fantasy such as McKillip's is envisioned as though the industrial revolution never occurred. It is infused with the pastoral as a longing for something that ought to have been but does not (and perhaps cannot) exist in the primary world. Clute argues in "Next" that "[f]antasy treats the present world as a *mistake* created by the engine of history, a mistake which must be refused through the creation of counterworlds and secret gardens as respite" (4). Pastoralism is important to much of fantasy in that it provides a mode for this secret garden of respite. The pastoral in McKillip is made up of Material world elements like landscape, but also aspects of the Social world, such as attitudes towards nature, and the city, and how the characters interact with both.

I employ a broad conception of pastoral as a mode of literature, focusing on nature and a past longing, rather than the more limited definitions of pastoral either as poetry or as dealing with the strictly agrarian. Terry Gifford states that "beyond the artifice of the specific literary form, there is a broader use of 'pastoral' to refer to an area of content," (2) and I continue that tradition here with an examination of McKillip's pastoral texts, and worlds.

Vernon Hyde Minor explains that it is "[a] peculiar character of the pastoral—its ability to propel the viewer into the work, to absorb him, and to make him a real part of a fictional space" (71). This "peculiar character" means that fantasy literature and the pastoral blend well (as Andy Sawyer also contends, 397), and it also means that it is another way of making the world feel authentic. By "propelling" the reader into the work, the pastoral is one of the key ways McKillip's worlds are able to "absorb" the reader.

Pastoral is not simply a category of literature; it encompasses everything, as does my own approach to world-building. Gifford claims that "[t]he reader recognises that the country in a pastoral text is an arcadia because the language is idealised. In other words, pastoral is a discourse, a way of using language that constructs a different kind of world from that of realism" (45). Both fantasy and the pastoral are modes full of longing and, in some respects, nostalgia. The pastoral landscape is, however, much more than mere setting. Like the larger worlds McKillip builds, it is as Gifford says, "a discourse." Part of McKillip's secondary-world pastoralism is the language, and not just the setting, of the pastoral, which means her worlds are further infused with the pastoral and its values.

Accordingly, this chapter is a closer investigation of pastoralism as it is found in McKillip; the longing in literature for a Golden Age of rural tranquility, simplicity, and the strength found inherently in the natural. William Barillas observes that the "[p]astoral often entails a contrast between urban and rural life, usually but not exclusively in favor of rurality, to which special virtue is attributed; and a tone of nostalgia" (12). McKillip's pastoral contains aspects of this, especially virtue and nostalgia, but her pastoral is often more complex than the simple "contrast" Barillas usually finds between urban and country.

This analysis maintains that a particular view of the past and nature affects how McKillip's characters, cities, and the counterparts of cities are shaped, and thus how pastoralism shapes her worlds as a whole. Chris Pak neatly condenses some of Sawyer's views when he notes "the pastoral and sf are dynamics rather than genres whose interplay within a given text help generate its meaning" (57). While I am not engaging in the same debate about science fiction (nor will I make the same argument for fantasy), I do employ the conception of the pastoral as a dynamic, and one which generates meaning as it interacts with all aspects of a world, which is why I focus less on actual, physical aspects of setting in this chapter, and more on how the characters and worlds themselves have an impact on and experience the sense of the pastoral.

As Lore Metzger explains in *One Foot in Eden: Modes of Pastoral in Romantic Poetry*, aspects of the pastoral include stylized landscape, independent soul, and Golden Age allusions. McKillip's texts exhibit all three of these attributes. Indeed, McKillip is often praised for her lyrical tone (as Ringel does in "Art" 187–188, as well as Mains in "Having" 24). This in turn lends itself to stylized landscapes, in that landscape is beautifully, if briefly, pictured. The enchanted wood from *The Book of Atrix Wolfe* is accordingly illustrated: "[he] rode away from them to a silver stream into which Oak, during one of the wood's arbitrary seasons, had dropped gold leaves to lie like coins at the bottom of the clear water" (8). The poetic description, though concise, fits the magic of the place, giving it beauty and a character all its own. I would also suggest that with the splendor of the description comes a value judgment, with "silver stream," "gold leaves," and "like coins." The richness of the landscape is stressed, and that in turn emphasizes the value. Jane Darcy, in her article "The Representation of Nature in *The Wind and the Willows* and *The Secret Garden*," suggests that *The Wind in the Willows* and *The Secret Garden* "[invest] the natural world with moral significance and with a quasi-religious mysticism," (214), and the same can be seen in the quotation from McKillip above. Certainly, the proper name given to an oak tree, "Oak," invests the passage with hints of paganism and a sort of mysticism, but the sentence as a whole emphasizes the beauty and cleanliness ("clear water") of the natural world. Sawyer declares that "a detailed attention to *language*" (404) is a key mark of the pastoral; this can come from anywhere in McKillip but we see it in *The Riddle-Master* trilogy where "[t]hey stopped beside a narrow stream under a stand of three oaks. The late sun in the clear, dark-blue sky glanced off the red faces of rocks pushing up in the soil, and turned the hill grass gold" (75). The actual setting is vague and follows long passages of action but no physical description. However, when it is given detail, the landscape is described with the careful grandeur displayed in the sentence above. The use of "clear" for the sky and "gold" for the grass imbues the passage with a sense of purity and wealth, and the sentence as a whole conveys raw beauty in the careful choice and order of words.

McKillip's landscapes are varied, and because she does not seem to go back to invented worlds often, it means that each of her worlds is carefully fashioned, with character and landscape interacting in variable and engaging ways. For example, in *The Cygnet and the Firebird*, the desert that the sorceress Nyx and her cousin Meguet have to contend with shapes and illuminates their characters. However, the first view of Nyx in the first of the *Cygnet* duology, *Sorceress and the Cygnet*, is as a swamp witch surrounded by decay calmly ignoring the horror of the other characters who must interact with her. The swampy landscape is described with precise, horror-laden language; "The trees thinned; water shunted into a slow side channel and from there bled into a wide lagoon" (40) the water does not flow, rather it bleeds. This is in stark contrast to the burning and nearly lifeless desert found later in the books. The same is true for various other McKillip novels. There is the territory that Cyan must contend with in *The Tower at Stony Wood*, for example: "If a road west took him across a mountain pass as narrow as a blade and so high he felt the cold starlight in his hair, he crossed it" (39). Forests, mountains, coastal regions, and even deserts all challenge him in distinctive ways. David E. Nye points out in *American Technological Sublime* that "[t]he North American continent possesses every feature that a theory of the natural sublime might require, including mountains, deserts, frozen wastes, endless swamps, vast plains, the Great Lakes" (1). The variety of terrain in McKillip's works indicates a connection to her American heritage. The importance of this landscape upon character (as upon people) is a characteristic of the sublime mentioned by Nye, and can be seen where McKillip's texts describe monumental landscapes, whether tall mountains or barren deserts.

Such variety shapes worlds that allow exploration not only of character, but also of different landscapes, which in turn affects characters.

The typical pastoral is likely to be set in gentle farmland, but Gifford contends that there are three types of pastoral: the historical form of shepherds and poetry, another pastoral that celebrates nature and "delight[s] in the natural," (2) and a more environmentally aware, eco-critical pastoral (1–2). McKillip's texts encompass some elements of all three of these modes.

Although a variety of landscapes are presented, from forests to desert, the difficulties encountered are more often manmade rather than natural in McKillip's books. This is slightly unusual, and means that her worlds are not always as straight forward as they seem. With such variety of landscapes it could be assumed that it would be used to foil the characters outright, such as by having characters forced to go under a mountain instead of over it, as is the case in *The Lord of the Rings*. However, in McKillip's worlds landscape is less physically challenging, and more mentally so. For example, in *The Tower at Stony Wood* the landscape seems to (but does not actually) change depending on who quests through it. Thayne finds by accident something Cyan has been searching months for: "They were not so far as they had looked; he came swiftly to the place where the river began its curve between the two closest hills" (81). Thayne easily finds, and rides to, the hills that Cyan must fight to reach. In McKillip the landscape shows character through adversity, but more importantly it is a tool of character illumination. As the witch Sidera notes in *The Tower at Stony Wood*, "[w]hat you need ... is not always what you are looking for" (99). And the same holds true for the landscape. It might not actively entangle the characters, but it does affect them, whether they see it or not. This means that the interaction between characters and their worlds is often less overt, and more internally focused, than could be expected with a large variety of landscapes. This works with the introspective nature of the pastoral that Metzger and others have described.

In addition, Metzger's independent soul can be found in many of McKillip's characters; we recognize this in Morgon, from *The Riddle-Master* trilogy, the ruler of the small agricultural island of Hed. Morgon refuses to do as is expected of him, and one of his subjects insists "you shouldn't let your private inclinations interfere with the duty you were born to.... It's not—it's not the way a land ruler of Hed should want to behave" (13). It is important to note that he says "should want" rather than "ought." It should be in Morgon's very nature to stay on his lands, but he has an independent, questing character. This is portrayed as a troublesome yet positive aspect in the book. Morgon should not want to leave his island nation, but he does. Morgon is a typical pastoral character in that he is a farmer in love with his lands and way of life, but the element of the independent soul is taken to an uncommon extreme. Pastoral is often linked to the role of the shepherd, which in turn can be used as a metaphor for kingship; that is, Morgon's dual nature as pastoral farmer and ruler are not in conflict. However, his independent nature causes him to roam away to school, and then journey again to find his destiny, even when that means leaving his true pastoral life, and kingship, behind.

Lastly, Golden Age allusions permeate McKillip's non-mechanized worlds. The system of governance found in all her books, such as monarchies, have a tinge of Golden Age. Only two of the novels that I am using in this study, *The Bards of Bone Plain* and *Kingfisher* have machines, and even then, the machines are rarely mentioned. Almost all McKillip's worlds included in this book are nostalgic for a non-mechanized Golden Age. This includes a fascination with the medieval and, in novels such as *Song for the Basilisk,* the Renaissance. Veldman is speaking of the Romantics, but could be arguing for the use of a sometimes idealized Middle Ages in McKillip's worlds: "Medievalism, however, was more than mere escapism or nostalgia; the Romantics may have created a utopia or social ideal out of the Middle Ages, but they utilized this social ideal in an effort to renew and recreate their social reality" (14). The use of medieval or Renaissance power structures and lack of mechanization is not only a way of escaping modern "social reality" but it is also a way to explore it in contrast with lands that are non-mechanized and the characters that are drawn to the land. Thus, Golden Age attributes in McKillip's works are not only a basic aspect of the pastoral but a way of exploring the pastoralism as well.

Simplicity

Pastoralism implies simplicity to many, with the city as vice and action, versus the country as straightforwardness and repose, and this does come across sometimes in McKillip's worlds. In *The Tower at Stony Wood*, for example, the rural kingdom of Ysse is contrasted with its more cosmopolitan neighbor, Yves. The character Thayne "thought of Craiche, who went to battle smelling of dung and whom Thayne carried home in his arms" (33). The brutality of war (a very young Craiche has been wounded and crippled for life) is contrasted with the innocence (or naiveté) of nature found in Craiche, who still smells of the peaceful farmyard he has left. The same can be found in *Song for the Basilisk*. The heir to the city's ruler, caught behind a wagon after spending time in the provinces, lashes out: "I've just spent six weeks smelling barns and eating sheep and listening to something that makes my teeth ache" (97), and when he spots a hapless Caladrius, he dismisses him as "[a]nother mutton eater," (97) each reaction a stereotypical one to the country from the city citizen.

The pastoral characters that reside in McKillip's worlds are not always accurate to true country living, emphasizing that this is often a genre of nostalgia and not "truth," per se. Morgon of *The Riddle-Master* trilogy refuses to kill because he is a farmer although one of the most necessary actions on a farm with livestock is to cull some of that livestock for food. *The Riddle-Master* trilogy is close to what Raymond Williams despairs of, books that idealize the pastoral too much, which, "[deceive] hardly anyone who really [live] and work[s] in the country, but ... in its way [is] a perfect weekending, rentier form" (*Modern Novel* 11). Characters (and in the primary world, people) from the countryside are often presented as rustic, unsophisticated, and sometimes deemed uninteresting as a result. Williams looked at literary novels and found that the people of the countryside were often diminished. In *Country and the City in the Modern Novel* he praises George Eliot for her ability to see country folk, but does so with a caveat:

> George Eliot reached out as far as the craftsmen and the small tenant farmers, though at the edges, even there, they are not always fully recognised as individuals, as invariably happens with more privileged persons, but are brushed in as a kind of chorus, or are given what some have called a quality of ballad, meaning that they are primarily seen as folk while others are seen as people [4].

This distinction is blurred in the better of McKillip's works, but in earlier worlds some of Williams' objections are realized. At the beginning of *The Riddle-Master* trilogy, Morgon's farmer friends have this aspect of "folk," in Williams's terms. Some of the names, such as that of Narly Stone, or the pig herder, seem "folk" and so are many of

Five. Pastoral Landscapes

the opening scenes and conversations. One of the farmers, upon hearing that Morgon has a crown, says, "Your father never had one. Your grandfather never had one. Your—" (5). They are presented as being plain and stuck in their ways. To have a crown is to have a symbol of rulership and the pageantry that goes with it. The people of Hed are not used to this sort of pageantry and view it and other forms of "civilisation" with suspicion. Life in the country in these worlds is not always the reality, but rather the wished-for perfection that someone looking in from the outside—or someone who only desires the pastoral life for a weekend—can envision.

McKillip's worlds also contain an idealized American sentiment in the form of landscape as Arcadia, as empty paradise. The United States was seen as virgin territory from the beginning (ignoring its indigenous inhabitants) and advertised as a land of bounty. Ashton Nichols notes that "Yellowstone National Park ... is a naturalistic theme park that relocated thousands of indigenous people ... to start using this land as self-described 'wilderness' for the benefit of mostly upper-middle class, mostly white, nature lovers" (17). Seen in this light, the American "wilderness" was false to begin with. Nevertheless, this American sense of the pastoral, as something wholesome, natural, and largely without people can be perceived in some of McKillip's works. McKillip's worlds are generally sparsely populated outside of the concentrated cities. There are great tracts of empty lands for the characters to quest across, very rarely coming across people. In *In the Forests of Serre,* for example, the Princess Sidonie is traveling to her betrothed, and does so for months without interacting with another soul besides her own retinue. There are occasional mentions of farmers in McKillip, for example in *Song for the Basilisk,* but even when they are the main characters, as is the case with Morgon in *The Riddle-Master* trilogy, it is not about the reality of being a farmer but about the illusion of being one. An argument between Morgon and another character, Lyra, demonstrates this after an incident when Morgon has had to physically defend himself. "You had good aim with that rock" notes Lyra, and Morgon responds "That's a good enough weapon for me. I might kill someone with a spear." Lyra's answer is a puzzled, "That's what it's for." And Morgon's response is "Think of it from a farmer's point of view. You don't uproot cornstalks, do you" (85–86). Lyra is disgusted because Morgon refuses to defend himself, and in turn his arguments about why do not ring true. A farmer would be very familiar with the killing of both plants and livestock. Defending his land from predators would be a natural preoccupation, as would using animals for sustenance. For him to disavow killing altogether is a false and nostalgic characterization, especially with "You don't uproot cornstalks," as that is exactly what is done once the corn crop has been harvested. (Morgon goes on to say that you do not do so before harvest, but the corn crop is still killed, as the animals on his farm would be.)

Leo Marx contends that "The soft veil of nostalgia that hangs over urbanized landscape is largely a vestige of the once dominant image of an undefiled, green republic, a quiet land of forests, villages, and farms dedicated to the pursuit of happiness" (6). Fantasy literature allows this "veil of nostalgia" to be embodied. Sawyer notes, "A 'pastoral' fiction may be unreal, escapist, nostalgic, sentimental, juvenile—all terms loaded with negative connotations—just as we dismiss fantasy novels for their reliance on dragons, dark Lords, Halflings and other post–Tolkienian borrowings.... 'Pastoral' in this sense, is pejorative" (397) and this is not without basis. There is no famine, and very little of the hard work involved in food production is mentioned in McKillip, for example. However, I argue that the nostalgia inherent in pastoral need not always be a negative concept.

Complications

Though at times sentimental, McKillip's version of the pastoral allows for more "contemporary" preoccupations, such as cities, as well as an exploration of the power that can be found in the wild. The pastoral is often presented as a mode of literature that is no longer relevant but McKillip's worlds prove that it is still. In *The Pastoral Vision of William Morris: The Earthly Paradise* Blue Calhoun suggests that by the eighteenth century the pastoral, though always an important genre, had begun to find its limits (5). And yet, Calhoun goes on to argue for the relevance of pastoral writing in the works of writers after the eighteenth century, those like William Morris who "use the pastoral contrast to evaluate the possibilities of life within what Morris calls 'a more complete civilization'" (9). Just as Lord Dunsany, John Ruskin, and William Morris found the pastoral a useful mode from which to critique the modern, so too does McKillip.

Five. Pastoral Landscapes

In later works, especially *The Tower at Stony Wood*, the loneliness and difficulty of the rural lifestyle is more accurately portrayed. This "reality" does not lessen the nostalgic impact of the pastoral, nor does it change the import of these pastoral works because, realistic or not, it still examines a lifestyle that predominated in the past in a mostly positive fashion. The "country" people in *The Tower at Stony Wood* are treated individually. It is Sel, the rural baker, who in the end sees the problem that the king and other nobles have not been able to discern. Sel, who might have been a one-dimensional, undescribed character in another work, is drawn, given an intimate connection to the world at large of *The Tower at Stony Wood*, and as a result, she is raised in importance. The characters of the countryside are lifted from their parts in traditional stories and shown to be people with real, and changeable, motivations instead, creating richer worlds for McKillip's books.

McKillip's works cannot be considered environmental in the strict sense of the term. They do not include manifestos about the evils of pollution or global warming. However, they are about nature and about the power it can lend to the human spirit when allowed to be wild. Nichols registers his displeasure that too often Thoreau is misquoted as saying "In wilderness is the preservation of the world," when in actuality it is "wildness" that Thoreau says can save the world (3). McKillip's worlds are built so that they champion both the urban and the natural, wilderness and civilization, and both can fit alongside one another when it is wildness that is viewed as the positive. Lawrence Buell argues in *The Environmental Imagination: Thoreau, Nature Writing, and the Formation of American Culture* of the "tendency ... to want to represent the essential America as exurban, green, pastoral, even wild" (32). The United States as untamed wilderness was a blatant fiction, and perhaps McKillip's works lean too much on this ideal; however, there is still a strong sense throughout her books of the wonder of nature and its improving influence on man. Morgon in *The Riddle-Master* trilogy, for example, though a "simple" farmer, has outwitted the greatest riddler in his world: "He said great lords of Aum, An and Hel—the three portions of An—and even riddle-masters from Caithnard had challenged him to a game, but never a farmer from Hed" (9). The riddle that has won Morgon a crown from the riddler is one from his homeland. The rest of the world ignores Hed because it is peaceful, and full of sheep and grain. Yet this is proven a mistake.

The independent and strong spirit of McKillip's pastoral characters is clear. In *Od Magic* Yar and Brenden are set up against the "city" (and thus, tame) wizards, who have been trained without imagination or hardship in what has become the king's (and therefore the capital city's) school. The degree to which the city has been sealed off from wild magic will be discussed at length in the next chapter, but the same can be applied to the people. Country-born Yar has left his wildness behind—along with his wonder and much of his power—in order to be a teacher in the wizard's school. He tells the story of how, from humble, rural beginnings, he came to be in the school and the reactions from his students are telling: "Some looked at him with wonder, as though he must have walked out of a tale instead of an obscure village.... Others seemed skeptical, unable to imagine either hunger or a hero who had not been brought up to become one" (91). Yar is thus presented almost as a creature of fable to the well-cared-for wizarding students of the city. The humor in the moment pokes fun at the tendency to see everything (and everyone) not of the city as backward and incapable of heroics. Wendell Berry suggests of the focus on the city evident in modern life and literature:

> there was the assumption that the life of the metropolis is *the* experience, the *modern* experience, and that the life of the rural towns, the farms, the wilderness places is not only irrelevant to our time, but archaic as well, because unknown or unconsidered by the people who really matter-that is, the urban intellectuals [7].

Pastoralism has this aspect—the feeling that it is something to be moved away from—to contend with. However, McKillip has astute characters defend the rural life. For example, in the midst of the turmoil in which he is embroiled in the city, Caladrius, in *Song for the Basilisk*, thinks of the land where he was brought up: "He felt a moment's helpless longing for the singing of the restless autumn seas, for the simplicity of fire, water, stone" (196). Though he is drawn to the city and its politics, Caladrius is still affected by what he thinks of as the peace of the countryside. When he and the music teacher Guilia are speaking of love, she says that, "[t]he subject makes me provincial," and Caladrius replies, "[b]ecause it goes to the heart of the matter" (198). The countryside then is presented as not only provincial (and therefore all that goes with it such as "backward" and out of date) but it is also where the truth can be spoken outright. The provincial is portrayed as both a positive—somewhere where truth is valued and as a negative—provincial is set in contrast to the city. Barillas notes that "[a]t the heart of modernist-derived attitudes about pastoral literature is confusion (perhaps at times willful) between regionalism and provincialism" (16). Provincial implies backward and uneducated. What Barillas describes as "regional" is the tendency of pastoral literature to feature concentrated areas, or a certain type of nature or area. McKillip generally avoids this in her disparate range of settings. Thus, although there are moments in McKillip's worlds where the pastoral is a bit too sentimental—that is, too full of might-have-beens rather than the reality of rural life—there is power to be found in this type of literature, and in turn the worlds that it helps to build.

The countryside is a large part of the pastoral, but so is the nostalgia tied into (usually idealized) memories of past landscapes and lifestyles. It is the combination of memories of the past with landscape that creates the particular settings McKillip's worlds include, and is one of the many ways McKillip's landscape are tied into far more than just the Material world. Though removed from the Romantics in time, criticism about some of Romanticism's values can be usefully applied to McKillip's worlds because the pastoral was a strong feature of both the literature and the art of the Romantic movement. Veldman contends that the Romantics "viewed human reason as essentially limited, and they endeavoured in their efforts to connect with nature and the past, to offer an expanded vision of experience and existence" (14). McKillip's books have a strong feel of the Romantic, of a movement which also sought to use the past and nature as counterpoint to modern sentiment and mechanization. Veldman contends that the Romantics, far from shunning change, acknowledged its use while still looking to the past for values that could help in the present (14). Although Veldman is speaking about a past Britain, her assertions can be used to explore more modern pastoral sentiments as well. The nostalgic aspect of pastoralism is one rooted in the glorification of the past, of golden ages. At its most positive, pastoral is a plan to move forward using the best of the past. Mains claims that there is a "[t]endency of fantasy writers such as McKillip to look backwards, into the pre-technological past, when the roles allowed to women were fewer and more restricted than in the present and, hopefully, in the future" ("Having" 118). This is true, to an extent, but McKillip's positive, progressive pastoral means that this aspect too can be challenged, as was explored in Chapter Three. This can be seen in all of McKillip's pre-industrial worlds. Patrick Curry champions an "emotionally empowering nostalgia, not a crippling one," (15) and this is what McKillip's texts contain. The problems of modern, primary world Earth are not to be found in McKillip's works. Without issues such as global warming or pollution, the texts focus on personal interactions both between characters, and between characters and the natural world. A reconnection with nature, and with the wildness which that allows, is one of the "lessons" that can be found in McKillip's pastoral combinations of the Material, Temporal and Social worlds.

Consequently, the pastoral can be a simple construct rooted in a past that never was as well as a guide forward. Barillas claims that "[w]hile this nostalgic tendency can lend itself to sentimentality and a false idealisation of life in nature, the best pastoral writing acknowledges social complexities and conflicts invented in the individual's striving for a meaningful life" (12). Working from this definition of a literature of "social complexities and conflicts," the best of McKillip's pastoral works is *The Tower at Stony Wood*. Though part of a typical fantastic monarchy, the lands in *The Tower at Stony Wood* are in conflict. The secondary world equivalent of serfs have been ground down long enough, as the baker, Sel, explains to the king: "It's not the Lord of Skye you would face…. It's all the folk whose faces you have never seen. Like the folk in the North Islands, they have names, and lives they think important" (278). The hardship of rural life is acknowledged and not glossed over. Farmers, shepherds, fishermen, all are given character and not minimized as is so often the case. Williams, in *Country and City in the Modern Novel*, proposes that Jane Austen's books are but one example where a seemingly sparsely populated land "[is] an actually crowded countryside, with most of the people in it faded to anonymity or to landscape" (4). The detailed descriptions of a variety of characters throughout the countryside in the more accurate of McKillip's pastoral works ensures that her worlds contain a whole populace rather than a few characters interacting. Hardship is acknowledged, even if but briefly. The village in *The Tower at Stony Wood*, for example, is sketched out, but with sympathy: "Half the villagers fished. The others raised sheep and goats on the wild land, which grew grass or rocks indiscriminately, but little else" (58). This is not a land full of plenty, but rather one where subsistence means toil of one kind or another, and this is acknowledged.

People and the Landscape (Nostalgia)

The nostalgia evident in McKillip's pastoral can work both as a way of becoming caught in the past, but also as transformative for her characters. Gayle Greene, in "Feminist Fiction and the Uses of Memory," contends that "nostalgia and remembering are in some sense antithetical, since nostalgia is a forgetting, merely regressive, whereas memory may look back in order to move forward and transform disabling fictions to enabling fictions" (9). While it is true that nostalgia can contain a notion of being frozen in time, and letting growth stall, I prefer Greene's slant on memory, and think that nostalgia need not be so different from memory in Greene's definition after all. Not being fixed in the past, but rather using it as a way to look forward, is an important part of the growth of several of McKillip's characters. All of *The Tower at Stony Wood* could be said to be focused on this dynamic. The web of intrigue that is set up to entangle the various characters is done precisely in order to enable them to move forward from their versions of the past. At the end of his journey, Cyan realizes he has accomplished "nothing," but a witch tells him, "[y]ou rode out of Gloinmere to rescue the woman in the tower. What you truly did, while you searched for me, was to rescue Thayne Ysse and the North Islands from seven years of bitterness and hardship. You rescued Sel from her dark tower" (289). The witch explains further: "If I had asked you to outface a dragon, catch a selkie in the sea, persuade Thayne Ysse to trust a knight of Gloinmere, face death by water, sword and sorcery, and survive to bring magic into Yves, what would you have said?" (289). Convinced his quest is something else, Cyan is able to heal the whole world of *The Tower at Stony Wood* "by accident." Thus, even though *The Tower at Stony Wood* is a book without machines, with medieval power structures, and pastoral all the way through, it still maps a way out of bitterness and power struggles and into hope.

Nostalgia, like the pastoral as a whole, is often held as a negative, something that prevents people from moving forward. A nostalgic view of the past, however, is not always damaging. Paul Gruchow suggests in *Grass Roots: The Universe of Home* that "Nostalgia is the clinical term for homesickness, for the desire to be rooted in a place—to know clearly, that is, what time it is" (7). Nostalgia is a natural part of the pastoral, and both are "rooted" in concepts of the past, and home. Many of McKillip's characters interact with their world through a lens of nostalgia in the sense of homesickness, and this once again ties her landscapes and characters together into integrated worlds.

Nostalgia as homesickness is powerful in McKillip's works, not only in the clear longing for rural life that runs through her books, but also within particular characters and how they are tied to the lands they are from. Brenden, in *Od Magic*, and Sel, in *The Tower at Stony Wood*, are not just examples of this nostalgia, they are embodiments of it. As a selkie Sel was discussed in Chapter Two, but there is another element to her that ties into the pastoral as well as to tropes. Sel is described by her daughter:

> [Melanthos] frowned absently, studying the tall, bulky, swaying figure. It was her private belief that her mother had once been a seal, who had swum too close to humans without her sealskin on and had been taken. She was shaped like one, she barked, and she knew some very strange things [58].

This characterization is blunt. Most of McKillip's turns of phrase are less forthright than this, but it does sum up the character quickly and brings her association with the seals to the forefront. Sel waits to return to her seal form, but so early in the novel she is not entirely aware of this. The characterization of her as something natural and non-human is important, but so is the sense of homesickness that her daughter senses from her mother's demeanor. Vijay Agnew, in his introduction to *Diaspora, Memory and Identity: A Search for Home*, contends that "the individual living in the diaspora experiences a dynamic tension every day between living 'here' and remembering 'there,' between memories of places of origin and entanglements with places of residence, and between the metaphorical and the physical home" (14). This tension is found in many different characters, and the characterization with the natural is one way in which the character's affinities and longings that tie them into the world around them are shown.

Both landscape and character are connected, and are often in symbiosis in some way. This is echoed and amplified with the descriptions of McKillip's character and this is one of the ways that McKillip's worlds feel drawn together. Donaldson contends in *Epic Fantasy in the Modern*

World: A Few Observations that "in fantasy the world is an expression of the characters" and in McKillip this is often literally true. Several of her characters—Sel and Brenden are but two examples—are attempting to return to nature in some way. Her descriptions of them echo and amplify this. One example of many can be found in *Od Magic* where Brenden's empathy with nature is illustrated when Brenden is described as "standing quietly as a tree in an ancient, weathered grove" (314). Portrayed here are the unmoving age of the tree as well as the sense of age outside of the few physical years Brenden has lived, together with his affinity to nature. His stillness is contrasted with the busy city he has been thrust into, and his wild nature is underscored as well. Brenden's link to the world he lives in is made abundantly clear; he does not simply live in a landscape, he is *of* it. Phrases are used to describe characters in ways that make the association between character and nature plain.

Within McKillip's worlds the natural is equated with a source of power and learning that are in line with nature-study advocates for whom "the green world was a source of delight, instruction, and nourishment for the soul" (Armitage 1). In Chapter Six I explore the duality between wild and tame magic in *Od Magic*. This can be seen in several of McKillip's works, and not just within her cities. Natural magic, the magic that is found away from civilization, is praised and shown to be powerful. In *Od Magic* two characters converse about the main character, Brenden: "'What are you saying? ... That he's more powerful than you?' 'At that moment he was.' 'And he learned this where?' 'From the bog lilies, by the sound of it. Earth. Rain. Seeds.'" (311). Brenden's "natural" way of learning has led him to be superior to those wizards that have been trained in the city, away from nature.

Wild and natural magic equates to power in many of McKillip's worlds. This dichotomy is an extension of the pastoral. It is a furtherance of the notion that the natural can be superior to the man-made. Both Nyx and Sybel are the same: they needed to leave civilization to find their strength. This aspect of the pastoral, "some form of retreat and return" (1), that Gifford argues is crucial is a drawing away from but also coming back to. When civilization and its power games have overcome Sybel, she returns to the wilderness, where the wise woman Maelga describes what she will find there:

> Come with me tomorrow through the forest; we will gather black mushrooms and herbs that, crushed against the fingers, give a magic smell. You

will feel the sun on your hair and the rich earth beneath your feet, and the fresh winds scented with the spice of snow from the hidden places on Eld Mountain. Be patient, as you must always be patient with new pale seeds buried in the dark ground. When you are stronger, you can begin to think again. But now is the time to feel [*Forgotten* 209].

Sybel can find the solace she needs only in nature, which is healing. However, it is also a place to remember—and to learn and overcome—what knowledge she has acquired and the actions she has performed in civilization. Gail David contends that:

> Women writers have ... turned to the pastoral genre, to depict in that mode's rural and urban dialectic—a recurring female figure, whose journey between "simple" and "complex" settings and whose objective to master both cast her firmly into an heroic mold [xiii].

David's argument that women writers use the pastoral to explore movement from simple to complex describes Sybel. However, the countryside in *The Forgotten Beasts of Eld* is presented as healing, but not as providing amnesia; it is not a complete escape from the urban and politics. Nor is it a world without men, or without male heroes.

In this sense, McKillip's worlds suggest a broader focus than some other feminist writers who have written about healing nature. Sally Gearhart's *The Wanderground: Stories of the Hill Women* (1978), for example, draws a strict dichotomy between male/female, evil/good, and city/country. This romantic view of nature, as something always healing and meant for woman alone, is complicated in McKillip. The distinctions are not so clear cut, and, as a result, her books are more accepting and more complex. David claims in *Gender and Genre in Literature: Female Heroism in the Pastoral,* that "[f]emale heroism, for example, seems an unlikely attribute of the pastoral, a genre which traditionally presents nature from the perspective of the white male author and according to literary convention, images the rural landscape as a submissive female" (xviii). McKillip's pastoral allows for the female as well as the male hero. Sybel, Nyx, Meguet, and others are all the heroes of their books. This does not, however, preclude a male engagement with nature as is presented in the conflation between men and evil in *The Wanderground.* The concept of "land-rule" (where a ruler is metaphysically connected to the land he rules) in *The Riddle-Master* trilogy, for example, means that Morgon is deeply, literally entwined with the land and its welfare. The lands in McKillip are also not presented as

Five. Pastoral Landscapes

something waiting to be conquered. Indeed, in *Od Magic* it is this tendency to see the wilderness as something that needs to be controlled and tamed that is presented as a problem.

Od Magic explores the dichotomy of trained versus natural as it follows the untrained but extremely powerful Brenden as he goes to be a gardener at the School of Magic. There he meets the wizards Yar (also originally from the countryside) and Valoren (completely a man of court) who attempt to help him and are afraid of him respectively. Brenden is different from the sorcerers in others of McKillip's books in that both nature and his longing to return to it lend him power: "Home drew him, the bare, windswept hills, the marshes where he could sit for an entire day watching a bog lily open and never hear a human word. The stark longing fueled his magic" (237). Other characters, such as Nyx, are lent power and knowledge by nature, but are not drawn to it in the same homesick way. The need to return to nature is a common sentiment. As Marx notes, it is a "familiar impulse to withdraw from the city, locus of power and politics, into nature," (22) but the way that characters are attached to their worlds lends an extra dimension to this. Not only does Brenden want to withdraw, this very nostalgia gives him power. Thus, something often presented as a negative can be (sometimes literally) powerful in McKillip. It is the character's feelings towards his home, his connection with his world, that gives him power, rather than the formal training that might otherwise be advocated.

There is also a sympathy for nature outside of landscape, as expressed through the characters in McKillip's pastoral worlds. Aldo Leopold claims in his *A Sand County Almanac and Sketches Here and There* that "wild things ... had little human value until mechanization assured us of a good breakfast" (vii). By this he means that only when humans had leisure did they look to nature. However, McKillip's worlds are largely non-mechanized and there is still space for the natural. In *Od Magic*, caring for other creatures and plants is presented as a clear virtue. Brenden explains, "[w]ell no one ever told me that plants couldn't speak and that I couldn't see what they said. It was something I just did" (68). Without someone to tell him that plants are important and have a (literal) voice of their own, he has noticed and acted upon this knowledge to help the plants themselves in addition to the animals and people who need the knowledge he has gained from the plants. Thus an understanding of, and sympathy with, nature is encouraged throughout McKillip's worlds.

"Countless Cultural Environments"

Though pastoral is at times assigned a pejorative meaning (as Gifford contends in his chapter on the "Anti-Pastoral Tradition"), and is at times idealized, it still holds positive values useful to highlight in a pre-industrial society, like most of the secondary worlds in McKillip. Like Hazel Sheeky Bird I believe the pastoral can be used in a "vital and dynamic way"; (48) a way to face challenge rather than avoid it (49). McKillip's books have varying combinations of cities, countryside, and populated or unpopulated landscape. Minor's contention that "[t]he pastoral endures the ages and adapts to countless cultural environments," (64) applies to McKillip's pastoral as well as the pastoral as a whole. Pastoral can be used as a variable concept, as I do here. The "countless cultural environments" usually encompass the agrarian, but can also include modern phenomena such as cities, as well as being able to celebrate the power that can be found in the natural. Thus, although the pastoral is an old concept, it continues to be used in innovative and compelling ways, and to create new worlds with old sensibilities. Gifford proposes that "[t]his is the essential paradox of the pastoral: that a retreat to a place apparently without the anxieties of the town, or the court, or the present, actually delivers insight into the culture from which it originates" (82). The pastoral as seen in McKillip allows for a myriad of relationships between man and nature, as well as an interrogation of the dichotomies inherent in the modern view of city versus country. This permits something inherently old-fashioned to provide fresh insight for the present.

McKillip's worlds contain a more complicated notion of the pastoral than that which regards it as a regressive genre of shepherd poetry, and McKillip's fiction is also not without the political. Pak takes Leo Marx's ideas and extends them, noting:

> The pastoral design is a more complex ordering of meaning referring to "the larger structure of thought and feeling of which the *ideal* is a part" (Marx, 1964, 24). The pastoral design adds complexity by introducing ambiguity into pastoral chronotopes; it manages "to qualify, or call into question, or bring irony to bear against the illusion of peace and harmony in a green pasture"

(25). It "embraces some token of a larger, more complicated order of experience" by "bring[ing] a world which is more 'real' into juxtaposition with an idyllic vision" (25) [Pak 58].

McKillip, "embraces ... [a] more complicated order of experience" by bringing politics into the natural world. As noted by Mains in "For Love or For Money: The Concept of Loyalty in the Works of Patricia McKillip" power relations seem to be of fundamental importance to McKillip (219), and this is indicated in the world-building. Her pastoral worlds are just as full of complex notions of power as her cities, and ensures they are more multifaceted than a pastoral/city dichotomy indicates. This keeps McKillip's pastoral world's contemporary, even when medieval or Renaissance in influence.

McKillip's worlds are largely fixed in an imaginary past that is neither true past, possible future, nor actual present but rather entirely apart in time as well as space. This allows for a less didactic examination of the natural and its values than is sometimes possible in the primary world. The pastoral is often set in opposition to the city and modernity, but, as Williams in his *The Country and the City* claims, "[i]t is significant, for example, that the common image of the country is now an image of the past, and the common image of the city an image of the future. That leaves, if we isolate them, an undefined present" (297). Many of McKillip's books seem to reside in this imaginary past. Even her cities are not images of the future such as science fiction might envision, but rather are inspired by the Renaissance or by ideas of medieval cities.

A critical examination of her characters suggests that McKillip argues for the power of the wild and the natural (as Le Lievre notes too of *The Riddle-Master* trilogy 241), but she does not do so at the complete exclusion of the city and the organized. This leaves her pastoral in a less conservative mode than is usually presupposed. Lawrence Buell summarizes the problem in Barillas's book when he asks "whether pastoral ideology and art 'ought to be looked at as conservative and hegemonic' or 'as a form of dissent from an urbanizing mainstream'" (3). Both are possibilities available within the pastoral. It seems McKillip's worlds strive for the latter; her pastoral is sometimes a little naive, but it leaves the possibility for city life open. In *Od Magic*, the wizard's school is superior when wild talent is allowed inside, but the school is not abolished in the end. Od wants "[p]ower shaped by wonder and curiosity, even love. Not by fear and laws that shut out rather than inviting in" (305). In the end, the school is not even moved out of the city. When the king asks, "[t]hen why bother with walls? Why books, teachers—," Od replies, "Most are the better for them. A few can do without" (311). Both the city and the country are allowed in McKillip's version of the pastoral. This is further conflated by the fact that power and politics are blended in all of McKillip's worlds. The countryside is not a refuge from power but is often equally embroiled in struggles. *In the Forests of Serre*, for example, is entangled in politics and power, and very little of the action takes place in a city but rather within the forest of Serre or in an isolated castle within the forest. Thus, Williams' argument in *The Country and the City*, that both country and city encompass more than their stereotypes, is given credence in McKillip's worlds. Williams claims:

> On the actual settlements, which in the real history have been astonishingly varied, powerful feelings have gathered and have been generalised. On the country has gathered the idea of a natural way of life: of peace, innocence, and simple virtue. On the city has gathered the idea of an achieved centre of learning, communication, life [1].

This is one of the ways that McKillip's pastoral worlds are more powerful than a simple nostalgic exercise, and one of the many ways she adds depth to her worlds with her iterations of nature and the city, and the characters who do not just reside, but are entwined, in both.

Both fantasy and the pastoral can be seen as simple concepts, rooted in a past that never was. McKillip's worlds subvert this expectation both within fantasy, and the pastoral. As Williams explains, country and city are varied but are often simplified into a dichotomy. Country can be wilderness, yet it also contains farmers as well as hunters. The city can be a capital, religious base, market or port. Putting them in strict contrast creates a false polemic. As fantasy literature is not striving to be realistic in all things, this is not a problem within the framework of fantasy. It does perpetuate the idea that this polemic exists, however, and that the difference between country and city is vast. Leo Marx argues for "[t]he stock literary contrast between the happiness and innocence of a bucolic golden age and the corrupt, self-seeking, and disorderly life of the city (or court)" (97). McKillip's worlds are often confused in these distinctions, allowing each sphere to bleed into the other, and both are richer as a result.

Five. Pastoral Landscapes

This richness too means that their attitude towards any mechanization is not a simple one. Colin Manlove contends that pastoralism is hostile to technology (58). However, when modernity is displayed in one of McKillip's books, there is no antipathy towards it. Spivack claims that "[t]hese fantasies are ecology-minded, often with an attendant bias against technology which is usually regarded as exploitative" (15) but even in the few McKillip books that are not pastoral, among them *The Bards of Bone Plain* and *Kingfisher*, McKillip's characters show no ire towards machinery. McKillip's pastoral worlds are therefore a celebration of the pastoral rather than a condemnation of the modern, the mechanized and, in turn, the city. John F. Lynen, in *The Pastoral Art of Robert Frost*, argues that "[t]he pastoral poet's real power springs from his ability to keep the two worlds in equilibrium" (12). Lynen here speaks of the worlds of country and town, and McKillip's worlds, though not written in poetry, keep these two elements in balance, with neither becoming the superior force.

One of the biggest differences between the literature of the city and the country is often that the city character is treated as an individual atom, floating through the city with no contact, no community. The country character is often part of a network, whether that network is family, neighbors, or even the natural world around him or her. However, both McKillip's city and country characters have networks that surround them. As Mains explores in her essay "The Use, Misuse, and Abuse of Power: The Wizards of Patricia A. McKillip," McKillip seems to have a fascination with power, and in her worlds this is often explored through the dynamics between people. McKillip's city characters are shown within networks and communities, somewhat against type. Examples from McKillip's work include Brenden in *Od Magic* and Caladrius in *Song for the Basilisk*. They are country strangers, but they are immediately enveloped in communities within the cities they come to inhabit. Brenden, though solitary, has the community of other gardeners of the school, as well as the protection of the wizard Yar, also a country boy. Caladrius stumbles upon a group of friendly musicians soon after entering the city and is followed by his son. He too has an immediate community. Therefore, neither of these characters, though thrust into the strange environs of the city, is isolated as is otherwise typical.

The pull between civilization and other is a strong tension in many of McKillip's worlds, but it is not a competition with a clear victor. In *The Forgotten Beasts of Eld* Sybel has to learn how to interact with people and to decide whether she wants to remain wild and powerful or join in with fellow humans. Nyx, in the *Cygnet* duology, feels a similar pull between her duty as an heir in the seat of power and the call to power out away from civilization. Likewise, Melanthos in *The Tower at Stony Wood* feels the tension between the wild and civilized. She has her own concerns and does not understand why others should be worried about her. Ready to follow the knight Cyan because she is curious, she thinks, "[o]ne of the wild horses roaming the plain might be in the mood to let her ride it. She bounded a step after the knight and then a voice wound around her ankle and pulled her motionless" (54). The voice is another human, a "civilized" one, calling her back to her responsibilities. This passage not only demonstrates Melanthos's power (she is able to communicate with wild animals) but it also establishes how her priorities are clearly different from more ordinary humans. Marx contends that "[a]n inchoate longing for a more 'natural' environment enters into the contemptuous attitude that many Americans adopt toward urban life" (5). This sense of yearning infuses McKillip's worlds. Nyx, Sybel, and Melanthos all feel pulled between duties to loved ones and the power that they can see in natural things, away from people and rules. It is an interesting value judgment, and more complex than it first appears. McKillip's texts do not seem to say that in the end wilderness is superior to civilization. There is a more moderate message: the wilderness is powerful and bewitching, but people need other humans. The wilderness is not presented as clearly superior in and of itself, nor is it denigrated. A character in *Song for the Basilisk* asks why the bards' school is out beyond even the province of farmed lands: "Why this lonely place? What possessed the first bard to build his school here, instead of some civilized place where you don't have to climb down off the edge of the world to buy an apple?" and Caladrius answers, "I suppose because that long ago no one had invented the word 'civilized' yet" (46). The phrasing is quite careful here. Civilized is in scare quotes, as if to question what that means. It is also prefaced by saying that it is merely a word, and therefore not a true concept. This means that the worlds are built so that they neither deny the power of the city, nor present civilized as a real concept, nor even display civilization as a superior force. The blending of city and country in McKillip's worlds allows for a more open, and positive, consideration of the pastoral.

As with her use of tropes and gender or age expectations, McKillip's texts take the traditional values of the pastoral and sometimes alters their expected course. Gifford notes that the pastoral is almost always presented in contrast to cities (2), but McKillip's worlds are less rigorously defined than this suggests. Gifford claims that the key to the pastoral is its connection between man and nature (especially the countryside), and many of McKillip's books exemplify this. McKillip's worlds complicate the standard narrative of the perfect, idyllic, quiet rustic life, separate from the city and all commonly entailed therein. Leo Marx makes a distinction between two different kinds of pastoral "one that is popular and sentimental, the other imaginative and complex" (5). McKillip's books do not hold with one or the other; her pastoral and landscapes can be sentimental at times, but they are also "imaginative and complex." McKillip's worlds show a sometimes idealized countryside, but they are blended with traditionally urban values and culture in a way that is somewhat atypical. Ekman notes that "[m]any scholars maintain that the principal cause of today's many environmental problems ... is the way in which Western society perceives there to be a difference between nature and culture" (129). This difference between nature and culture is softened in McKillip's worlds, and often done away with altogether.

Like Nichols, I would suggest that McKillip's worlds are not set up so that the city is antithetical to nature. Nichols argues that "[c]rucial to the *urbanature* is the idea that human beings are never cut off from wild nature by human culture" (vx). In other words, cities are just as much a part of the natural environment as wilderness, and McKillip's texts integrate both types of environments into her worlds, connecting characters, story, and environment to showcase united worlds. The approach to the countryside and cities, in fact, to landscape and the people who inhabit them as a whole, is one of inclusion rather than exclusion in McKillip's work. In the next chapter this theme will be covered in more depth, but it is important to keep in mind with respect to pastoralism as well.

Six

Cities

McKillip's cities are exemplary world-building in that their detail and organic-seeming growth imply a past and a development of the worlds in which they occur. Cities are an integral part of the modern human environment; as such they must play a role in how a world is built, and thus are important to its Material world. In the following pages I explore how McKillip's cities are intricate; full of history and past that add to the richness of her created worlds by combining both the Temporal and the Material world.

Just as the pastoral is the illusion of the absence of human intervention, so too are cities the misapprehension of a lack of nature. Rather than set them up in opposition, I continue the notion that the country and the city are not distinct entities in McKillip's texts, and that this is one of the many ways her worlds are integrated wholes. Cities are not as separate from nature as they appear in many ways but I will focus on two: first, cities are natural occurrences of human nature and therefore not entirely antithetical to the pastoral, but secondly, they also grow, and though this is not organic in the sense of living tissue, it is a development both influenced by humans and outside any one direct influence too. McKillip's cities are built with various eras layered on top of one another to create places with complex histories and complicated political machinations. Each is an accumulation of history, different eras, and distinctive politics and I will explore what their concentrated form entails, how they are cities of mystery, and how politics have influenced them.

Concentrated City

In general McKillip's works are geographically sprawling affairs, taking place over large tracts of land. *Kingfisher*, for example, takes place in tiny sea villages as well as the capital, and long stretches of land in between. Even when they do not, such as in *The Changeling Sea, The Bell at Sealey Head*, and *Winter Rose* (all of which take place in a village and its close surrounds), the setting is largely rural. When McKillip does feature cities, as in *Song for the Basilisk, Od Magic, Ombria in Shadow*, and *The Bards of Bone Plain*, they are city-centric novels, and this is what makes them unique in her oeuvre.

The cities that McKillip's books focus on are varied, but retain similar features. Sometimes they are walled, like Kelior in *Od Magic* or Berylon in *Song for the Basilisk*. Occasionally they are ringed by more natural fortifications such as the river in *The Bards of Bone Plain*. What they all have in common, however, is that they are old, with layers of past and political eras impacting on the current form of the city, thus implying a past and history both turbulent and realistic.

McKillip's cities are part of a European tradition in that they are built in and around their pasts. Older variants confuse and complicate the modern versions of the cities; streets are twisting, labyrinthine affairs. Marilyn Faulkenburg claims that "*The Wings of the Dove*, another novel that pits America against Europe, depicts the European city as a stone colossus, a labyrinth which imprisons and deadens rather than frees or gives life" (7). While my argument does not center on the deadening effect that Faulkenburg sees, I do propose that European cities, and therefore McKillip's in this sense, are labyrinthine in contrast to American cities. There is not the ordered regimentation that American cities typically exhibit. This is indicative of civilizations (and therefore cities) that have complicated pasts. They have grown slowly and organically instead of being planned in one moment in a regimented fashion. This is one of the many ways in which McKillip's worlds are convincing. They contain layers of past and history, with the result that a reader is assured that there is more world not only around the corner, but also under the ground, and in the past.

Nearly all the cities in McKillip rise from nothing, surrounded by agricultural hinterland, but without the spread of modern, primary-world suburbia. The effect of their placement means that the cities are concentrated, cylinders of time and space. This adds to the cities' confusion, as they are dense, with history and the present in close, sometimes indistinguishable, proximity. The novels with cities in them are very definitely set in the cities. In some of the books, a part of the plot will take place out in the hinterland, such as in *Song for the Basilisk* or *Od Magic*, but the parts set in the city are placed firmly within the city's walls and are where the central plot happens. What is noteworthy is that though a great deal happens within the confines of the city, and much of the lives of the characters within it are presented, external details such as trade are hardly mentioned, concentrating the texts into a smaller space. Although the city being enclosed is sometimes a metaphorical closure (Ombria, for example, certainly feels enclosed though no walls are mentioned), other cities in McKillip's works are literally enclosed and the past and history of the city are therefore layered in a dense and enclosed space.

The containment of McKillip's cities means that politics, and action, are also concentrated. They are more like the city-states of Greece, the polis, rather than anything modern. This adds to a sense of the fantastic in that it is a formation of ages past, and slightly exotic in contrast to the suburban sprawl of many cities in primary world Earth. As Arthur W.H. Adkins and Peter White note in their introduction to *The Greek Polis*, "[g]eographically, the polis consisted of a political and religious center and a tract of countryside. The center was usually a fortified town" (1). McKillip's cities are generally the entire country and if they are not, as seems to be the case in *Od Magic*, they are still self-contained units of governance that have very little to do with the outside world. The walls of the cities signify a boundary and demarcation of the state/country. Unlike McKillip's quest-type fantasies that range over a wide area of an invented world, her cities tend to be very centralized like the polis. Adkins and White note that the polis were autonomous communities (1), and McKillip's cities follow in this tradition. The countryside is barely explored in these books, and McKillip's cities seem to be self-contained and self-governing, with very little or no outside influence.

This enclosure is often important to the story. For example, the city of Berylon, though poorly described in general, does have the one characteristic of medieval and Renaissance cities that both *The Bards of Bone Plain* and *Ombria in Shadow* seem to lack: it has fortified walls. This is a city obsessed with power, and it is germane that it is described as a walled city. This is an example of where elements of the world can be examined for ideas about what the world contains, and how it functions. The addition of walls to the city of Berylon, an unremarkable addition in the primary world, and a little-mentioned marker in McKillip's cities, is significant. There seems to be very little real threat from the provinces, and yet it is a fortified town. The ruling families inside the city are more dangerous to the general populace and themselves than the countryside, but it is the countryside that the city is guarded against. The Basilisk uses the walls to keep arms out of the city (and out of the hands of his enemies), but presumably this was not their original function as it seems to be a relatively new decree. Even though docks are mentioned, there is no word of trade from other lands. Berylon seems like a tenuous city-state, on its own with no real connection to the surrounding lands, and yet there are walls.

There are several possible explanations for this. One of the ways a critic examines world-building is through the order in which details are provided, and story made clear. In this instance, the shape of the city, and by extension, the world, are revealed before why it is shaped as it is is investigated. In fact, speculation must take the place of fact as no definitive answer is provided within the story. Either the history of the city is so well known as to be unvoiced, or, the characters are not interested in what this might say. The critic, however, has several possible explanations open to them, and each changes the nature of the world in which the story is set. One is that the citizens have so much to fear from each other that they are paranoid about anyone else and so have built fortifications. Or, perhaps the walls were built more to keep the populace in, rather than anyone out. This occurs at the end of *Song for the Basilisk* when the population of the city is locked in to keep rebels from escaping. A third possible explanation is that the city of Berylon has walls because, in spite of the great power inside the city, the populace fears the wild and mysterious magic of the hinterlands. Perhaps they are right to do so; in the end it is this magic that overthrows the Basilisk in his own lair. In each of these scenarios, the walls serve to highlight power, its use and strength, all without anything overt being said by the characters, or directly written in the text.

The worlds are entire (or as entire as something written and not experienced can be), because everything ties into everything else. Like the legends and even the countryside of many of McKillip's worlds, cities are influenced by their pasts, even if this is below the character's notice. Mains compares *Ombria in Shadow* and *Song for the Basilisk* to Renaissance Italy in her article "For Love or For Money: The Concept of Loyalty in the Works of Patricia McKillip": "Two of McKillip's fictional worlds, the worlds of *Ombria in Shadow* and *Song for the Basilisk*, evoke the city-states of Renaissance Italy, a time and place characterised by intense violence and inter familial conflict, both within and between the city-states" (219). The choice of Renaissance Italy is interesting both for the reasons Mains cites, but also because Italy is a country rich in history. Italian cities such as Rome and Florence are conflations of past and present. The past and present are constantly in collision, especially in light of the physical remains left by previous eras. George Nelson remarks on this combination of times in Rome, where:

> You would be walking down a street past a fifteenth-century palazzo and sticking out of the wall of the palazzo would be a ruin of an arch; the palazzo was built around the ruin centuries older than the palazzo. Then because business wasn't good in Rome either, a corner of this palazzo had been remodelled and somebody had put in an ultramodern candy shop [viii].

Modern and ancient are conflated and are built upon in primary-world cities, just as in McKillip's fantastic ones, and this adds a further air of realism to McKillip's worlds. This also re-emphasizes that her worlds are integrated ones, seemingly inconsequential details are often important to the city, but also the world that contains the city as well as to plot and characters, as explored in the following section.

Mystery

Many of McKillip's books contain mysteries (Morgon's secret destiny in *The Riddle-Master* trilogy, for example) but those that are also placed largely in cities, like *The Bards of Bone Plain* and *Ombria in Shadow*, result in cities that are themselves mysterious. Mysterious cities are part of the primary world as well, and examples like the modern Mexico City invite illuminating parallels with *The Bards of Bone Plain* and *Ombria in Shadow*. The ancient Aztec city of Tenochtitlan is still buried beneath the present incarnation of the city. Things are speculated, some archaeology has been done, but the exact nature of the city and its citizens remains a matter for myth and legend, just as in *The Bards of Bone Plain* and *Ombria in Shadow*. As in *The Bards of Bone Plain*, the modern Mexico city began with the remnants of the older city and expanded so boundaries are no longer clear and eras are mixed together indiscriminately. *Ombria in Shadow* is a slightly different case in that the past is still living (in the form of Faey) beneath the newer incarnation of the city. Like the pastoral, the characters in the city-centered books entwine with their environments, and each provides clues to the other.

In all of McKillip's cities, there are characters more aware of their history than others. In *Invisible Cities*, Italo Calvino writes "[b]eware of saying to them that sometimes different cities follow one another on the same site and under the same name, born and dying without knowing one another, without communication among themselves" (27). Calvino warns that some people do not wish to know that the city they see as theirs has other forms and other incarnations. Those who do pay attention to this are rare. The past speaks to only a few characters in McKillip's books, while the general population moves through the cities without awareness of former incarnations. To most of the inhabitants of *The Bards of Bone Plain*, for example, their city's past is of little importance. To select characters, such as the Princess Beatrice, it is interesting, yet it is also, to characters such as the immortal Nairn, full of clues and mystery. It is this interweaving of mystery with indistinct clues that makes McKillip's cities work so well as ciphers. They provide clues without speaking, just as archeological evidence provides clues to the mute past in the primary world.

Cities like Caeuru, in *The Bards of Bone Plain*, serve as ciphers for mysteries in McKillip but they also work as believable cities. Fantasy, especially fantasy like McKillip's, is often accused of inaccuracy, and being "fluff" (as Melissa Thomas, along with many others have pointed out), but McKillip's books work against this allegation even though cities are not McKillip's primary settings in most of her books. The city of Caerau, for example, is a plausible city. Its history is similar to that of thousands of primary world cities. An encampment was set up beside a river. Merchants arrived to supply this encampment. Buildings grew to house the town, and at last a castle was built to fortify and rule it. This ordinary past is evidenced by the ruins buried beneath the city and the new ways in which older parts of the city are used. The Princess Beatrice shows an un-princess-like interest in archaeology:

> The smoke-stained walls, their stones dug out of field and river, still spoke, she thought, of a time so long ago that the school on the hill with its broken tower and the tiny village called Caerau was surrounded by grass and fields

and the great standing stones so old nobody remembered when or how they had come to the plain [63].

The city's past is a seemingly regular one, but Beatrice's last comment about the standing stones shows that Caerau has its mysteries. It is with the smallest details that McKillip's worlds are filled in, allowing them to stand as whole creations. The characters like Beatrice who are the most interested in the city's past are the ones most likely to notice and, perhaps, solve its mystery. All of these clues, built into the city and into the text itself, cue readers as well as characters into the mysteries surrounding them.

Caerau has characters, like the Princess Beatrice, who are interested in its mysteries, but it also has many ordinary citizens who seemingly are not (including, largely, one of the main characters—Phelan). In *Rhetorics of Fantasy* Mendlesohn talks about the "blinkered gaze of the urban inhabitant" in *Perdido Street Station*, *The Etched City* and *Titus Groan* (90). It is this "blinkered gaze" that the citizens of Caerau, Ombria and Berylon have in common, but in *Song for the Basilisk* history is ignored in a more purposeful way. The history that the victorious Pellior House has tried to erase is left to the evidence of buildings in *Song for the Basilisk*. Caladrius notes that "he could look down at the griffins still intact on their egg-shaped shields on either side of the front doors. The basilisk had destroyed the House, but had let the stones survive. A gesture for history, Caladrius guessed. A token to the dead" (115). Presumably, the Basilisk does not see the buildings as a threat, unlike the human children he slaughtered along with their parents. Mark Crinson explains Aldo Rossi's idea that "[a] city remembers through its buildings" (xiii), so it is noteworthy that the Basilisk has allowed the building to remain. The obvious presence of the Tormalyne building, but its dangerous place in history, leaves it in a curious space between seeing and unseeing:

> Tormalyne Palace lay in the bright, drenching light like the immense, blinded, sun-bleached corpse of some fabled animal. Caladrius tried to pass without looking at it, afraid he might stop in the middle of the jostling crowds and howl like a dog, tear cobbles from the street to wring sorrow out of stone. It loomed beyond his lowered eyes, insisting, until he finally looked and was stopped [*Basilisk* 119].

It is in "bright" light, almost spot-lit, and described as both "immense" and looming. Yet, it is a building dangerous to pay attention to because of its history. No one wants to seem too interested in the Tormalyne family, and so the "corpse" of their house is ignored. Caladrius's inability to look away regardless of his fear is a stark reminder of the power his traumatic past still holds over him.

Buildings are tied into the politics of the world in which they appear, and how the characters see, or do not see them, is vital. The music building in *Song for the Basilisk* is significant in that it is the one remainder of Tormalyne House that has been permitted to survive intact. It has been allowed to retain its name, its griffin carvings, and its sculptures of the dangerous but brilliant Tormalyne family. Music is what defeats the Basilisk in the end; music is what the story hinges on and is the one thing the Basilisk almost overlooks (for a longer discussion of this see Ringel's "Art"). Caladrius must "[learn] the history of Tormalyne House through its music" (*Basilisk* 179). In Berylon history is so dangerous it can only be navigated through music so, as a consequence, music is made dangerous. And yet, it is the music school that has been allowed to survive intact, providing clues to both the reader and the characters about how the Basilisk may be defeated.

Some of McKillip's cities, such as Berylon, have their history loudly proclaimed by the state of the city, but Ombria is more of a mystery. Physical clues are available but harder to read than a blatantly burned-out mansion, as is the case in Berylon. The physical past, though more difficult to read in *Ombria in Shadow*, is just as important as it is in other books, and characters (for example, the court historian and tutor Camas Erl) ignore the clues it provides to their detriment. When Camas Erl seeks to understand Ombria's past he is brought to the sorceress Faey by her helper Mag. Faey presents Camas Erl with a series of historical figures who lead him deeper into the underworld as a means of getting him out of the way. It is curious that he does not seem interested in the fact that there is another city sunk beneath the present one. Calvino writes that "[t]he city, however, does not tell its past, but contains it like the lines of a hand, written in the corners of the street" (13). Ombria keeps its secrets but, if looked for, they are there to be read. Bewitched or not, the under-city is physical evidence of the story Camas Erl seeks to prove, of Ombria's story. Physical evidence cannot be distorted in the same way that a historian's treatise can. Camas Erl is described as deep into books several times, but he never seems to notice the history that physically surrounds him. It is this physical presence that gives the best clue to what happens—and what has happened—to Ombria, and it is perhaps why Camas Erl never fully pieces everything together.

These clues are presented in both large and small form. McKillip's little details are a hallmark and one of the reasons her world-building is so successful. One of the many ways in which small details are in evidence in her cities is that there are empty rooms. Empty rooms, without purpose or sometimes even content are scattered throughout primary world cities, and it is one of the peculiarities of literature that there seem to be very few truly empty rooms in novels. The empty rooms found scattered throughout Ombria are important. Empty rooms can be a sign of great wealth but also of decline. (In *Cities of Tomorrow* Peter Hall argues in "The City of Dreadful Night" that empty rooms were a sign of wealth in contrast to the late 1800s and earlier when whole families sometimes lived in one room.) Ombria, unlike Rome, has not, for the most part, re-appropriated the old rooms for new uses. Neil Christie claims, in his essay "Lost Glories? Rome at the End of Empire," that starting in the fourth century, and perhaps even earlier, many cities in Italy were abandoned as populations fell and people moved back out into the countryside (314). Ombria, under Domina Pearl's rule, is a similarly failing city. The docks have become grown over, and descriptions of the empty rooms tell of mold, sagging, and disuse. The empty rooms all over Ombria are an unremarked upon, but important, sign of the city's death. They are also clues to Ombria's past, rooms have fallen into disuse as their uses (or even presence) are forgotten in the magical turning of Ombria into a new incarnation. Ombria is complicated by its shadow city and by its own regeneration. Both phenomena have left physical clues on the city, but only some of the characters are aware of these. The physical presence of the city and the corporeal marks that its past has left are important but often ignored. This cues the reader into the importance of unspoken, physical clues scattered through McKillip's worlds.

The way that characters fit into their environment can also give important clues. The manner in which McKillip's characters are integrated with their environments is one of the key ways her world-building is holistic, and in which the Material world is tangled with the Social world. The sorceress Faey is a reflection of the city. To her, each era is much like the next; her domain is similarly mixed. All times blend together, and neither she nor the city remembers where she came from, or even what she, or it, must have looked like originally. The underground mansion Faey lives in is a collection of multiple and shifting eras. Her house is an accumulation of the past, and none of it is ordered, or sequential, as it ought to be. Lydea feels as though "she moved backwards in time, wandering haphazardly through layers of history that changed at random and were never consecutive" (*Ombria* 161), but this could be referring to either Faey or Ombria. The full path of Ombria's past is a mystery. Faey's mansion reflects this in that though it is full of history, it is disordered and hidden: "Faey, who had been born in Ombria before it had a past, had sunk gradually underground along with it" (22). Faey and Ombria are simultaneous entities, and each is an accrual of times past that must be paid attention to.

Power

Like cities in the primary world McKillip's metropolises have multiple layers of different eras, history, and power ensuring that the Material world is entwined with the Cultural and Temporal worlds. The political eras that each city experiences are important to the overall form they take, again demonstrating how McKillip's worlds are integrated near-wholes, with elements impacting upon one another. Primary world cities, too, are influenced in this way, and useful comparisons may be drawn. Rome is an especially pertinent comparison because of the impact of various regimes. During the Roman Empire various emperors built, rebuilt, and destroyed monuments, palaces, and public spaces. In the declining years of the empire, buildings were taken apart for their materials and restructured for new uses. In more recent years, the dictator Mussolini created great changes in the physical structures of the city of Rome. With quick archaeological work, he sought to show the continuing glory of Italy. He also cleared great sections of the city for triumphal marches and other projects he considered important; as Borden W. Painter, Jr., notes "sometimes Rome's buildings and churches would have to fall to the piccione, or pickax, of progress as the regime destroyed the old to create the new and uncover the glories of the imperial past" (3). Thus, by "improving the flow of traffic, preserving and 'liberating' ancient monuments, tearing down buildings of little or no historical value, and above all demonstrating the fascist ability to carry out projects that others had only talked about," a modern city considerably different in shape and with different political purpose than it had had in the past was created (8). Politics are ingrained both in a city's past, as evidenced in its monuments, and in a city's present; in what still remains, what is ignored, and what is destroyed. The powerful characters of McKillip's cities have an impact on their physical space as much as their real-world counterparts do. McKillip's cities have also been torn down and built over; their political history is written in the physical spaces. Each city has its political past marked out in the concrete spaces of the city. It is perhaps curious then that it is only the mundane details of a city, such as how people live, that are overlooked or not deemed important enough to be described in detail. This seems to indicate that the power dynamic when people live in close proximity to each other is more interesting to McKillip than how the cities work as cities. The power dynamics between characters are worked out in detail, but important things such as markets, food importation, or water sources are not commented on. Unlike, for example, K.J. Parker's *Colours in the Steel*, where details such as markets are crucial, McKillip's work is more focused on her characters and on the buildings they use or need rather than the actual structure of her cities.

This focus gives clues to the books' themes. It is McKillip's lack of detail that is interesting in *Song for the Basilisk*, for example. In contrast to Ombria, and Caerau, both of which are described in detailed prose, Berylon is hardly fleshed out at all. Only certain buildings and structures are described in any depth, and which buildings are chosen for this detail is telling. Werner Wolf contends that description is "**implicated in the construction of meaning of the artefact or text** as a whole as well as in guiding various responses to the recipients" (18). That is, detail can be used to focus the reader's gaze: it can act as a marker, as is the case here. The buildings described in detail are all important to the plot: the music school and the palaces of the ruling Pelliors and the deposed Tormalynes. Other than these key buildings and certain markers (such as pubs important to the conspirators or the bridges leading in and out of the city) very little is explored. From a readerly perspective the city itself is left as a haze, and were one to attempt to map it out, certain buildings would be drawn clear and the rest a blank. From a critical perspective, where details focus is where the action, and the power, are centered. Unlike Kelior and Ombria, which are full of mystery involving the city, the action and mystery of *Song for the Basilisk* are centered on the people and a few buildings connected to those characters.

As Gary Westfahl (1) and others have argued, fantasy is often set in the past. It comes as no surprise then that the past of McKillip's cities development is described in more detail than its current form. A map of the cities in McKillip's works would be virtually impossible because space is not clearly defined in terms of how the cities work as cities. In and of itself this is interesting because fantasy literature is infamous for its inclusion of maps of the invented terrain (see Jones's lampooning of the topic in *The Tough Guide to Fantasyland,* or Ekman's extensive work on the subject: *Here Be Dragons: Exploring Fantasy Maps and Settings*). City maps are far less common in fantasy literature, but this perhaps points to the lack of interest in structurally defining cities. In one of her early secondary world fantasies, *The Riddle-Master* trilogy, there is a map, but none of McKillip's subsequent books has had one, and *The Riddle-Master* trilogy only has dots for the cities; there are no details. The cities themselves are imprecise; however, the power dynamics, the past and history of a city, and how these influence the physical look of the city are all explored in depth in McKillip's novels.

Buildings can be "read" for their past in McKillip's worlds. The past is not just part of the Cultural world with story and history; it is also an occupied, Material space in some of McKillip's works, such as *Ombria in Shadow,* where

> Faey lived, for those who knew how to find her, within Ombria's past. Parts of the city's past lay within time's reach, beneath the streets in great old limestone tunnels: the hovels and mansions and sunken river that Ombria shrugged off like a forgotten skin, and buried beneath itself through the centuries [14].

Part of Ombria's past is a physical manifestation. There are a number of primary world cities where the same physical remnants of the past are significant. For example, Jon Coulston and Hazel Dodge claim in their introduction to *Ancient Rome: The Archaeology of the Eternal City* that "[w]hen the economic tide receded from the 3rd Century, AD onward, the urban fabric remained for future generations to live in, adapt, and continue to marvel at. The skeletons of massive buildings, their original functions often forgotten, remained" (2). Like in Rome, the past in Ombria is something not only found in history lessons but lived in. Unlike in Caerau, where much of the past is buried beyond usability or integrated into the present city, Ombria's past is distinct from the modern city, even if its "original functions" (like in Rome) have been forgotten.

The people of Caerau, while just as careless of their history as the common people of Ombria, have built around buildings left by the past, which indicates how the history of Caerau is safer to explore, and how its past is more regular: "The servants got used to finding the princess anywhere at all: in the laundry room examining water pipes, following the line of an ancient wall into the butler's pantry" (*Bards* 37). As this line demonstrates, new buildings have accumulated around old sections. In Caerau, people live in history in a practical manner: what is not buried deep beyond usability is incorporated. There is no under-city as in Ombria, and this points to the difference in how the cities have developed and who has had control. This is an example of the way McKillip's cities are built into the worlds around them in complete ways; the histories of the cities are different so their present physical shapes are different too. Caerau has been built in a more ordinary fashion, with older structures buried or incorporated, while in Ombria the city's turning has meant that sections go unused suddenly, sinking out of use and forgotten without warning.

In *Ombria in Shadow* the shadow city, the underground remnants of past Ombrias, and Ombria's current incarnation are all part of the same physical space, but not completely. At times they intersect but they also have their own distinct characteristics as well. This adds to the confusion and mystery, especially because the laws of how the worlds work are not fully explained. From a readerly perspective the reader must conjecture exactly what differentiates each part from the other because the processes are not fully explored. This might be considered a weakness in McKillip's world-building (creative-writing manuals often expound on making the world consistent, for example) but, it is yet another aspect of the mystery that surrounds Ombria and its characters, it is un-knowable, even to the reader.

Unlike *Ombria in Shadow* and *The Bards of Bone Plain*, where the past is ignored or just forgotten, most of the characters in *Song for the Basilisk* are ordered to forget the past, and this willful ignorance has physical consequences for the city. As explored earlier, Tormalyne

Palace, a distinct reminder of the city's past, is ignored by the denizens for their own safety. The main character Caladrius, dismissed as "the librarian," "lingered beside the iron fence, studying the ruined palace, the monument to the dead, that those born in Berylon scarcely noticed when they passed" (*Basilisk* 189). The clues to history and the past are available for everyone to see, but ignored. The same can be found in primary world cities such as Budapest, where communists changed street names and erected monuments which then needed to be changed again once the regime ended. Richard S. Esbenshade proposes that the blank pedestals where the monuments used to stand and the crossed-out old street names (still found above the new versions) remain as examples of "'under-erasure' in the Derridean sense, neither truly there nor fully absent" (72–3). The palace in Berylon, too, is "neither truly there nor fully absent" because it is a huge building, an entire palace, but one that the populace tries their best to ignore.

History is ignored by the general populace, sometimes in ironic fashion, as when in *Song for the Basilisk* "[a] basilisk unfurled, black on red, in a silken cascade that did not quite touch the marble griffin crouched beside the door" (195). The basilisk and the griffin are the emblems of the two opposing houses, but the basilisk and griffins are forced into close proximity during the city's festival. History is erased with banners and celebrations, but the buildings themselves remain as mute testimony to the city's violent past. In Berylon there is a "consensus memory," to use Jenny Barrett's term (202). The past that the Basilisk has tried to suppress is still evident in physical structures, and so a state in between knowing and yet ignoring the past is evident. Barrett suggests that "consensus memory" is "a manufactured and agreed-upon perception" (202). It is a forced "agreed-upon" perception by the despot of Berylon, but it is a manufactured view, or rather un-view of the past to which the citizens of Berylon seem to subscribe.

In Berylon it is not safe to remember. The mystery of *Song for the Basilisk* (and to an extent *Ombria in Shadow*), is enhanced by the seeing/unseeing dichotomy. Noticing what is not meant to be seen is more than impolite—it is dangerous. This unseeing is deliberate and takes an act of will. The spaces of her worlds, and how they are controlled, is one of the ways characters, politics, story, and space are all entwined in McKillip, as will be explored further in the next section.

Politics

Cities reflect their past and this is often inescapable from their politics. Andrew Ballantyne contends that "[b]uildings are always symptomatic of larger and smaller forces, operating at different levels of influence, from the personal to the global" (11). Mussolini, for example, cleared great swathes of Rome to make room for triumphal marches, as the Nazis did in Germany. As Painter Jr. asserts, "[f]ascism transformed Rome. The city has a fascist imprint that has changed the way we experience the city today" (xv). Similarly, the Nazis, in addition to the Communists in the former USSR, had strict building codes that dramatically changed the landscape of the cities they dominated. Paul B. Jaskot notes, "[a]s with the Party Rally Grounds, building in Berlin was used both as a symbol for specific ideological policies as well as means of asserting Party (and specifically Hitler's) control over an existing administration" (82). Just as various regimes have deep impacts on the physical aspects of primary world cities, so, too, do politics impact cities in McKillip's books.

Fantasy is often accused of escapism (as Wolf *Imaginary Worlds* 33; and Mains "For Love" 219, also point out), and were this true, an easy way to truly escape the troubles of the primary world would be to build a world devoid of politics. But this is neither generally true for fantasy, nor for the worlds of McKillip. As Mains emphasizes in "For Love or For Money: The Concept of Loyalty in the Works of Patricia McKillip":

> Critic Rosemary Jackson, following the lead of Tzvetan Todorov, argues that narratives of the pure marvellous (32), to use her terminology for Tolkienesque high fantasy set in an idealized past and making use of magic and supernatural forces, are at best harmless escapism and at worst work to reconcile readers to the status quo [219].

In the chapter on the pastoral I investigated how McKillip's countryside's are unusual in that they are not refuges from politics and power. Similarly, McKillip's cities are deeply influenced by politics and this is demonstrated both with what is focused on, and with what is not. Ombria, Kelior, and Berylon all have power structures physically demarcated in their streets and palaces. Berylon in *Song for the Basilisk*, for example, experiences a coup, the remnants of which can be found tangibly manifest on the city in various ways. Some are obvious, such as the burnt-out husk of the Tormalyne family palace, allowed to remain a destroyed shell in full view, but some are subtler. These signs thus tie in the action, or past, of the books to the settings in which they occur.

Kelior (located within the unexplored kingdom of Numis) in *Od Magic* also has areas where politics are manifest. The Twilight Quarter is an area where politics have been physically marked on the city. The entrance is described as "the Twilight Gate, an archway through the thick wall which led to the upside-down world within" (33). It is a section of the city forbidden to wizarding students, and one that is looked after closely by guards. Even though the area has been walled off and isolated, it is still presumed too dangerous to ignore entirely. Walling off a part of the city means that the ideas coming in from other lands are carefully contained. As in Berylon, walls serve to contain the populace and also to keep external influences (especially those considered threatening) out. The Twilight Quarter is described as "dangerous, bewitching" (48), and because of this vice as well as ideas are cordoned off physically from the rest of the city, creating problems. The same can be said of primary world cities, such as nineteenth-century London. Jerry White notes that "[e]xtremes of deprivation and discomfort and pain provoked extremes of anticipation and enthusiasm and pleasure" (258). The excesses caused when large numbers of people are packed into small spaces can be just as volatile in fantastic cities as in the primary world. London needed outlets for pleasure, just as Kelior does. The power of such extremes can become explosive, just as it did with mobs and rioting in London, and with revolution in Kelior.

In *Od Magic* certain areas have been appropriated for political reasons, and this is reflected in the shape that the city takes. Both the Twilight Quarter and the School of Magic are carefully enclosed because they are places of naturally unruly power. Yar bitterly notes that "[y]ou will be taught how best to use your powers for Numis. You will never leave Numis to go roaming out of curiosity and wonder as Od does. You will be considered too valuable a weapon" (21–2). Through the years the wizards have been turned into weapons of the king, and with this process came the merging of the school building with the king's palace: "The very walls of the school are owned by the rulers of Numis. Why should they not train wizards to their own advantage?" (32). Somehow the wizards of Numis have become shaped to the king's will, just as their school became the king's. Through the centuries the school—first the subjects and how they were taught, and later the building itself—was overtaken by the kings. As Yar teaches, "[s]o, you can see, from the very beginning there was that strong bond between wizard and ruler which strengthened through the centuries until Od's school became, in Cronan's reign, part of the king's palace" (20). The coherence of McKillip's world is again emphasized with the intertwining of character, politics, and space. The school that began as a separate entity, eventually merged with the palace, literally and figuratively beneath the king's gaze.

This intersection is not necessarily a positive one within the book. The balance of power that sees the king ruling both kingdom and school is one that seems beneficial to the king yet is detrimental for the wizards. Yar notes, "I didn't realize, as the years passed, how these walls that keep us safe and comfortable have also put such limits on our vision" (28). The wizards have been physically attached to the king's house, walled in, and in the process their powers and vision have been walled in as well. Knowledge is controlled by the king, because "[b]oth rulers and wizards [crave] power; to avoid contention and chaos one must be bound by the other" (48). The kings have decided that power cannot be shared, that it must be leashed, and this vision of power shapes how the city looks: "He couldn't get lost; the king's high towers overshadowed everything" (71). The king's palace is the ultimate building in Kelior, as he is the ultimate power, and both the Twilight Quarter and the School of Magic are in its shadow.

The king nearly spells his own doom with the separation of the Twilight Quarter from the city and of the School of Magic from creativity. The king is wrong in his assumptions that the wizards seek power like his and must be kept in check. The Twilight Quarter is less dangerous than expected, so too those who simply want knowledge. The characters in the novel who seek to subvert the king's rules do so for their own sake, for their own dream of knowledge, not for power itself. As Yar explains, "[g]reat wizards pursue knowledge and magic, not power.... They are not confined by the boundaries of a king's power, nor by any law except the laws of magic, which are exacting and compelling as any king's" (*Od* 129). All that those with untamed magic really seek is freedom from walls and strictures, not anarchy. This is reflected in the fact that those rebelling do not enact any physical violence on the city itself (at least not on purpose); it is an intellectual rebellion, not a physical one.

The kings have sought to protect themselves and their kingdom, but instead they have stagnated it. By closing off the Twilight Quarter, which is creativity, fun, and inspiration, and the school, which should be the same but is no longer, the monarchy impedes the progress of its citizens without knowing it. The hero of Kelior, Od, was not formally taught, but used wind and water to defeat an impending army only because she did not know she could not. So, too, the wizard Yar, who as a young man on his way to the school saved the palace from destruction by a Beast because he thought to ask it what it wanted, and listened. Compassion and curiosity win, not structured, sanctioned power. The careful interplay between past politics and the modern shape of the city is another example of where McKillip's world-building is at its best. Each aspect reflects and builds on the other so that the present, past and politics are all entwined as in primary world cities. By physically marking off space as dangerous, or regimented, the kings have cut off the flow of ideas as well.

To drive the point home that control has stifled, rather than improved the city, the most powerful characters in the story are those with "wild" magic who still think outside of what is allowed by the king and try to escape the physical, as well as mental, confinement of the school. "I had a dream of magic ... somehow, within the walls of Od's school, I lost sight of that dream" (96), laments Yar. Magic is tamed by the king, and the characters who wish to break free of this are treated as dangerous. The king's own daughter is one such character, and when told she is to be married to a complacent wizard, and thus never free again, "[a] helpless despair rose in her, that she would never see past the walls the Kings of Numis had placed around magic; she would never know how much more, if anything, there was to know" (57). Her first response is to lament the lack of knowledge. Crucially, she immediately thinks that she "would never see past the walls" that the kings have put around magic. She thinks of walls because they go beyond metaphor in the city of Kelior and into physical reality. Knowledge is corralled with physical as well as metaphorical walls.

The Twilight Quarter, though forbidden, is clearly presented as a positive, somewhere where knowledge is to be found. When the gardener Brenden needs to know what a plant is, he is directed to the Twilight

Quarter. When the Princess Sulys wants to know if there is more small magic, like that of her mother's family, she tries to go to the Twilight Quarter. The Twilight Quarter has forms of knowledge not available in the rest of the city, which creates problems. As a young student notes, "[b]ut if the wizards in other lands learn different ways of magic that are forbidden here, they could attack the king, and no one could stop them" (128). The kings have created their own destruction with the enclosure of school and Twilight Quarter and thus the stifling of knowledge.

A similar political shaping is shown in *Ombria in Shadow*, but the inherent mystery of *Ombria in Shadow* gives form to a subtler form than that found in *Od Magic*. The two greatest forces in the city are the powerful women Domina Pearl and Faey. Each has her own domain and her own secrets. That neither of their realms is easily accessible gives clues to their personalities and to the mystery surrounding the two women. Domina Pearl's regime in Ombria imposes her will on the landscape of town in addition to castle. In the city of Ombria her influence is seen in the rotting timber and weed-filled docks. At one point the wharf's disintegration is described: "On the end of a weedy pier, where they could see the waves though rotting wood.... The warehouse facing the water was empty; so was the harbor except for a few fishing boats and a black-sailed pirate ship" (*Ombria* 58). Hints are dropped throughout of an embargo. An imprudent former merchant toasts to "[t]he Black Pearl and her sea scum that closed the ports of Ombria" (56). Domina Pearl has closed the town's free shipping, and only her black-sailed ships go in or out. Her rule has caused Ombria to decline, which is shown tangibly in the deteriorating state of the city's docks and the empty rooms discussed earlier.

Like in the pastoral characters are influenced by and influence their surrounds in the worlds in which they live in McKillip's integrated worlds. For instance, Domina Pearl's secret dominance of the city in the past and her blatant dominance of it in the present are both reflected in her physical surroundings. She has two places of power: her secret chamber and her secret library. The publicly acknowledged library of the castle was purged long before of anything to do with magic or poison. Domina Pearl sees to it that only she has the knowledge, and the space, to rule. Mag stumbles upon the lesser of the two rooms, the library: "She had chanced across the Black Pearl's library.

The knowledge she found important, her spells, perhaps her history" (*Ombria* 127). Even this already secret room is hidden well, with its "stairs hidden behind a warped, flecked mirror in the back of a room" (126). Domina Pearl's library is hidden behind a mirror, in the back of an empty room, in the secret and disused part of the palace. This triple layer of deception shows her cunning, her imagination, and her ability to shape the castle to her needs. The need for a room of one's own, as described in Virginia Woolf's eponymous manifesto on what women writers need in order to succeed—including space of their own and the luxury to use time as they want—seems to apply to sorceresses just as much as to women writers.[1] The powerful characters in McKillip's cities are similarly in need of space and time, and their secret domains accomplish this by allowing them to hold and wield power from secure bases. It could be supposed Domina Pearl is powerful not only because she is ruthless but because she has carved herself this space and time away in which to work.

Secret rooms are important to someone looking for power regardless of gender. Like Domina Pearl in *Ombria in Shadow*, the prince from *Song for the Basilisk* has a secret room to do sorcery, also without a door. Unlike Domina Pearl's sanctuary, however, there is not even a whisper of the Basilisk's room's existence. According to the definition in the *Encyclopedia of Fantasy* the Prince of Berylon is a true "secret master," someone who is the "guiding will" behind events. He manipulates events from a secret room: "In Pellior Palace, the Prince of Berylon's dragon-eyed daughter stood beside him in a chamber without a door. The chamber was the heart of the palace, a secret only known to the two of them, for the prince, having discovered it, had eliminated those who helped him furnish it" (*Basilisk* 48). This room of power is important both because it helped him to overtake Tormalyne house with poisons and magic, but also because he and his daughter are the only ones who have found it. The uses of the chamber illuminate the power dynamic. It is interesting that the room has not only been used to deal with outsiders but with family as well: "The chamber, built of massive blocks of white marble behind the walls of other rooms, had been the last refuge of rulers of Pellior House who had exhausted every other method of dealing with troublesome neighbors or relatives" (51). As with *Ombria in Shadow*, the power struggles in *Song for the Basilisk* can be within a family as well as without. This is yet another way the worlds of *Ombria in Shadow* and *Song for the Basilisk* are similar to the primary world's Renaissance Italy, where family feuds had significance in the outside world.

Ombria in Shadow too deals with family subterfuge. Domina Pearl is the great Aunt and regent of the boy king, and Ducon Greve is her great-nephew. Domina Pearl's secret chamber is reminiscent of the Basilisk's secret chamber in *Song for the Basilisk*. Here her secrets are kept and her poisons brewed. It differs from the Basilisk's private space in that it is a space that a few intuitive characters, such as Mag, guess must be there. This reflects other aspects of the world and stories. In *Song for the Basilisk* magic seems to be a hidden, mysterious part of the world, and poison as well. The Basilisk's use of both is thus a secret, and so the room he concocts them in is as well. In *Ombria in Shadow* magic and poison seem to be un-discussed but natural parts of the world. Thus Domina Pearl, who uses both magic and poison to good effect, is supposed to have somewhere where she prepares them. But, in the end, none of the characters of Ombria actually find this secret domain; it has to be shown to them. Ducon exclaims, "[s]he opened the door for me ... and I went in. I've been searching everywhere for that door" (*Ombria* 230). It is important that although Ducon suspects Domina Pearl has such a space, she has to show it to him. It is as well concealed as Domina Pearl herself has been, hiding in Ombria's past of and manipulating its future: "It was Domina Pearl's most closely guarded secret, the center of the she-spider's web. That she had permitted Mag to see it, Mag found profoundly disquieting" (268). Mag is "disquieted" because being shown the room means she is un-likely to ever leave it; this is a secret too precious to be shared. Domina Pearl's closely guarded sanctuary is within the palace, but seemingly outside it as well since no one has ever been able to find it without her help. Just as she has been able to hide herself from notice and time's ravages, her secret chamber is within the castle, yet separate. In the *Encyclopedia of Fantasy*, the entry on "wainscots" maintains that "invisible or undetected societies [live] in the interstices of the dominant world." Ombria and Berylon both contain these "wainscots," or people (sometimes groups as with the conspirators in *Song for the Basilisk*) who work invisibly in secret chambers and hidden rooms to manipulate events to their satisfaction.

Just as the holding of space displays power, the appropriation of space displays power dynamics. McKillip's worlds are a connected ecology—each part influences the other segments, physically but also psychologically. How each section of a city has dealt with its past makes for contrasting but connected areas in many of her books. *Od Magic*, for instance, has the opposing structures of the School of Magic, and the Twilight Quarter. Both are blocked-off sections of the city where particular acts are performed by particular types of people. They are both concerned with magic, but one is creativity and the other is regime. They are part of the same city, the same problems and solution, but in superficially different ways. In *Ombria in Shadow* Domina Pearl seeks to take over the underground, to commandeer all the spaces of Ombria, and thus to hold all the political power as well. Faey is complete mistress of the underground city and, to an extent, Ombria's past as well. The disuse of the underground is a reflection of the power Faey holds over the unconscious city. She suffers no one to be underground without her knowledge, and since the general townsfolk have no curiosity about Ombria's past, the only ones she chases out are the street urchins. Faey does not even allow people to die in peace in the under city: she says to Lydea, "I wish ... that people wouldn't die down here. I can usually send them back up before they get too far" (*Ombria* 133). Thus, the only members of the under-city are those Faey has allowed to be there, demonstrating her complete dominance.

Faey holds complete control of the underneath Ombria, the one place Domina Pearl has taken no notice of until the end of the book, when she notes, "[s]he has grown too free and unpredictable in her underground city. I want her here, under my control" (*Ombria* 271). Domina Pearl seeks to control Faey not only by removing Faey from her own domain but also by physically putting Faey into Domina Pearl's realm of influence. Thus space is important in a multitude of ways.

In *Song for the Basilisk* as well there is an appropriation of space. Arioso Pellior does not just want to destroy the Tormalyne family, he takes everything that was associated with it, including "the music school, which Prince Arioso had appropriated, down to its last demisemiquaver, for the good of the city, though he at least allowed it to keep its three-hundred-year-old name" (71). Later in the novel Caladrius notes that in Tormalyne House "[h]e recognized racks for bottles and kegs, though they were empty. Pellior House must have appropriated the wine cellar along with the music" (159). Taking the wine is a small example, but shows the completeness of the ruination of Tormalyne House. The Basilisk torched the house and killed all the family, but also appropriated the wine and music. It was a complete, and callous, appropriation, one that displays the extent of Pellior's power and ruthlessness.

How characters move through space as well as how it is used is an indicator of relationships as well as movement, and reflects the detail with which characters are integrated with their world. Caladrius follows Luna through the palace that should be his by right:

> She moved ahead of him through the dark; he saw her easily, moving surely, gracefully across damp, sagging flagstones, through the maze of rooms. He felt the blood pound again behind his eyes. She knew the place where he had been born as if she had claimed it for her own [295].

That she moves so easily through what should be her enemy's palace is interesting, but so, too, is the fact that she dominates the space (even "claims" it) over and above Caladrius with her ease of movement. The blood pounding behind his eyes is a sign of his shock; this is a space that has been forbidden since Luna was a very young child, and yet she moves through it with confidence, "easily," more so than Caladrius whose family and childhood home it was. This creates interesting implications. Perhaps Luna has explored the forbidden space as she has done other secret spaces. Perhaps it is simply a talent. Whatever the answer, and the book is not forthcoming with any, what is clear is that space and how characters move within it is important for more than just travel from point A to point B.

Luna's ability to get into her father's secret chamber as a small child is a secret test and another example of how space can expand beyond the physical and into the psychological. Here she enters the room for the first time: "[she] had seen an unfamiliar expression on his face when she joined him in his secret place. He looked, she realized later, as if he had seen her for the first time in their lives; he had finally recognized her as part of him" (52). The Basilisk's relationship with his daughter is important, and it is equally important that they are the two who can enter the chamber and have managed to do so without formal teaching or anyone pointing out that it can even be done. Arioso discovered it by paying attention to lore, but without actual guidance: "According to family history, it had last been used two centuries before. Then it had passed into family lore until Arioso had discovered a need for it, and, in his methodical fashion, discovered it" (51). In the same methodical way, Luna, too, discovers it when she needs her father. They find the space and privacy they require within a busy household and their dominance of this space reflects their dominance over the rest of the family and city.

The use of space can be both subtle and important and its further exploration in *Song for the Basilisk* is provided at the end of the book with a small moment where Luna allows Caladrius to see her come out of the secret room. Her father would have allowed no one to do so, and, at this point, Luna knows that Caladrius is quite dangerous. The opening of a secret door openly displays trust but serves as a warning as well. The fact that Caladrius has already noted the eyehole where a tapestried animal's eye should have been shows his own cunning. The fact that he has noticed a keyhole where no one else has combined with the fact that she allows him to see the secret provides a hint at the balance of power that occurs at the end. Caladrius uses his own nerve and cunning, and Luna allows a balance of power to be restored for the sake of peace. These power struggles are played out silently, all with the simple opening of a door, but they are an important hint and yet another understated way clues are found subtly in McKillip's worlds.

The past and its few visible remnants the stones speak to Caladrius and Luna, linking them again, both with their special importance to the novel, and their affinity with the past and the world they inhabit. When Caladrius goes into Tormalyne Palace; "[d]ark and stone closed around him ... he heard the sounds within the register of its silence; the forgotten screams of pain and despair that had seeped into the stones through centuries of Tormalyne history" (158). Both he and Luna hear the past in the stones. If it were not a fantasy, it is entirely possible that it would be a figure of expression. As it is, it can be taken literally: "[Luna] walked curiously through the vast, empty rooms, their walls charred black like chimney stones. Cries followed her, seeped out of the past around her" (274). Both she and Caladrius can hear the past, not just in their own imagination, as we would in the primary world, but in reality. This deep connection to the past is far more intimate than the usual figurative use of "hearing the past." Perhaps this shared affinity is partially why they are the two rulers left at the end of the book. They do not ignore the past; the past—and its pain—speaks to them both and gives them a level of empathy their parents likely lacked.

The physical effects of tyranny are obvious in Berylon and must, like the emotional wounds, be healed after the regime changes. As in the primary world action has consequences, and this is explored in McKillip's worlds. In *Song for the Basilisk,* at the height of the conflict, "[t]he doors of the school were chained shut; guards stood at every corner. Someone had pounded the faces of the stone griffins flanking the doors into dust" (266). The griffin is a symbol of the Tormalyne family; the griffins on the school's steps (and the school's name) are some of the few reminders of the Tormalyne family, and they have been disfigured purposefully. Though the name cannot be maimed physically, the other symbol of the house is. This means that there is more than psychological reparations to be made at the end. Berylon must begin the mundane task of picking up after peace: "Around her students and magisters picked up books, mopped mud and spilled water off the floors, repaired battered doors" (313). These are not great acts, but they are important to physically setting the city to rights and to returning it to the state it was in during more peaceful times. It is also important that Luna provides furnishings and other necessities for the destroyed Tormalyne House. They are unlooked-for reparations that point the way to future interaction between the two houses (Mains points out in "For Love" that Luna retains loyalty and fosters peace, unlike her father 228). Thus the complete cycle of rebellion is displayed—both the initial, fighting, stages through to the resolutions, physical as well as mental. The characters, their actions, and the events that have happened around them are thus all tied together.

Ombria, too, must be repaired. All that Domina Pearl has physically done to stamp her power on Ombria must be undone. In the end, the physical manifestations of power must be changed when the regime comes to an end. Politics are physically imprinted on the city with a reminder that Ducon Greve, the new Regent, must see that "[a]ll the broken piers he had wandered over must be fixed; the troubled, dangerous streets he had roamed at all hours must be made safe" (*Ombria* 293). The metaphysical repairs are created with the forgetting that is cast by Ombria's turning into a new version, but the physical damage must be undone as well. The wharves that Domina Pearl allowed to rot need to be fixed, even if her dangerous secret rooms have crumbled in Ombria's change. Faey, whose power goes on forgotten, but undiminished, is left undisturbed in her underground domain, with her power intact and her domain untouched by the newest ravage of history. The framing device that was explored in Chapter Four is thus reinforced by a cycle of renewal that takes place physically within the city itself, connecting elements of McKillip's worlds once again.

The nature of McKillip's cities reflects the general tone of her writing: even though she has placed these tales in mostly self-contained cities, she seems more interested in the power dynamics of people than in how the cities function as cities. In Chapter Five it was explored how McKillip's characters are integrated with their environment so that neither is unaffected by the other, which gives the sense of a more complete world, and the same is true of her cities, the other side of the landscape coin from her pastoral settings.

Reflections

I have been blessed to work with an author whose works can be read again and again, gaining rather than diminishing upon each reading. The worlds Patricia A. McKillip invites one to enter have always held the promise of being so much wider than what was on the page, and when I began to study them as a literary scholar, I was fascinated by how her worlds grew even more when subjected to the tools of critical reading. The aim of this book has therefore been to analyze critical world-building by examining this in the works of a single author, the under-studied McKillip.

Each chapter in this book has been informed by an overall feeling that each part is adding to the collective sense of a critical discourse on McKillip's world-building. When observed through the lens of critical world-building, it becomes clear that a particular set of McKillip's texts, though fairly different, can all be grouped together. Each of these books provides a nexus of a number of distinct elements, all brought together and entangled in different ways, but always with the result that a sense of depth and a fully realized world is brought to life in each.

The topics and themes of the preceding chapters interlock in (sometimes surprising) ways, and, as a result, numerous examples could have been used in multiple chapters. Selecting which example to use in what chapter became a challenge, as many examples proved to exemplify multiple themes. This, of course, was part of my overall point: world-building can and should be studied holistically and thus all aspects of its examination are bound to intertwine. But the selection of examples also led to certain titles, especially *The Changeling Sea, The Bell at Sealey Head, Winter Rose,* and *Kingfisher,* not receiving the concentrated attention that could have been paid to them, in favor of other works that more closely fit with the themes under examination. Ultimately, however, every book of McKillip's could (and indeed should) be analyzed and interpreted with a basis in their world-building elements, and my choices have been if not random then at least highly idiosyncratic.

Although grouped loosely as secondary world fantasies, the books I have used in this text could be differentiated just as often as compared. Few of them seem to return to lands or characters previously explored, but each has a depth and breadth that leaves no doubt but that the worlds that McKillip constructs are fully realized. How this is construed, interpreted, and presented has all been probed, with the result that I hope McKillip's worth as a world-builder is clear. I also hope that I have broadened the conception of world-building so that it not only encompasses what the reader sees, or writer does, but what its affects are, how these are constructed and construed, among a myriad of other considerations. World-building is a complex subject and this book is just the beginning.

I propose a particular approach to world-building, an approach that focuses on the way a world is constructed by critical activity rather than on the work of an author or reader to bring the fictional world to life. Such critical world-building, I argue, is the result of a dynamic interplay between all the various elements of the world as well as the theoretical and methodological tools introduced by the scholar. In the first chapter, I provide a background to world-building in general and lay out the basis for critical world building. With this as a springboard, the rest of the book is then a demonstration of how a number of thematic areas can be analyzed through critical world-building in McKillip's works, and how this results in interesting insights on the texts in question.

Tropes and other fantasy expectations can be used to build a world, as well as to disrupt the assumed shape of the narratives that can play out in it. Every genre develops its own conventions and standardized forms, and how the tropes of the fantasy genre and the expectations that fantasy conventions create affect world-building is the topic of Chapter Two. Using examples from a number of texts including *The Throme of the Erril of Sherril*, *The Tower at Stony Wood*, and *The Forests of Serre* I show how McKillip uses expectations to surprise, and subvert assumptions, enriching her worlds into far from formulaic places.

Characters can be affected by age and gender much the same way that people are in the primary world, but they can also react differently, and when they do so they subvert many of the "rules" that bind people. McKillip's worlds are rich in terms of age ranges and gender roles, and this is the focus of Chapter Three. As a vital part of the Social world characters are often how a world is observed, and moved through, and as a result are an integral part of world-building. When characters are allowed out of the roles that people can be constrained to, a vision of a more inclusive world is celebrated.

Legends build a richer world by adding a feeling of culture and history to works. McKillip uses legends in the traditional way, as stories of heroes, but she also uses them to point at the mutability of story. Culture, in this case the legends that are evoked or built in a world, are part of world-building just as much as more tangible considerations like setting. The perceived depth that is a hallmark of McKillip's worlds is largely a result of the legends that populate, and enrich, them, and I explore this aspect of the Mythological world in Chapter Four.

Location is often all that is considered when examining world-building, and this is naturally an important part. McKillip's primary landscapes, pastoral countrysides (Chapter Five), and ancient cities (Chapter Six), are complete ecologies, tied into other aspects of McKillip's works. What sorts of landscapes and settings are used is important, but so too is how the characters interact with them, and what they are designed to show about the world as a whole, thus the exploration of the Material world is tied into considerations of the Temporal, Cultural, and even, at times, the Mythological world.

Critical world-building is a long overdue tool, but it is also a difficult one to master. I was surprised how easy it was to slip into an authorial, or readerly viewpoint. But I think it important to try, at times, to separate out critical world-building from other functions, and to see what is said as a result.

My main argument is that McKillip is an exemplary world-builder within a particular framework, and the dynamic interplay style of critical world-building was used to show why and how she is. Mendlesohn proposes in *Diana Wynne Jones: Children's Literature and the Fantastic Tradition* that "[t]he immersive fantasy requires the author to convince the reader of the existence of a whole world" (101). It is this that McKillip has accomplished in all of her books, whether immersive or not.

That does not mean I focused entirely on the successful. I pointed out some of the instances when she was not quite as careful—even Tolkien allowed an express train through now and again. McKillip follows in the Tolkienian tradition, in the sense that she works to give her secondary worlds believability, and she does this through her exemplary world-building. James contends that "[w]hat Tolkien did to give readers that necessary sense of belief in Secondary World was to provide enormous historical and cultural depth to Middle-earth," (66) and McKillip does something similar with her characters, her landscapes, and the trappings of fantasy literature that she uses, twists or discards altogether. Poul Anderson argues that "[b]y bringing in this detail and that, tightly linked, the writer makes his imaginary globe seem real" (106). My aim was to explore these details, to explore how they were linked, and in what way this could be surprising, novel, or expected; whether they did, in fact, make the "imaginary globe seem real."

Patricia A. McKillip has been the focus of this work but she is not the be-all or end-all of world-building, nor is her type of world-building "the best." It would be interesting, for example, to take a novel like China Miéville's *Perdido Street Station*, almost as far from McKillip in the fantasy genre as possible, and subject it to the same critical lenses that I have used to examine, for instance: *In the Forests of Serre*, *Ombria in Shadow*, and *The Tower at Stony Wood* in McKillip. Or to use that lens to scrutinize the two fantasy-versions of London featured by Tom Pollock in his *Skyscraper Throne* series; or as a critical basis for a comparative analysis of the epic worlds of Steven Erikson and Stephen R. Donaldson. The fantasy genre offers a surfeit of topics for scholarly attention. What each reader, critic, or author considers to be the best in world-building is largely subject to opinion, though I hope I have succeeded in introducing some critical metrics. I have not sought to provide an answer to what is world-building, when it is done "best," but to offer multiple answers and open up new avenues of exploration along the way. The lens deserves more sharpening than I have been able to provide; there is room for more critical investigation and further investigation into the uses to which world-building has already been put within creative writing and media studies.

Far more work needs to be done on world-building in general, but also on world-building as a critical tool. All authors, all genres, all individual works can be explored in the light of world-building, and I hope some of the tools and angles that I have used might spark interest in others. Similarly, McKillip's complex, innovative, and well-crafted fantasies deserve wider, and, above all, more careful attention. In this book, I have roamed through some of her worlds, untangled some of their themes, and uncovered some of their mysteries, but so much more remain to be seen, untangled, and uncovered. The work I have done is only a beginning, in examinations of McKillip and of critical, fantastic world-building, but hopefully it inspires further work.

Chapter Notes

Preface

1. Although the edition of *The Riddle-Master* trilogy that I use is entitled *Riddle of Stars*, I have retained the tradition of recent editions and scholarship, that refer to the trilogy as a whole, as *The Riddle-Master* trilogy. I also treat it as a single text, though it is sometimes sold as three different books. This is because the world remains the same throughout the trilogy.

2. The edition of the Cygnet duology that I use has both books together. However, I generally treat them as two separate novels, and label them as such when I do.

Chapter One

1. This is where I differ from Wolf, who works with imaginary worlds outside of books and therefore sans stories as well.

2. None of McKillip's worlds are named (which is why I call them all by their book's title) thus it is possible (though unlikely) that at some future date McKillip herself might indicate that they were all in one world.

3. Largely taken from reader-response theory.

4. Credit must be given to Chrissie Mains for this idea, and for help with this chapter as a whole.

5. Thanks to Stefan Ekman for his help generally with this chapter, but specifically for bringing this point to my attention.

Chapter Two

1. Thanks to Brian Attebery for bringing this concept to my attention.
2. Thanks to Chris Pak for his observations on this.

Chapter Four

1. See Martha Hixon's "'The Lady of Shalott' as Paradigm in Patricia McKillip's *The Tower at Stony Wood*." Also, Robert M. Tilendis's "Patricia A. McKillip *In the Forests of Serre* (Ace Books 2003)."

2. Thanks to Stefan Ekman for pointing this out.

Chapter Six

1. Christine Mains also explored McKillip and *A Room of One's Own* at ICFA 37.

Works Cited

Adkins, Arthur W. H., and Peter White, eds. *The Greek Polis*. Chicago: University of Chicago Press, 1986.
Agnew, Vijay. "Introduction." *Diaspora, Memory and Identity: A Search for Home*, ed. Vijay Agnew. Toronto: University of Toronto Press, 2005.
Anderson, Poul. "The Creation of Imaginary Worlds: The World Builder's Handbook and Pocket Companion." *Writing Science Fiction and Fantasy*, ed. Gardner Dozois et al. New York: St. Martin's Press, 1991.
Armitage, Kevin C. *The Nature Study Movement: The Forgotten Popularizer of America's Conservation Ethic*. Lawrence: University Press of Kansas, 2009.
Attebery, Brian. *The Fantasy Tradition in American Literature: From Irving to Le Guin*. Bloomington: Indiana University Press, 1981.
_____. *Stories about Stories: Fantasy and the Remaking of Myth*. Oxford: Oxford University Press, 2014.
_____. *Strategies of Fantasy*. Bloomington: Indiana University Press, 1992.
Ballantyne, Andrew. *Architecture Theory: A Reader in Philosophy and Culture*. London: Continuum, 2005.
Baltasar, Michaela. "J.R.R. Tolkien: A Rediscovery of Myth." *Tolkien and the Invention of Myth: A Reader*, ed. Jane Chance. Lexington: University Press of Kentucky, 2004.
Barillas, William. *The Midwestern Pastoral: Place and Landscape in Literature of the American Heartland*. Athens: Ohio University Press, 2006.
Barrett, Jenny. "Glory, Glory: Hollywood's Consensus Memory of the American Civil War." *Reconfiguring the Union: Civil War Transformations*, ed. Philip John Davies and Iwan W. Morgan. New York: Palgrave Macmillan, 2013.
Barry, Elizabeth. *Beckett and Authority: The Uses of Cliché*. New York: Palgrave Macmillan, 2006.
Berry, Wendell. *The Art of the Commonplace: The Agrarian Essays of Wendell Berry*, ed. Norman Wirzba. Berkeley: Counterpoint Press, 2002.
Bettelheim, Bruno. *The Uses of Enchantment: The Meaning and Importance of Fairy Tales*. Harmondsworth: Penguin, 1978.
Bird, Hazel Sheeky. "The Pastoral Impulse and the Turn to the Future in *The Hobbit* and Interwar Children's Fiction." *J.R.R. Tolkien*, ed. Peter Hunt. New York: Palgrave Macmillan, 2013.
Bloom, Harold, ed. *Falstaff*. William Shakespeare. New York: Chelsea House, 1992.
Bolintineanu, Alexandra. "'On the Borders of Old Stories': Enacting the Past in *Beowulf* and *The Lord of the Ring*." *Tolkien and the Invention of Myth: A Reader*, ed. Jane Chance. Lexington: University Press of Kentucky, 2004.

Boyer, Robert H., and Kenneth J. Zahorski. "The Secondary Worlds of High Fantasy." *The Aesthetics of Fantasy Literature and Art*, ed. Roger C. Schlobin. Notre Dame: University of Notre Dame Press, 1982.
Brooks, Terry. *The Sword of Shannara*. New York: Del Ray, 1977.
Buell, Lawrence. *The Environmental Imagination: Thoreau, Nature Writing, and the Formation of American Culture*. Cambridge: Harvard University Press, 1995.
Butler, Catherine. "Tolkien and Worldbuilding." *J.R.R. Tolkien*, ed. Peter Hunt. New York: Palgrave Macmillan, 2013.
Calhoun, Blue. *The Pastoral Vision of William Morris: The Earthly Paradise*. Athens: University of Georgia Press, 1975.
Calvino, Italo. *Invisible Cities*, ed. W. Weaver. London: Pan Books, 1979.
Campbell, Joseph. *The Hero with a Thousand Faces*. New York: Pantheon Books, 1949.
Card, Orson Scott. *How to Write Science Fiction and Fantasy*. New York: Writer's Digest Books, 1990.
Carter, Lin. *Imaginary Worlds: The Art of Fantasy*. New York: Ballantine Books, 1973.
Chandler, Daniel, and Rod Munday. "Tropes." *A Dictionary of Media and Communication*. Oxford: Oxford University Press, 2011.
Christie, Neil. "Lost Glories? Rome at the End of Empire." *Ancient Rome: The Archaeology of the Eternal City*, ed. Jon Coulston and Hazel Dodge. Oxford: Oxford University School of Archaeology, 2000.
Clute, John. "Canary in the Coalmine." *Pardon this Intrusion: Fantastika in the World Storm*. Harold Wood: Beccon Publications, 2011.
_____. "Next." *Pardon this Intrusion: Fantastika in the World Storm*. Harold Wood: Beccon Publications, 2011.
_____. "Notes on the Geography of Bad Art in Fantasy." *Pardon this Intrusion: Fantastika in the World Storm*. Harold Wood: Beccon Publications, 2011.
_____. "Pardon this Intrusion." *Pardon this Intrusion: Fantastika in the World Storm*. Harold Wood: Beccon Publications, 2011.
Clute, John, and John Grant, eds. *Encyclopedia of Fantasy*. London: Orbit, 1999.
Clute, John, and Peter Nicholls, eds. *Encyclopedia of Science Fiction*. London: St. Martin's Press, 1995.
Coffin, Tristram Potter. *The Female Hero in Folklore and Legend*. New York: Seabury Press, 1975.
Copper, Baba. *Over the Hill: Reflections on Ageism Between Women*. Freedom, CA: Crossing Press, 1988.
Coulston, Jon, and Hazel Dodge. "Introduction: The Archaeology and Topography of Rome." *Ancient Rome: The Archaeology of the Eternal City*, ed. Jon Coulston and Hazel Dodge. Oxford: Oxford University School of Archaeology, 2000.
Crinson, Mark. "Urban Memory—an Introduction." *Urban Memory: History and Amnesia in the Modern City*, ed. Mark Crinson. London: Routledge, 2005.
Curry, Patrick. *Defending Middle-Earth: Tolkien, Myth and Modernity*. New York: Houghton Mifflin, 2004.
Darcy, Jane. "The Representation of Nature in *The Wind and the Willows* and *The Secret Garden*." *The Lion and the Unicorn* 19.2 (1995).
David, Gail. *Gender and Genre in Literature: Female Heroism in the Pastoral*. New York: Garland, 1991.
Delany, Samuel R. "About 5,750 Words." *The Jewel-Hinged Jaw: Notes on the Language of Science Fiction*. Middleton, CT: Wesleyan University Press, 2009.
Donaldson, Stephen R. *Epic Fantasy in the Modern World: A Few Observations*. Kent: Kent State University Libraries, 1986.
Doughty, Amie A. *"Throw the book away": Reading versus Experience in Children's Fantasy*. Jefferson, NC: McFarland, 2013.

Works Cited

Eagleton, Terry. *How to Read Literature*. New Haven: Yale University Press, 2014.
Eco, Umberto. *The Role of the Reader: Explorations in the Semiotics of Texts*. Bloomington: Indiana University Press, 1979.
Ekman, Stefan. *Here Be Dragons: Exploring Fantasy Maps and Settings*. Middletown, CT: Wesleyan University Press, 2013.
Ekman, Stefan, and Audrey Isabel Taylor. "Notes Toward a Critical Approach to Worlds and World-Building," *Fafnir* 3 (2016).
Elliott, Kate (KateElliottSFF). "When I see a lack of older women characters I see girls being told they have no future to grow into even if they are the kickass heroine now," 21 November 2014. https://twitter.com/KateElliottSFF/status/535672144798416896, Accessed 22 January 2017.
Emmerichs, Sharon. "Straddling Genres: McKillip and the Landscape of the Female Hero-Identity," *Journal of the Fantastic in the Arts* 16.3 (2005).
Esbenshade, Richard S. "Remembering to Forget: Memory, History, National Identity in Postwar East-Central Europe," *Representations* 49 (1995): Special Issue: Identifying Histories: Eastern Europe Before and After 1989.
Eynat-Confino, Irene. *On the Uses of the Fantastic in Modern Theatre: Cocteau, Oedipus, and the Monster*. Basingstoke: Palgrave Macmillan, 2008.
Farrant, Anthony. *Longevity and the Good Life*. Basingstoke: Palgrave Macmillan, 2011.
Faulkenburg, Marilyn Thomas. *Church, City, and Labyrinth in Brontë, Dickens, Hardy, and Butor*. New York: Peter Lang, 1993.
Friedan, Betty. *The Fountain of Age*. New York: Simon & Schuster, 1993.
Gearhart, Sally M. *The Wanderground: Stories of the Hill Women*. London: Women's Press, 1985.
Giebert, Stefanie. "A Place for the Silver Horde or No Country for Old Men? Age and Aging in Fantasy and Science Fiction." *New Directions in the European Fantastic*, ed. Sabine Coelsch-Foisner and Sarah Herbe. Heidelberg: Universitätsverlag Winter, 2012.
Gifford, Terry. *Pastoral*. London: Routledge, 1999.
Greene, Gayle. "Feminist Fiction and the Uses of Memory." *Signs* 16.2 (1992).
Grimm, Jacob. *Deutsche Mythologie*. Dieterich, 1844.
Gruchow, Paul. *Grass Roots: The Universe of Home*. Minneapolis: Milkweed Editions; Distributed by Publishers Group West, 1995.
Hall, Peter Geoffrey. *Cities of Tomorrow: An Intellectual History of Urban Planning and Design in the Twentieth Century*. Oxford: Blackwell, 1996.
Harrison, M. John. "Very afraid." Uncle Zip's Window, 27 January 2007. http://web.archive.org/web/20080410181840/http://uzwi.wordpress.com/2007/01/27/very-afraid/. Accessed 22 January 2017.
Herman, David. *Basic Elements of Narrative*. Malden, MA: Wiley Blackwell, 2009.
_____. *Story Logic: Problems and Possibilities of Narrative*. Lincoln: University of Nebraska Press, 2002.
Hixon, Martha. "'The Lady of Shalott' as Paradigm in Patricia McKillip's *The Tower at Stony Wood*." *Journal of the Fantastic in the Arts* 16.3 (2005).
Hourihan, Margery. *Deconstructing the Hero: Literary Theory and Children's Literature*. New York: Routledge, 1997.
Howey, Ann F. "Changing Self, Changing Other: Patricia McKillip's *The Changeling Sea* as Feminist Fairy Tale." *Journal of the Fantastic in the Arts* 18.1 (2008).
Hume, Kathryn. *Fantasy and Mimesis: Responses to Reality in Western Literature*. London: Routledge, 1985.
Iser, Wolfgang. *The Act of Reading: A Theory of Aesthetic Response*. Baltimore: Johns Hopkins University Press, 1980.

James, Edward. "Tolkien, Lewis and the Explosion of Genre Fantasy." *The Cambridge Companion to Fantasy Literature*, ed. Edward James and Farah Mendlesohn. Cambridge: Cambridge University Press, 2012.
Jaskot, Paul B. *The Architecture of Oppression: The SS, Forced Labor and the Nazi Monumental Building Economy*. London: Routledge, 2000.
Jones, Diana Wynne. *Dogsbody*. London: Methuen Children's, 1988.
_____. *The Tough Guide to Fantasyland*. London: Vista, 1996.
Jung, C.G. "Civilization in Transition." *Collected Works*. Princeton: Princeton University Press, 1970.
Kavey, Alison B. *World-Building and the Early Modern Imagination*. New York: Palgrave Macmillan, 2010.
Knapp, Bettina L. *A Jungian Approach to Literature*. Carbondale: Southern Illinois University Press, 1984.
Lacey, Lauren J. *The Past That Might Have Been, The Future That May Come: Women Writing Fantastic Fiction 1960s to the Present*. Jefferson, NC: McFarland, 2014.
Lauter, Anne, and Carol Schreier Rupprecht. "Introduction." *Feminist Archetypal Theory: Interdisciplinary Re-Visions of Jungian Thought*, ed. Anne Lauter and Carol Schreier Rupprecht. Knoxville: University of Tennessee Press, 1985.
Lee, Alison. "Bending the Arrow of Time: The Continuing Postmodern Present." *Fictions Anglaises Contemporaines*, ed. Max Duperray. Aix-en-Provence: Publications de l'Université de Provence, 1994.
LeFanu, Sarah. *In the Chinks of the World Machine: Feminism and Science Fiction*. London: Women's Press, 1988.
Le Guin, Ursula K. *The Earthsea Trilogy*. New York: Bantam, 1972.
Le Lievre, Kerry. "'I will play no games with you': Riddlery, Narrative and Ethics in 'The Riddle-Master's Game.'" *Journal of the Fantastic in the Arts* 16.3 (2006).
Leopold, Aldo. *A Sand County Almanac and Sketches Here and There*. Oxford: Oxford University Press, 1968.
Little, T.E. *The Fantasts: Studies in J.R.R. Tolkien, Lewis Carroll, Mervyn Peake, Nikolay Gogol, and Kenneth Grahame*. Amersham: Avebury Publishing, 1984.
Lynen, John F. *The Pastoral Art of Robert Frost*. New Haven: Yale University Press, 1960.
Mains, Christine. "Bridging World and Story: Patricia McKillip's Reluctant Heroes." *Journal of the Fantastic in the Arts* 16.1 (2005).
_____. "For Love or for Money: The Concept of Loyalty in the Works of Patricia A. McKillip." *Journal of the Fantastic in the Arts* 16.3 (2006).
_____. "Having It All: The Female Hero's Quest for Love and Power in Patricia McKillip's *The Riddle-Master* Trilogy." *Extrapolation* 46.1 (2005).
_____. "The Quest of the Female Hero in the Works of Patricia A. McKillip." MA, University of Calgary, 2001.
_____. "The Use, Misuse, and Abuse of Power: The Wizards of Patricia A. McKillip." *Fantastic Odysseys: Selected Essays from the Twenty-Second International Conference on the Fantastic in the Arts*, ed. Mary Pharr. Westport, CT: Praeger, 2003.
Malmgren, Carl Darryl. *Worlds Apart: Narratology of Science Fiction*. Bloomington: Indiana University Press, 1991.
Manlove, Colin. *From Alice to Harry Potter: Children's Fantasy in England*. Christchurch: Cybereditions, 2013.
Marx, Leo. *The Machine in the Garden: Technology and the Pastoral Ideal in America*. Oxford: Oxford University Press, 2000.
McArthur, Tom. "Cliché." *The Concise Oxford Companion to the English Language*. Oxford: Oxford University Press, 1998.
McDonald, George. *The Light Princess and Other Fairy Tales*. New York: G.P. Putnam's Sons, 1893.

McKillip, Patricia A. *Alphabet of Thorn*. New York: Ace, 2004.
———. *The Bards of Bone Plain*. New York: Ace, 2010.
———. *The Bell at Sealey Head*. New York: Ace, 2008.
———. *The Book of Atrix Wolfe*. New York: Ace, 1996.
———. *The Changeling Sea*. New York: Firebird, 2003.
———. *Cygnet* [*The Sorceress and the Cygnet* (1991), *The Cygnet and the Firebird* (1993)]. New York: Ace, 2007.
———. *The Forgotten Beasts of Eld*. New York: Berkley, 1986.
———. *In the Forests of Serre*. New York: Ace, 2003.
———. *Kingfisher*. New York: Ace, 2016.
———. *Od Magic*. New York: Ace, 2006.
———. *Ombria in Shadow*. New York: Ace, 2002.
———. *Riddle of Stars* [*The Riddle-Master of Hed* (1976), *Heir of Sea and Fire* (1977), *Harpist in the Wind* (1979)]. Garden City, NY: Nelson Doubleday Inc., 1979.
———. *Song for the Basilisk*. New York: Ace, 1998.
———. *The Throme of the Erril of Sherrill*. New York: Tempo, 1984.
———. *The Tower at Stony Wood*. New York: Ace, 2001.
———. *Winter Rose*. New York: Ace, 1996.
———. "Women in SF&F Month." Blog Post. *Fantasy Café*. FantasyBookCafe, 15 April 2013. http://www.fantasybookcafe.com/2013/04/women-in-sff-month-patricia-a-mckillip/. Accessed 22 January 2017.
Mendlesohn, Farah. *Diana Wynne Jones: Children's Literature and the Fantastic Tradition*. New York: Routledge, 2005.
———. *Rhetorics of Fantasy*. Middletown, CT: Wesleyan University Press, 2008.
Mendlesohn, Farah, and Edward James. *A Short History of Fantasy*. Enfield: Middlesex University Press, 2009.
Metzger, Lore. *One Foot in Eden: Modes of Pastoral in Romantic Poetry*. Chapel Hill: University of North Carolina Press, 1986.
Middleton, Peter, and Tim Woods. *Literatures of Memory: History, Time and Space in Postwar Writing*. Manchester: Manchester University Press, 2000.
Miéville, China. *Perdido Street Station*. London: Pan, 2001.
Minor, Vernon Hyde. *The Death of the Baroque and the Rhetoric of Good Taste*. Cambridge: Cambridge University Press, 2006.
Moorcock, Michael. *Wizardry & Wild Romance: A Study of Epic Fantasy*. London: Gollancz, 1987.
Nelson, George, and Yale University School of Architecture. *Building a New Europe: Portraits of Modern Architects: Essays by George Nelson, 1935–1936*. New Haven: Yale University Press, 2007.
Neubauer, John. *The Fin de Siècle Culture of Adolescence*. New Haven: Yale University Press, 1992.
Nichols, Ashton. *Beyond Romantic Ecocriticism: Toward Urbanatural Roosting*. Basingstoke: Palgrave Macmillan, 2011.
Nye, David E. *American Technological Sublime*. Cambridge: MIT Press, 1994.
Overall, Christine. "Longevity, Identity, and Moral Character: A Feminist Approach." *The Fountain of Youth: Cultural, Scientific, and Ethical Perspectives on a Biomedical Goal*, ed. Stephen G. Post and Robert H. Binstock. Oxford: Oxford University Press, 2004.
Oziewicz, Marek. *One Earth, One People: The Mythopoeic Fantasy Series of Ursula K. Le Guin, Lloyd Alexander, Madeleine L'Engle and Orson Scott Card*. Jefferson, NC: McFarland, 2008.
Painter, Borden W, Jr. *Mussolini's Rome: Rebuilding the Eternal City*. Basingstoke: Palgrave Macmillan, 2005.

Pak, Chris. *Terraforming: Ecopolitical Transformations and Environmentalism in Science Fiction*. Liverpool: Liverpool University Press, 2016.
Parker, K. J. *Colours in the Steel*. London: Orbit, 1998.
Pilinovsky, Helen. "The Mother of all Witches: Baba Yaga and Brume in Patricia McKillip's *In the Forests of Serre*." *Extrapolation* 46.1 (2005).
Pollock, Tom. *Skyscraper Throne Omnibus*. London: Jo Fletcher Books, 2015.
Pringle, David, ed. *The Ultimate Encyclopedia of Fantasy*. London: Carlton Books, 2006.
Propp, Vladimir. *Morphology of the Folk-Tale*. Austin: Texas University Press, 1968.
Ringel, Faye. "The Art of Patricia McKillip: Music and Magic." *Journal of the Fantastic in the Arts* 16.3 (2006).
____. "Women Fantasists: In the Shadow of the Ring." *J.R.R Tolkien and His Literary Resonances: Views of Middle-earth*, ed. George Clark and Daniel Timmons. Westport, CT: Greenwood Press, 2000.
Roberson, Jennifer. *Sword Dancer*. New York: Daw, 1986.
Rochelle, Warren G. *Communities of the Heart: The Rhetoric of Myth in the Fiction of Ursula K. Le Guin*. Liverpool: Liverpool University Press, 2001.
Rowland, Susan. *Jung: A Feminist Revision*. Malden, MA: Blackwell, 2002.
Russ, Joanna. "The Image of Women in Science Fiction." *Vertex* 1.6 (1971).
Salmon, Phillida. *Living in Time: A New Look at Personal Development*. London: Dent, 1985.
Salter, Jessica. "Game of Thrones's George RR Martin: 'I'm a feminist at heart.'" www.telegraph.co.uk. 1 April 2013. http://www.telegraph.co.uk/women/womens-life/9959063/Game-of-Throness-George-RR-Martin-Im-a-feminist.html. Accessed 22 January 2017.
Sawyer, Andy. "Ursula Le Guin and the Pastoral Mode." *Extrapolation* 47.3 (2006).
Schmid, Astrid. *The Fear of the Other: Approaches to English Stories of the Double (1764–1910)*. Bern: Lang, 1996.
Sellers, Susan. *Myth and Fairy Tale in Contemporary Women's Fiction*. Basingstoke: Palgrave, 2001.
Senior, William. A. *Stephen R. Donaldson's Chronicles of Thomas Covenant: Variations on the Fantasy Tradition*. Kent: Kent State University Press, 1995.
Shippey, Tom A. *The Road to Middle-earth*. Boston: Houghton Mifflin, 1982.
Sibley, Brian. "Foreword." *The J.R.R Tolkien Handbook: A Concise Guide to His Life, Writings, and World of Middle-earth*, ed. Colin Duriez. Ada, MI: Baker Books 2002.
Stableford, Brian. *Historical Dictionary of Fantasy Literature*. Lanham, MD: Scarecrow Press, 2004.
Spivack, Charlotte. *Merlin's Daughters: Contemporary Women Writers of Fantasy*. New York: Greenwood Press, 1987.
Stockwell, Peter. *Cognitive Poetics: An Introduction*. London: Routledge, 2002.
Swinfen, Ann. *In Defense of Fantasy: A Study of the Genre in English and American Literature Since 1945*. London: Routledge & Kegan Paul, 1984.
Sword in the Stone. Dir. Wolfgang Reitherman. Movie. Walt Disney, 1963.
Tatar, Maria. *The Hard Facts of the Grimms' Fairy Tales*. Princeton: Princeton University Press, 1987.
Tennyson, Lord Alfred. "The Lady of Shalott." *Tennyson's The Lady of Shalott and Other Poems*. London: Macmillan, 1909.
Thomas, Melissa. "Teaching Fantasy: Overcoming the Stigma of Fluff." *The English Journal* 92.5 (2003).
Thoreau, Henry David. *Walden*, ed. Zdene Franta. Praha: Laichter, 1902.
Tilendis, Robert M. "Patricia A. McKillip *In the Forests of Serre* (Ace Books 2003)." *Green Man Review*, 15 September 2013.

Works Cited

Timmerman, John H. *Other Worlds: The Fantasy Genre*. Bowling Green: Bowling Green University Popular Press, 1983.
Tolkien, J. R. R. *The Lord of the Rings*. London: HarperCollins, 2011.
_____. "On Fairy-Stories." *Tree and Leaf*. London: Unwin Paperbacks, 1979.
Townley, Roderick. *The Great Good Thing*. London: Simon & Schuster, 2003.
Tuttle, Lisa. *Writing Fantasy and Science Fiction*. London: A&C Black, 2002.
Veldman, Meredith. *Fantasy, the Bomb and the Greening of Britain: Romantic Protest, 1945–1980*. Cambridge: Cambridge University Press, 1994.
Walker, Steve. *The Power of Tolkien's Prose: Middle-earth's Magical Style*. New York: Palgrave Macmillan, 2009.
Waller, Alison. *Constructing Adolescence in Fantastic Realism*. London: Routledge, 2009.
Webb, Caroline. *Fantasy and the Real World in British Children's Literature: The Power of Story*. London: Routledge, 2015.
Wehr, Demeris S. *Jung and Feminism: Liberating Archetypes*. Boston: Beacon Press, 1987.
Westfahl, Gary. "Introduction: The Quarries of Time." *Worlds Enough and Time: Explorations of Time in Science Fiction and Fantasy*, ed. Gary Westfahl et al. Westport, CT: Greenwood Press, 2002.
_____, ed. *The Greenwood Encyclopedia of Science Fiction and Fantasy: Themes, Works, and Wonders*. Westport, CT: Greenwood Press, 2005.
White, Jerry. *London in the Nineteenth Century: 'A Human Awful Wonder of God.'* London: Jonathan Cape, 2007.
Williams, Raymond. *The Country and the City*. London: Hogarth, 1985.
_____. *Country and City in the Modern Novel: W.D. Thomas Memorial Lecture: Delivered at the College on 26 January 1987*. Swansea: University College of Swansea, 1987.
Wolf, Mark J.P. *Building Imaginary Worlds: The Theory and History of Subcreation*. New York: Routledge, 2012.
Wolf, Werner. "Description as a Transmedial Mode of Representation: General Features and Possibilities of Realization in Painting, Fiction and Music." *Description in Literature and Other Media*, ed. Walter Bernhart and Werner Wolf. Amsterdam: Rodopi, 2007.
Wolfe, Gary K. *Critical Terms for Science Fiction and Fantasy: A Glossary and Guide to Scholarship*. London: Greenwood, 1986.
_____. "The Encounter with Fantasy." *Evaporating Genres: Essays on Fantastic Literature*. Middletown, CT: Wesleyan University Press, 2011.
Woolf, Virginia. *A Room of One's Own*. Hogarth Press, 1929.

Index

age 30–1, 61–3, 65, 67, 83, 110, 113, 129, 137, 166; effects of 69–79; expectations of 62, 66, 68, 80; *see also* world frames
Agnew, Vijay 128
allegory 47, 55, 57, 60
Alphabet of Thorn 49, 67–8, 73–7, 87, 91–2, 95, 98–9, 101, 103–7, 109, 113; Gavin 73, 75–6, 99; Kane 68, 98, 104–5, 108, 112; Tessera 68–70, 74, 77–9, 99; Vevay 66, 68–9, 73–5, 77, 79, 99, 113
Anderson, Poul 167
animals 8, 57, 70, 122, 131, 136; in *The Forgotten Beasts of Eld* 91, 94, 100, 112; *see also* world frames
archetypes 35–7, 40, 62–3
Armitage, Kevin C. 129
Attebery, Brian 3, 4, 15–7, 28, 34, 88, 90–1
authorial world-building *see* world-building

Baba Yaga 2, 49, 56, 91–2, 175
Ballantyne, Andrew 152
Baltasar, Michaela 109
The Bards of Bone Plain 5, 72, 87, 98–109, 119, 135, 139–40, 142–3, 150; Beatrice 143–4; Caerau 143–5, 148, 150; Jonah/Nairn 72–3, 103–4, 107, 112, 143; Phelan 72, 107, 144
Barillas, William 115, 125–6
Barrett, Jenny 151
Barry, Elizabeth 37, 43
The Bell at Sealey Head 5, 17, 85, 139, 164; Gwyneth 85; Judd 85
Berry, Wendell 124

Bettelheim, Bruno 97
Bird, Hazel Sheeky 132
Bloom, Harold 79
Bolintineanu, Alexandra 104
The Book of Atrix Wolfe 4, 38, 56, 74–80, 92, 110–1, 116; Atrix Wolfe 74–6, 110–3; Talis 74, 78–9
Brooks, Terry 81
Buell, Lawrence 123, 133
building-blocks *see* elements

Calhoun, Blue 122
Calvino, Italo 143
Campbell, Joseph 35–6
casual reader *see* reader
The Changeling Sea 2, 5, 33, 59, 85, 91, 139, 164; Peri 59, 85
city *see* setting; urbanity
city-state *see* polis, Greek
cliché 29, 35, 37–8, 43, 76, 83, 86
Clute, John 2, 17–8, 28, 55–6, 58, 94, 101, 114
Coffin, Tristram Potter 93
consistency 19–20
Copper, Baba 74, 77
Coulston, Jon 149
creative writing 17, 19, 150, 167; *see also* world-building, authorial
culture 3, 20, 25, 27, 31, 87–9, 97, 132, 137, 166; *see also* world frames
Curry, Patrick 126
The Cygnet and the Firebird 4, 43–5, 66, 92, 95, 117; Meguet 45–7, 117, 130; Nyx 43, 45–6, 85, 92, 117, 129–31, 136
Cygnet duology 3–4, 117; *see also The Cygnet and the Firebird; The Sorceress and the Cygnet*

Index

Darcy, Jane 116
David, Gail 130
Delany, Samuel R. 20–1, 55
depth, world 27, 31, 38, 54, 60, 63, 86–7, 91–2, 96, 101, 106–7, 113, 134, 164–7
detail 9–10, 21–8, 38–9, 41–2, 47–8, 65–8, 76, 81, 100–1, 116–7, 126, 138, 140–9, 160, 167
Diski, Jenny 63
Dodge, Hazel 149
Donaldson, Stephen R. 2, 128, 167
dragons 15, 34, 36, 43–7, 64, 122, 127
dynamic interplay 21, 23, 25, 165, 166; see also elements, interplay of

Eagleton, Terry 74
Eco, Umberto 52
Ekman, Stefan 7, 90, 137; on maps 149; on *Ombria in Shadow* 3; on worldbuilding 10, 12, 18, 22–3, 25–6, 29, 33, 87
elements 3, 10–1, 29, 33, 35, 56, 58, 77, 110, 114, 118, 135, 140, 163; interplay of 12–3, 23–5, 30, 147, 165; order of 21–3, 110, 117, 141; speculative 9, 15–6, 29, 34
Emmerichs, Sharon 2, 82
Esbenshade, Richard S. 151
expectations *see* age, expectations of; gender, expectations of; reader expectations
Eynat-Confino, Irene 65

fairy-tale 2, 26, 35, 37, 56, 88–93
fantasy, definitions of 4
Faulkenburg, Marilyn Thomas 139
feminism 2, 41, 54, 63, 74, 82, 84, 91, 130
The Forgotten Beasts of Eld 1, 3–4, 42, 57, 62, 82, 85, 87, 91–4, 98–101, 107, 114, 130, 136; Coren 29, 42, 98–100; Sybel 29, 42, 85, 93–4, 99–100, 129–30, 136
Friedan, Betty 73

Gearhart, Sally M. 130
gender 30–1, 42, 61, 72, 77, 86, 130, 137, 157, 166; expectations of 2, 10, 62–3, 66, 81–5
Giebert, Stefanie 67
Gifford, Terry 115, 118, 129, 132, 137
Golden Age 115–6, 119, 134

Greene, Gayle 127
Gruchow, Paul 127

Hall, Peter Geoffrey 146
Harrison, M. John 19, 61
Herman, David 8, 10, 19, 20; *see also* storyworld
hero 36, 41, 56, 65, 75, 79, 80–1, 124, 155, 168; females as 2, 37, 43, 63, 66, 74, 82–5; legend of 88–95, 99; reality of 110–1
history 27–9, 31, 71–2, 87–94, 96–101, 104–9, 113–4, 138–51, 166; *see also* world frames
Hixon, Martha 3, 39–40
holistic approach 12, 28, 81, 146, 164
homesickness 38, 40, 128, 131
Hourihan, Margery 49, 66, 82–3
Howey, Ann F. 2, 33–4, 91
Hume, Kathryn 15
humor 22, 59–60, 76, 85, 100, 124

In the Forests of Serre 2, 5, 48–9, 52, 56, 58, 75–6, 91–2, 110–14, 121, 134, 167; Brume 2, 48–53, 56–7, 91–2, 110 (*see also* Baba Yaga); Euan the scribe 52–3, 75, 111; Gyre 52, 58, 64–5, 75; Prince Ronan 49, 52, 56, 64, 110; Serre 52–3, 56–8, 64–5, 110, 113, 134; Sidonie 52–3, 58, 110, 121; Unciel 75–6, 110–3
interplay, dynamic *see* dynamic interplay

James, Edward 3–4, 27, 93, 100, 167
Jaskot, Paul B. 152
Jenkins, Henry 9
Jones, Diana Wynne 64, 97; *see also* The Tough Guide to Fantasyland
Jung, C.G. 35–6, 62–3; *see also* archetype

Kavey, Alison B. 13
Kingfisher 5, 22–5, 119, 135, 138, 164; Carrie 23–5; Pierce 22–3
Knapp, Bettina L. 36

Lacey, Lauren J. 48
landscape *see* setting
laws 8–9, 20, 67, 85, 134, 150, 154
Le Guin, Ursula K. 90
Lee, Alison 108
LeFanu, Sarah 42, 54, 65, 82, 84
Leopold, Aldo 131

178

Index

literalization 30, 33, 39, 41, 44, 45–7, 54–60
Little, T.E. 40
The Lord of the Rings 4, 27, 37, 81, 89, 95, 104, 118; *see also* Tolkien, J.R.R
Lynen, John F. 135

magic 17, 41, 45, 47, 49, 68, 74, 77, 84, 108, 110–2; element of fantasy 15, 18, 34, 42, 88, 90, 152; wild 38–9, 124, 129, 131, 133, 141, 155–8
Mains, Christine 2, 28, 35, 61–2, 116, 125–6, 152; duomyth 2, 71, 82–3; female wizards 42–3; Luna 50, 162; nature of story 57, 94, 96; power 133, 135; Renaissance Italy 141–2
Malmgren, Carl Darryl 16
Manlove, Colin 135
maps 148–9; *see also* Ekman, Stefan
Marx, Leo 122, 131–2, 134, 136–7
McDonald, George 20
memory 38–9, 105, 127–8, 151; *see also* world frames
Mendlesohn, Farah 3–4, 14, 27, 77, 100, 144, 166
metaphor 3, 34, 39, 46, 55, 57, 119, 155
Metzger, Lore 116, 118
Middleton, Peter 108
Miéville, China 167
the mimetic 13, 15–6, 18, 25, 28, 55
Minor, Vernon Hyde 115, 132
Moorcock, Michael 11–2
music 3, 145, 160
myth 8, 20, 25, 29–31, 35–7, 63, 83, 87–93, 100, 109, 142; *see also* world frames

nature 3, 20, 29, 31, 59, 95, 114–38, 158; *see also* landscape; world frames
Neubauer, John 78
Nichols, Ashton 121, 123, 137
nostalgia 115, 119–20, 122, 126–32
Nye, David E. 117

Od Magic 5, 80, 124, 128–9, 131–3, 135, 139–40, 153, 156, 159; Brenden Vetch 80, 124, 128–9, 131, 135, 155; School of Magic 80, 124, 131, 134–6, 153–6, 159; Twilight Quarter 153–6, 159; Valoren 131; Yar 80–1, 124, 131, 135, 153–5
Ombria in Shadow 3, 5, 48, 50–1, 102–3, 106–9, 139–45, 149–51, 156–9; Camas Erl 108–9, 145–6; Domina Pearl 48, 50–1, 146, 156–62; Ducon Greve 48, 108, 158, 162; Faey 48, 50–1, 143–9, 156, 159, 162; Kyel 48, 102; Lydea 48, 102–3, 147, 159; Ombria 48, 51, 102–3, 108–9, 140–52, 156–62
"On Fairy-Stories" 8–9, 93; *see also* Tolkien, J.R.R.
Overall, Christine 78
Oziewicz, Marek 101

Painter, Borden W., Jr. 147, 152
Pak, Chris 116, 132–3, 169
pastoral, American 117, 121, 123, 136, 139; *see also* setting
perspective *see* world-building
Pilinovsky, Helen 2, 56, 91, 94
polis, Greek 140, 170; *see also* world frames
politics 31, 50, 104, 124, 130–1, 133–4, 138, 140, 145, 148, 151–63

reader: casual reader 21, 24, 28; fan reader 19, 21
reader expectations 2, 29–37, 40–3, 47–54, 56, 61–4, 66, 68–9, 75, 84, 92–3, 137, 165
readerly world-building 19–21, 51, 97, 148, 150, 166
The Riddle-Master trilogy 2–4, 9, 38, 43, 57–8, 68–71, 82–3, 114, 116, 118, 120–3, 130, 133, 142, 149; Morgon 2, 57–8, 68–72, 83–4, 118–23, 130, 142; Raederle 2, 58, 71–2, 83–5
Ringel, Faye 2–3, 28, 34, 37, 62, 83, 116, 145
Rochelle, Warren G. 106
Rowland, Susan 36, 63

Salmon, Phillida 73, 80
Sawyer, Andy 115–6, 122
Schmid, Astrid 51
science fiction 16, 54, 67, 81, 116, 132
selkies 38–40, 59, 128
Sellers, Susan 36, 63, 96
Senior, William A. 15–7
setting 3, 10, 11–2, 27, 29–31, 88, 166–7; city 143, 153 (*see also* urbanity); landscape 9, 17, 43, 45–7, 56, 71, 78, 81, 97, 118–21, 128–9, 132; pastoral 114–7, 125, 130, 137, 139 (*see also* pastoral, American); shaping of 152, 156; *see also* world frame

Index

Shippey, Tom A. 55
Sibley, Brian 20, 27–8
Song for the Basilisk 5, 49–50, 58, 86, 119–21, 124, 135–6, 139–52, 157–62; Arioso Pellior 49, 157, 159–60; Berylon 49, 139–41, 144–5, 148, 151–3, 157–8, 162; Caladrius 49, 58, 120, 124, 135–6, 144–5, 151, 160–1; Guilia 86, 124; Luna 49–50, 58, 160–2
sorceress 38, 48, 50–1, 66–8, 85 104, 145–6, 157; *see also* wizard, female
The Sorceress and the Cygnet 4, 42, 92–8, 109–12; Corleu 95–8, 109–10; Nyx 42–3, 85, 92, 95, 98, 117, 129–31, 136
speculative fiction 10, 13–6, 65
Spivack, Charlotte 3, 48, 82–4, 135
Stableford, Brian 42, 48
storyworld 8, 20; *see also* Herman, David
Swinfen, Ann 91

Tatar, Maria 49, 89
Thoreau, Henry David 123
The Throme of the Erril of Sherril 4, 26–7, 53–4, 65, 84, 95; Cnite Caerles 26–7, 54, 84, 95; Damsen 27, 53–4, 57, 84
time abyss 94
Timmerman, John H. 17
Tolkien, J.R.R. 2, 4, 8, 19–20, 26–7, 29, 34, 55, 82–3, 89–90, 93, 95, 101, 109, 122, 152, 167; *see also* "On Fairy-Stories"; *The Lord of the Rings*
The Tough Guide to Fantasyland 17, 47, 149; *see also* Jones, Dianna Wynne
The Tower at Stony Wood 3, 5, 38, 40, 42, 43–4, 46, 49, 59, 79, 83, 85–6, 91, 117–9, 123, 126–8, 136; Cyan Dag 38–45, 59–60, 79, 83, 117–8, 127, 136; Melanthos 38, 40–1, 85, 128, 136; Sel 38–40, 44, 59, 83, 85–6, 123, 126–9; Thayne Ysse 38, 44–5, 83, 118, 120, 127
tropes 10, 29–30, 33, 54; damsel in distress 40–1; definition of 34–37; dualism 31, 48–51; subversion of 62–3, 80, 165; *see also* dragons; selkies; wizard; world frames
Tuttle, Lisa 11, 19, 36

underground 51, 146–7, 150, 159, 162; *see also* world frames
urbanity 115, 122–4, 130, 133, 136–7, 140, 144, 149; *see also* setting; world frames

Veldman, Meredith 95, 119, 125

Walker, Steve 26
Waller, Alison 68–9
walls 36, 134, 139–43, 153–7; *see also* world frames
Webb, Caroline 37
Westfahl, Gary 18, 149
Williams, Raymond 120, 126, 133–4
Winter Rose 4, 37, 92, 139, 164
wizards 34, 75, 112, 124, 129, 131, 133, 135, 154–6; female 2, 42–3, 82 (*see also* Mains, Christine; sorceress); *see also* magic, wild
Wolf, Mark J.P. 7–10, 13–5, 19–20, 22, 28–30, 34, 47, 61, 152, 169
Wolf, Werner 148
Wolfe, Gary K. 3–4, 10, 15–6, 26, 57, 88–9
Woods, Tim 106
Woolf, Virginia 157
world: definition of 7–9; primary 9, 17, 24, 26–7, 31, 40, 61, 67, 77, 81, 87–8, 90, 92–3, 95, 97, 105–7, 126, 133, 140–3, 146–55, 158, 161–2, 166; secondary 17, 40, 87, 90, 92–3, 97, 107, 126, 165, 167; *see also* depth, world; elements; storyworld; world-building
world-building: authorial perspective 7, 19, 20, 24, 62, 67, 73, 75, 78, 80, 82–3, 89, 90, 99, 103; critical world-building 1, 4, 7–8, 11–1, 17–9, 21–6, 28–9, 33, 62, 67, 90–2, 103, 133, 148, 164–6
world frames: cultural world 3, 10, 31, 147–9, 166–7 (*see also* culture); social world 29–30, 61, 96, 100, 115, 146, 166 (*see also* age); material world 29, 31, 97, 103, 114, 125, 138, 146, 166 (*see also* animals; nature; polis, Greek; setting; underground; urbanity; walls); mythological world 30–1, 92, 106, 166 (*see also* myth; trope); temporal world 29, 67, 78, 92, 103, 105, 114 (*see also* history; memory)

www.ingramcontent.com/pod-product-compliance
Ingram Content Group UK Ltd.
Pitfield, Milton Keynes, MK11 3LW, UK
UKHW042014140426
5217IPUK00015B/1163